Demystifying Intelligent Multimode Security Systems

An Edge-to-Cloud Cybersecurity Solutions Guide

Jody Booth
Dr. Werner Metz, PhD
Dr. Anahit Tarkhanyan, PhD
Sunil Cheruvu

Demystifying Intelligent Multimode Security Systems: An Edge-to-Cloud Cybersecurity Solutions Guide

Jody Booth
Intel, Chandler, AZ, USA

Dr. Werner Metz, PhD
Intel, Chandler, AZ, USA

Dr. Anahit Tarkhanyan, PhD
Santa Clara, CA, USA

Sunil Cheruvu
Intel, Chandler, AZ, USA

ISBN-13 (pbk): 978-1-4842-8296-0
https://doi.org/10.1007/978-1-4842-8297-7

ISBN-13 (electronic): 978-1-4842-8297-7

Managing Director, Apress Media LLC: Welmoed Spahr
Acquisitions Editor: Susan McDermott
Development Editor: Laura Berendson
Coordinating Editor: Jessica Vakili

Distributed to the book trade worldwide by Springer Science+Business Media New York, 233 Spring Street, 6th Floor, New York, NY 10013. Phone 1-800-SPRINGER, fax (201) 348-4505, e-mail orders-ny@springer-sbm.com, or visit www.springeronline.com. Apress Media, LLC is a California LLC and the sole member (owner) is Springer Science + Business Media Finance Inc (SSBM Finance Inc). SSBM Finance Inc is a **Delaware** corporation.

For information on translations, please e-mail booktranslations@springernature.com; for reprint, paperback, or audio rights, please e-mail bookpermissions@springernature.com.

Apress titles may be purchased in bulk for academic, corporate, or promotional use. eBook versions and licenses are also available for most titles. For more information, reference our Print and eBook Bulk Sales web page at http://www.apress.com/bulk-sales.

Any source code or other supplementary material referenced by the author in this book is available to readers on the Github repository: https://github.com/Apress/Demystifying-Intelligent-Multimode-Security-Systems. For more detailed information, please visit http://www.apress.com/source-code.

Printed on acid-free paper

Table of Contents

About the Authors

Jody Booth has been a systems architect and a systems-on-silicon architect focused on imaging and media-related processing for more than 30 years. After three years in secure video gateway cybersecurity architecture, he joined Intel's Internet of Things/Network and Edge group, returning to his greatest interest—vision systems. Jody has 40 patents spanning imaging, display, memory, and security systems. Jody served as an advisor to the Security Industry Association cybersecurity board, and Jody is also the co-chair of the Coalition for Provenance Authenticity AI/ML task force.

Dr. Werner Metz, PhD is a system architect with over 30 years of experience in architecting, developing, and implementing digital imaging systems. He has contributed at the level of image sensor architecture and design, conventional and deep learning imaging algorithms, digital image processor architecture, AI accelerator architecture and design and analog image signal processor design. He has architected a wide range of consumer, commercial, and industrial imaging systems spanning visible, IR, thermal, and UV wavelengths for both human viewing and computer vision. His current technical focus is the secure ML based E2E system architecture at Intel, spanning camera to gateway to data center, with an emphasis on edge devices. Werner has a PhD in Physics, holds a diverse set of patents and publications spanning a broad range of subject matter. Currently Werner is the Lead System Architect at Intel Foundry Services.

Dr. Anahit Tarkhanyan, PhD is a security architect who leads the security definitions for Intel's broad IoT/Edge products portfolio. Anahit has 20+ years of vast industry experience delivering end-to-end security solutions to the market. Her deep expertise includes hardware and software systems security applied to IoT/OT/ICS and AI/ML cybersecurity risks, principles, and practices. Anahit is a technical expert at ISO/IEC/JTC1 and a senior member of IEEE. She holds a Ph.D. in Distributed Computer Systems and Networks and authored several patents and publications in diverse areas of security technologies.

ABOUT THE AUTHORS

Sunil Cheruvu is Chief IoT/Edge Security Architect in the Network and Edge group at Intel Corporation. He has over 27 years of experience in architecting complex systems involving HW/FW/SW on multiple architectures, including Intel, ARM, and MIPS/PowerPC. At Intel, he leads security across all of the IoT/Edge vertical domains and he was the Content Protection and Trusted Data Path System Architect (end-to-end premium content protection within an SoC). He is the subject matter expert for IoT/Edge security across Intel and industry while serving as the co-chair of the TCG IOT WG. At Microsoft, as a software design engineer, he was the tech lead for vehicle bus networking stacks, threat modeling, and mitigations in the Windows Mobile for Automotive (WMfA) platform. At 3com and Conexant, he implemented the code for baseline privacy security in DOCSIS-compliant cable modems.

About the Technical Reviewer

Tinku Acharya, PhD a Fellow of IEEE, is a researcher, inventor, technologist, teacher, and entrepreneur. He is the inventor of 150+ US and international patents. He has contributed to 100+ technical papers and authored 4 books: (1) *Image Processing: Principles and Applications* (Wiley, 2005), (2) *JPEG2000 Standard for Image Compression: Concepts, Algorithms, and VLSI Architectures* (Wiley, 2004), (3) *Information Technology: Principles and Applications* (Prentice-Hall, 2004), (4) *Data Mining: Multimedia, Soft Computing, and Bioinformatics* (Wiley, 2003).

Dr. Acharya is the recipient of several prestigious awards: Most Prolific Inventor in Intel (1997, 2001), Engineer of the Year Award (IEEE – Phoenix, 2008), Outstanding Engineer Award (IEEE Southwest Region, USA, 2008), NASI-Reliance Industries Platinum Jubilee Award for Innovation in Physical Sciences (National Academy of Science in India, 2009), 1st Acharya P. C. Roy Memorial Award for Distinguished Achievements in Science & Entrepreneurship (Institute of Pulmocare & Research, 2010), and many others.

Videonetics, under his leadership, pioneered "Intelligent VMS" and video analytics applications for IP video surveillance and successfully deployed in over 200 installations worldwide. He led several R&D teams and initiatives in Intel Corporation, USA. He developed the key "image processing chain" to pragmatically map into silicon for the first low-cost dual-mode digital camera (Intel's first webcam). His works became the foundation of the MXP5800/5400 media processor, capable of processing 10 BOPS, and enabled a set of Internet-capable photocopiers from Xerox and Fuji. He made pioneering contributions in VLSI architectures and algorithms for JPEG2000 and Wavelet Transform.

He also served in AT&T Bell Labs, University of Maryland, Arizona State University, IIT-Kharagpur, and Intellectual Ventures and collaborated with many institutions worldwide including Xerox PARC, Kodak, etc. He served in the US National Body of ISO JPEG 2000 committee from 1997 to 2002.

About the Intel Reviewers

Dr. Richard Chuang is a Principal AI Engineer with Intel Corporation focusing on media, AI, algorithms, and workload accelerations in the Data Center and AI Group. He also has been in various architect roles in the Internet-of-Things Group developing platforms, systems, and solutions with CPU, FPGA, and VPU, in the video, safety, and security segments. Richard is an IEEE Senior Member.

Brent Thomas is a Sr. Principal Engineer focused on security architecture and initiatives targeting the enhancement of product security assurance at the system to IP levels. He has 30+ years of experience in the development, design and modeling of systems, in areas such as: mixed-signal Si, Pkg/Si power delivery, RF library characterization, and applied cryptography - spanning levels of abstraction. Currently, he is a security architect, product security expert (conducting threat model analysis), and contributing to Intel Security Development Lifecycle definition. He holds 10+ patents in areas ranging from image signal processing, mixed-signal circuits, security & computer systems. Brent holds MSEE and BSEE degrees from the University of Massachusetts, Amherst, Massachusetts.

Acknowledgements

Much of what I have learned on these topics came from my esteemed co-authors, so thanks to Werner, Anahit and Sunil for the tutelage. Of course. thanks to my coauthors for the countless hours they put into this. I also thank Stuart Douglas, our publishing coordinator, for his patient support. And special thanks to Sunil for encouraging me to write this book.

—Jody Booth

The authors also want to acknowledge the expert reviews we received from our Intel colleagues: Dr. Richard Chuang and Brent Thomas, who generously lent their experience in vision systems, data centers, and general system security to make this better than it would have been without their corrections and recommendations.

In addition to those already mentioned, we would like to acknowledge the many valuable and insightful discussions and knowledge from our many Intel colleagues over the years that have contributed to our knowledge. Among those are Richard Zhang, Ming Li, Heng Juen (HJ) Han, Dave Panziera, Wenjian Shao, Todd Matsler, Dian (Penny) Gu, Stewart Taylor, Ram Rangarajan, Soren Knudsen, and many others too numerous to name.

Finally deep thanks to Dr. Tinku Acharya for his insight into the industry and the technology. His feedback makes this more relevant to professionals specifying, designing, and maintaining Intelligent Multimodal Security Systems.

Legal Notices and Disclaimers

Intel technologies may require enabled hardware, software or service activation.

All product plans and roadmaps are subject to change without notice.

No product or component can be absolutely secure.

Your costs and results may vary.

Intel does not control or audit third-party data. You should consult other sources to evaluate accuracy.

© Intel Corporation. Intel, the Intel logo, and other Intel marks are trademarks of Intel Corporation or its subsidiaries. Other names and brands may be claimed as the property of others.

In this book we have provided references to laws and regulations that may apply to Intelligent Multimodal Security Systems. This is informational only and should not be considered as definitive or complete legal advice. The authors are not attorneys and cannot provide legal advice; your own attorneys should be consulted to provide legal advice.

We have provided copious footnotes to sources for the reader's convenience. Some of these references may be from subscribed information services or behind publication paywalls.

Abstract

There are nearly half a Billion active Security System cameras globally, with over 100M added annually. These systems are used across public and private enterprise (access controls, traffic monitoring, driver enforcement, etc.), mobile (situational awareness), and body-worn (monitoring). Intelligent Multimode Security Systems (IMSS) with a camera, a Network Video Recorder, and machine learning based intelligence all are becoming normal infrastructure for capturing, analyzing, and transmitting video content securely while protecting privacy. Most recently, Military, Aerospace, and Govt. entities are also embracing Intelligent Multimode Security Systems, and the security of those systems are becoming a vital function for their operations. And Video Analytics are increasingly used as evidence in legal proceedings. All these use-cases make a compelling case for bolstering the security within the intelligent systems at all levels, including leveraging Intel devices and software blocks as a multi-layered, in depth defense.

The original version of this book was previously published without open access. A correction to this book is available at https://doi.org/10.1007/978-1-4842-8297-7_9

CHAPTER 1

Introduction and Overview

Why You Should Read This Introduction and What to Expect

Reading and comprehending a technical text represents a substantial investment of time and energy on the part of the reader. Digital security systems are well-known in the industry and have been applied for decades, beginning with Closed Circuit Television (CCTV) and Video Recorders. What is driving the need for a new entry in the technical literature for Digital Security and Safety Systems?

Two megatrends are driving a revolution in the purpose and design of Digital Security Systems: the assets being protected and the rise of Artificial Intelligence (AI) as a pragmatic technology.

...Because That's Where the Money Is

Traditionally, the assets being protected consisted of physical items that could be touched – currency, gold, bearer bonds. When Willy Sutton, an infamous American bank robber, was asked why he robbed banks, his apocryphal reply was simply – "Because that's where the money is" (Though Mr. Sutton denied ever saying it). During his career from the 1920s to the 1930s, it is estimated Mr. Sutton stole $2M. Allowing for a bit of inflation, Table 1-1 shows the characteristics of $10M in assets of various forms.

The original version of this chapter was previously published without open access. A correction to this chapter is available at https://doi.org/10.1007/978-1-4842-8297-7_9

© Intel 2023, corrected publication 2023
J. Booth et al., *Demystifying Intelligent Multimode Security Systems*,
https://doi.org/10.1007/978-1-4842-8297-7_1

Table 1-1. *$10M in Assets*

Asset	Form	$10M Value	Description
Currency	$100 Bills	100,000 Bills	@1gm/bill = 100KG = ~250 lbs.
Gold	Gold Bullion	5,000 oz@ $2,000/oz	~310 lbs.
Platinum	Platinum Bullion	10,000 oz (about the volume of a bathtub) @ $1,000/oz	~620 lbs.
Diamonds	1 carat diamond	~$10,000/diamond	~ ½ lb.
Digital Data	Patents, Trade Secrets, Business Data, electronic funds	Megabytes to Gigabytes	No measurable weight, can be transported electronically

The physical assets lend themselves well to the traditional methods of guns, guards, and gates as all require physical transport to be stolen. In all but the case of gems, the physical characteristics for even a modest sum of $10M require transport of hundreds of pounds of material and substantial physical bulk. However, an increasing proportion of the world's assets are embodied in digital form as digital data. These digital assets take many forms – trade secrets, electronic currencies, business data related to customers, processes, and methods. These digital assets require no physical access to steal or corrupt. Guns, guards, and gates are of limited use in protecting these assets. Consequently, there is a fundamental shift in the types of threat models emerging to attack these new digital assets.

Cogito Ergo (Multiply and) Sum – Artificial Intelligence

The second megatrend impacting the Digital Security and Safety industry is the rise and widespread adoption of Artificial Intelligence (AI) techniques and methods for practical applications. AI experienced several cycles of enthusiasm and disappointment starting in the mid-twentieth century. In the early 2010s, the introduction of Convolutional Neural Networks combined with the evolution of the requisite compute power enabled practical demonstrations of computer vision-based AI. The subsequent decade saw the continued co-evolution of AI algorithms and specialized compute platforms. The immediate result was the ability to capture, analyze, and act upon vast quantities of data in real-time. Security systems progressed from being reactive to becoming proactive, real-time capabilities. Many of the functions that once required human observation and reaction are now being delegated to machines. So, while new and novel threat models are emerging, there are also new and novel techniques based on AI to counteract and mitigate these new threat models.

What This Means for You As a Security and Safety Professional

The world is changing rapidly – not only the assets being protected but also the tools and techniques used to protect both traditional and emerging assets. The purpose of this text is to assist security and Safety professionals in understanding and addressing these contemporary trends and techniques, to build on the skills and knowledge you already possess to extend to these new regimes. Our goal is to help you understand how to navigate this new landscape, introduce basic concepts and techniques, and enable you to collaborate with and incorporate these new techniques into your professional life.

It is also important to be clear about what is beyond the scope of this text. This is not intended to be a detailed investigation and exploration of the mathematical foundations of AI and Machine Learning (ML). There are a number of academic texts which cover these areas quite adequately. It is beyond the scope of this text to enable the reader to create novel AI algorithms or discuss in detail the current state-of-the-art algorithms. The reason is quite simply that the field is in a very fast state of evolution, often requiring less than six months from the creation of a new AI algorithm to productization and within a year or two – obsolescence. By the time this tome is published, much of such an attempt would be outdated. For the detailed current state of the art, we will defer to specialized conferences and journals on the topic. Fortunately, the vast majority of the intended readership will require the ability to make use of the outputs of the research and development, and those wishing to pursue an in-depth study will still find this a useful introduction.

What we will enable you to do, however, is intelligently converse with and collaborate with specialists in the field of AI-enabled Security and Safety technologies. Our intended audience includes, but is not limited to:

- Security executives responsible for protecting corporate and governmental assets

- Security system specifiers creating system Requests For Proposals (RFP)

- Security system architects are responsible for creating detailed systems architecture requirements

- Security system consultants guide clients in best practices and proposal evaluation

- Security system designers must ensure their systems protect the right assets with modern techniques

- Security system installers and Value Added Resellers who need to understand the systems being installed and verify the systems perform correctly

- End users who need to understand the security systems they have purchased and what those systems will and will not protect in terms of assets and threats

Every Journey Begins with a Single Step – Maya Angelou

If you have read this far, then you understand that the security world is evolving and you are ready to begin that journey with a single step, the first of the journey. This describes some of the main features and points of the journey we will take together.

The author's goal is to inform you about how intelligent multimodal security systems (IMSS) can help you sense the world to make the world more secure, especially the security you need in the system, to better assure that outcome. Note that while following these recommendations will make your systems more secure, no component, device, or system can be absolutely secure.

Chapter two is a system-level view of Intelligent Multimodal Security Systems. You will understand the history, current state, and trends of these systems. The basic system components are described, and you will get an introduction to the security of security from the devices at the sensor edge to the cloud.

In Chapter three, you will dive deeper into the evolution of security systems and learn what an Intelligent Multimodal Security System does and how it is done.

In Chapter four, you will gain detailed understanding of security analysis methods with a focus on the threats and assets for security systems, followed by the step-by-step elements necessary to build a secure system.

Chapter five gives you the detailed knowledge of security for the wave of the future: The intelligent aspect of Security Systems. Machine learning has a number of unique risks and challenges that must be understood and addressed for a security system that includes artificial intelligence or machine learning capabilities. You will learn about the unique assets and threats to machine learning, how to provide protection for the applications and the data, and ultimately, trust for this class of security systems.

In Chapter six, you will see these principles in practice through three system examples: a small business system, and edge server system, and a large system in a smart city. Through these examples, you will see the kinds of threats in these types of systems and how to mitigate them.

Devices and networked processing and content aggregation systems are evolving quickly. Laws and regulations and corresponding standards that impact these systems are another rapidly evolving element you need to stay abreast of. Perhaps the only things evolving faster are the attacks on those systems. Chapter 7 will guide you on ways to keep up with the change in the systems and how to defend those systems.

Indeed, there is so much change that we saved the last updates for a final "as we go to press" refresher in Chapter 8, so you will get the most recent updates we can provide.

CHAPTER 2

IMSS System Level View

It is necessary to know the typical topology and use cases for Intelligent Multi-Modal Security Systems (IMSS) to understand the security considerations.

Summary

The design of Intelligent Multi-Modal Security Systems (IMSS) has experienced major transformations from the age where Analog cameras were monitored by humans and stored on VHS tapes to today; an IP networked, Deep Learning-driven system can efficiently augment humans with insightful information and recommendations. Intel expects further developments in this space and is enabling game changing technologies that will usher us into the next generation of IMSS.

In this Chapter, we explore the various historical transformations of IMSS technologies and show you a glimpse of how Intel is changing the future by driving exponential changes end-to-end from endpoint sensor edge devices, at the network edge, and through the network infrastructure to the cloud.

Intel is making advances in new technologies in Machine Learning-based inferencing, computing devices, memory, storage, and security and show how they allow IMSS System Architects to design for various constraints around cost, performance, security, privacy, and public policy.

- Intel technology can add intelligence on the edge to optimize network bandwidth utilization, reduce storage and computing costs in the Data Center, and reduce human review time and fatigue.

- Intel technologies like the OpenVINO™ toolkit make it easy to develop, deploy, and scale analytics intelligence on a variety of hardware platforms that optimize for performance, power, and cost.

The original version of this chapter was previously published without open access. A correction to this chapter is available at https://doi.org/10.1007/978-1-4842-8297-7_9

© Intel 2023, corrected publication 2023
J. Booth et al., *Demystifying Intelligent Multimode Security Systems*,
https://doi.org/10.1007/978-1-4842-8297-7_2

- Intel OpenVINO™ security Add-on (OVSA) solutions can be used to protect valuable analytics applications in transmission, storage, and at runtime. In addition, OVSA can provide privacy protections for video streams and analytics results.

- Foundational Intel Security solutions ensure platform integrity, protect data, provide trusted execution environments, and accelerate end-to-end cryptographic operations.

- Overall security robustness and system efficiency can be improved by taking an end-to-end system approach to security.

- IMSS-using Intel Security technology helps to support new privacy and public policy requirements, laws, and regulations.

- Adding intelligent analytics to edge devices improves privacy protection in IMSS.

- Intel Corporation's advances in AI, memory, and compute device designs drive the future capabilities of IMSS by enabling the use of efficient sensor fusion technologies.

History of Intelligent Multi-modal Security System Solutions

Video 1.0 – Analog Video Technology

Over the past 15 years, new technology has profoundly changed the design of IMSS solutions. Before the 2000s, typical IMSS implementations were built around analog cameras; the recordings they made were spooled to VHS tapes on stand-alone systems. When an incident occurred, a security agent faced a time-intensive process of screening VHS tapes on a video monitor to find an incident. Sharing the video information with another investigator required a security team to manually retrieve a tape and transport it to the next agent, who would then spend even more time scrolling through the VHS tape.

In this analog camera era, security was simple physical security; systems were hardwired and the integrity of the wiring and the recorders and recording media was protected by limiting physical access to the system.

Video 2.0 – IP-Connected Cameras and Video Recorders

Starting in the early 2000s, Physical Security System technology adopted the Internet revolution with the Internet Protocol Camera (IPC), and with it a major shift in the digital recording process: the digital data was now stored on a local server (Networked Video Recorder – NVR) rather than on VHS tapes (Figure 2-1). A local security agent could quickly retrieve an incident while at their desk and decide what to do based on the screening. A digital clip could be forwarded electronically to the next agent in the investigation.

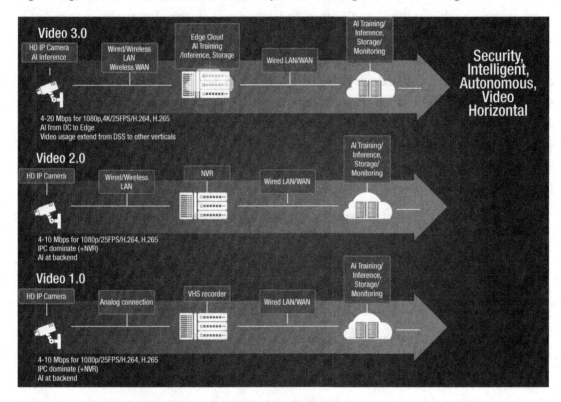

Figure 2-1. *Recent evolution in IMSS system designs*

These systems were installed and maintained mostly by consumers and physical security professionals, not Information Technology security experts. The shift to digital video and IP cameras went unnoticed by remote network attackers for many years, but in 2016, the video systems industry got a wake-up call. Starting in September 2016, the Mirai botnet DDoS attack took down the Akamai host service of Krebs on Security[1] with a

---

[1] https://krebsonsecurity.com/2016/11/akamai-on-the-record-krebsonsecurity-attack/

worldwide botnet of 620 Gbps from more than 600,000 networked devices, most of them being IP cameras and video recorders. This was followed quickly by a similar attack on the DYN servers (Hosting Twitter, Spotify, Reddit, and others) in October 2016. The Mirai botnet exploited IP connected devices with default or fixed remote login credentials.

The next innovation in IMSS brought basic cameras with intelligence in the form of traditional computer vision. However, these system designs placed higher demands on a Data Center for more intelligence and computing power. System designers off-loaded some of these demands by connecting basic cameras with intelligent edge servers, and then connecting those with Data Centers. Today, the new system designs include smart camera technology with intelligence at the sensor, at the edge, and in the Data Center.

The recent releases of Intel vision technology enable moving intelligence to devices at the edge. Intelligent edge devices make it possible to detect and properly annotate objects of interest in the video stream. Such objects (termed "annotated video data") are then transmitted to the Data Centers, where they receive more computationally intensive analysis and operation.

Intelligent edge devices bring four major benefits for system designers in optimizing the system operation:

- The optimal use of network bandwidth and storage resources, as only the relevant data is transmitted to the Data Center for further analysis by discarding irrelevant or redundant data.

- The optimal use of Data Center operators by reviewing only the annotated events, focusing attention on the important tasks.

- The optimal use for review. When an administrator reviews captured and annotated data at the data center, personnel can quickly zero-in on potential areas of interest. This use case does not optimize the use of network bandwidth and storage resources; however, it greatly aids a human reviewer in finding and screening important events.

- The ability to optimize for response latency through local analytics and accuracy through connected high-performance systems in the network edge for the best latency or in data centers for accuracy and performance.

Through the application of edge intelligence, video streams are now annotated with metadata that enables reviewers to find events of significance (e.g., a person of interest). However, as the number of cameras grows, and their resolution increases, more network capacity is required, raising the demand for more processing and storage resources in Data Centers.

In addition, performance and efficiency improvements in edge inferencing, bandwidth constraints and cost, and response latency constraints are driving the migration of analytics from the data center to on-premise edge video recorders, and even to edge cameras. Further bandwidth and storage benefits can be attained when only the frames or regions of interest can be upstreamed rather than the entire video stream.

Current Intelligent Multi-modal Security Systems Solutions

Video 3.0 – Intelligent Cameras and Video Recorders

Today, Intel offers the next evolution in this technology process: E2E Video 3.0. This innovation places compute intelligence in the form of Machine Learning (ML) inferencing at the edge of the Internet. Recent designs prove that the application of analytics to raw data streams at the on-premise edge creates a compelling advantage by improving compute efficiency, reducing latency, and reducing network bandwidth utilization.

Traditional computer vision algorithms worked well when both the target and the environment were well defined. In practice, however, real-life situations are often not clearly defined, and leave unacceptable gaps in certainty. The need for clear identification of objects of interest has driven recent developments in Intel compute systems. This has resulted in the development of hardware accelerators capable of deploying popular Convolutional Neural Network (CNN) models that have been trained to identify anomalies in targets and environments on the edge. Intel has invested heavily in these hardware accelerators to efficiently process computer vision workloads present in similar environments like Autonomous Vehicles, whenever changing environments and situations require close-to-100% certainty in environmental awareness.

Current system solutions employ network link protection, enabled via Open Network Video Interface Forum (ONVIF[2]) standards, to protect the video streams while in transit across the network. While this improves security, it does not address the security inside private networks or on the devices.

Bandwidth and Connectivity

Intel's Visual Computing accelerators for edge analytics have enabled new designs from edge to cloud that is faster and more efficient. Intel devices on the edge and in the Data Center offer a varying degree of power and performance to meet system constraints. This makes it possible for Intel to provide a suite of products that address customer design needs from edge to cloud (see Figure 2-2). With these intelligent edge devices, Intel has altered the type of data being transferred to a Data Center: metadata describing detected events can now be sent in place of or alongside raw data streams depending on design requirements. This pre-analysis and data pre-processing unlock several advantages: it unlocks the potential to reduce the amount of data to be transferred to a Data Center, increases the amount of network bandwidth for other functions or more metadata streams, and also increases the usefulness of the data at the Data Center.

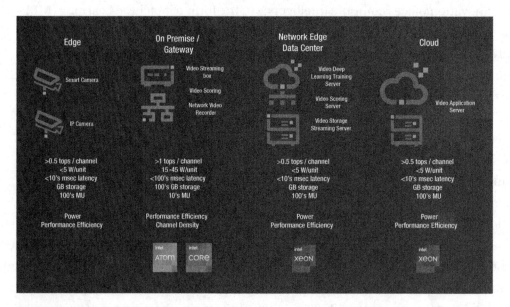

Figure 2-2. *Key performance improvements at each stage in an intelligent video system design*

---

[2]`www.onvif.org/`

It matters where the analytics are located in a computer system design. A system design with intelligent video system capabilities that is placed at the edge helps to balance the overall compute performance. Consider what happens when analytics are embedded into edge sensor compute devices; for example, in the form of a field programmable gate array (FPGA). When an analytics application is installed in an edge device, the device can reduce the raw data streams into actionable metadata for Data Center analysts. This changes the analyst's role from that of a performer of forensics analysis (searching data streams to analyze past events) to a decision maker (reviewing actionable metadata in near-real-time).

Cost/Power/Performance

Most Camera systems use Power over Ethernet (PoE) to minimize installation infrastructure complexity and cost. The lowest cost POE (type 1) supplies 13W to the camera. After power supply efficiency, there is about 10W available to camera electronics. Adding intelligence to these devices can be challenging to fit in the 10W constraint. As a result, many of the older designs require an extensive and expensive infrastructure redesign to be used in an edge device analytics environment.

Today's new edge-based camera designs require only about 4–6 watts of power for a system on a chip that includes onboard analytics, as Figure 2-2 shows. Networked video recorders at the network edge for processing more streams or networks that require more processing capacity use less power and therefore have a better Total Cost of Ownership. Being able to fit analytics capabilities in a camera or NVR power constraint results in a reduced workload in the Data Center. This can be counted as a reduction in power demand and corresponding cooling demand for the Data Center, reducing the Total Cost of Ownership (TCO). Power efficient analytics engines can also be used in the data center, reducing the TCO of data centers that run analytics or Video Analytics as a Service (VAaaS) in public cloud centers.

The efficacy of the current generation machine learning accelerators brings additional benefits in response latency and in security.

Time-sensitive applications such as access controls that depend on recognition from a video camera can be performed locally, reducing the latency for system response. This improves efficiency and safety by reducing action response latency in the system.

Security is also improved in cases where privacy is critical. Analytics and high efficiency cryptographic functions in the camera can now enable new modes of privacy protection where video is never seen outside of the camera in an unprotected form.

Ease of Development, Deployment, and Scaling

Intel offers several toolkits that streamline the effort required to develop and deploy an intelligent video system design at the edge. Intel's OpenVINO™ toolkit[3] enables software vendors and Original Equipment Manufacturers (OEMs) to easily and quickly deploy their pre-trained Vision-based CNNs to a variety of Intel-based accelerators: central processing units (CPUs), graphics processing units (GPUs), FPGAs, and visual processing unit (VPUs). The OpenVINO toolkit greatly reduces the time-to-deployment because it eliminates the need to redesign hardware and software architectures through its Inference Engine that does a load time compilation targeting existing Intel technologies with optimized kernels. The OpenVINO toolkit includes optimized calls for OpenCV* and OpenVX*, and provides support for the popular Deep Learning frameworks like Tensorflow* and Caffe*.

Today, the Intel OpenVINO™ toolkit (Figure 2-3) can be used to port a customer-pre-trained, Vision-based CNN (on supported frameworks and architectures) into OpenVINO's Intermediate Representation (IR). The model's IR can then be deployed at load time to a multiplicity of compute node types, including Intel® Xeon® processors, Core Processors, Atom processors, GPUs, FPGAs, and VPUs. Through the model's IR, the OpenVINO toolkit has the ability to automatically optimize the system for best performance. The OpenVINO toolkit offers several advantages to developers:

- Architecture agnostic: Operation with major frameworks

- Performance: High performance and high efficiency solutions for edge-based computing

- Portability: Cross-platform flexibility via hardware abstraction

---

[3] https://software.intel.com/OpenVINO-Toolkit

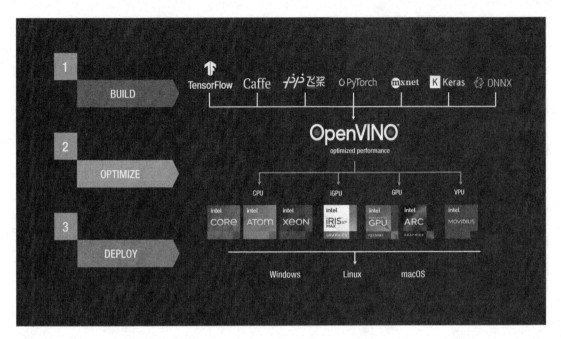

Figure 2-3. *Intel OpenVINO™ toolkit – visual inferencing and neural network optimization*

The Intel OpenVINO toolkit libraries are capable of mapping analytics applications to specific architectures quickly and in an optimal manner. It is not uncommon for a customer application running on an older machine to see a significant increase in speed when the application is ported onto a supported processing unit. The Intel OpenVINO toolkit is designed to survey the system environment, determine what inferencing compute resources are available, and customize the model deployment to gain optimal performance or maximize power efficiency.

Figure 2-4 shows a simple recipe for IMSS designs that include distributed inference at the gateway/edge/endpoint. Start with an Intel CPU, then add targeted acceleration for higher throughput and/or throughput per watt. Intel-integrated graphics processor boosts throughput and is generally available in Intel® Core processors. Specialized Intel processors, including the Intel® Movidius™ Vision Processing Unit,[4] are targeted for computer vision.

---

[4] www.intel.com/content/www/us/en/artificial-intelligence/hardware.html

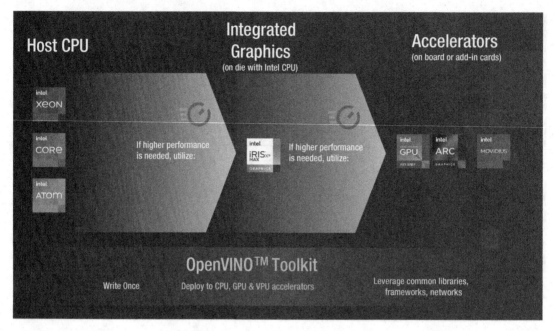

Figure 2-4. *Components and software support within the Intel OpenVINO™ toolkit*

Next-Generation Intelligent Multi-modal Security Systems Solutions

Intel expects IMSS system solutions in the future to continue moving analytics capabilities out to the edge of computing environments. As an example, a facial recognition application could run today on a system that uses edge-based analytics. The metadata generated by the edge-computing analytics could be fed into a series of mobile edge-based servers (see Figure 2-5). This design would give quick access to a database of information, equip security agents with near real-time access to facial recognition results, and allow for near real-time response through the network.

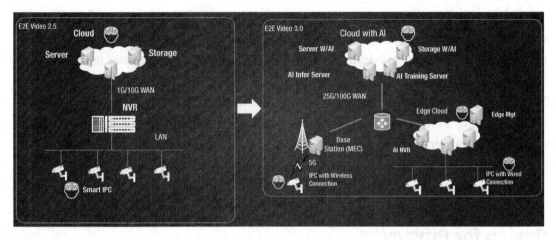

Figure 2-5. *Edge server networks will evolve as 5G networking takes hold*

There has been a robust discussion in industry circles concerning the optimal partitioning of intelligence at the edge as opposed to in the Cloud (Data Center). The results of some recent customer applications have suggested several key advantages in placing intelligence at the edge of the compute environment:

- Data Centers see a lower demand for power and, as a result, a lower demand for cooling.

- Time to actionable data is reduced; agents can make almost real-time decisions.

- Network communications traffic is minimized.

- Privacy and security are improved by reducing the exposure of content and personally identifying data.

Impact of Memory and Compute Improvements

New, high density, persistent memory and storage technologies are enabling new optimizations in IMSS implementations. Changes in data storage density and R/W energy make it easier to include storage in edge devices such as NVRs and Cameras. New optimizations in IMSS are being driven by the changes in the latency and bandwidth of memory access along with different R/W lifetimes and energy cost.

Dramatic improvements are being made in compute capabilities from edge to cloud with an increased emphasis on heterogeneous compute platforms that are specialized to perform certain tasks. In addition, these compute platforms will continue to push the limits of performance at lower power envelopes.

Combining heterogeneous compute with new memory hierarchies can further improve performance and power efficiency when the architecture of computation and memory are combined to provide reduced latency and higher bandwidth to memory. There is an additional security benefit to on-die memory storage when the data transfers are unobservable.

Design for Privacy

Data privacy remains a hot topic in many parts of society and is typically driven by regional regulations. Regulations like the EU General Data Protection Regulation (GDPR)[5] and privacy regulations in many US states enforce strict privacy rules protecting the rights of subjects whose images are captured on edge devices (often accompanied by stiff penalties for non-compliance). The GDPR, for example, stipulates that the data subject must give a consent to the processing of his or her personal data – in the IMSS use-case, images – for it to be a lawful basis for processing. In addition, the data subject is afforded the right to access and request the erasure of any personal data related to them within a given period.[6] GDPR also mandates that personal data is lawful for use by authorized personnel under specific circumstances. Hence IMSS must support both personal privacy and provide authorized access to personal identifying information under strict controls for the public's benefit. Failure to comply with the GDPR is punishable by fines of up to 4% of the violators' annual gross revenue.

Our opinion is that the GDPR stipulates the privacy framework well, plus much of the new legislation (for example, the UK data protection Act of 2018 and the California Consumer Privacy Act of 2018) is similar to the GDPR, therefore the GDPR definitions and text will be used here as a reference.

---

[5] https://eur-lex.europa.eu/legal-content/EN/TXT/HTML/?uri=CELEX:32016R0679&from=EN

[6] _

Personal data

Personal data is any information related to an identified or identifiable person (PII). This can be a name, identification numbers or tokens, location, physical, physiological, genetic, mental, economic, cultural, or social identity.

Processing

Processing means operations on personal data such as collection, organization, recording, structuring, storage, adaptation or alteration, retrieval, consultation, use, disclosure by transmission, dissemination or otherwise making available, alignment or combination, restriction, erasure or destruction. Processing also includes profiling; using personal data to evaluate personal aspects such as work performance, economic situation, health, personal preferences, interests, reliability, behavior, location, or movements.

Protection

The GDPR requires that appropriate technical measures with due regard to the state of the art are taken to ensure that data controllers and data processors are able to fulfill their data protection obligations. Under the definitions of GDPR, video streams and images captured from video streams are the input data for analytics processing which extract biometric data for the purpose of uniquely identifying a natural person. These biometric data are a special category of personal data. The GDPR requires personal data to be protected against unauthorized or unlawful processing.

Protection Security guidelines

The following is a summarization of the security requirements regarding the protection of personal data. These have been collated and simplified from the GDPR text.

- Data protection by design
- Data protection by default
- Minimizing processing of personal data
- Pseudonymizing personal data as soon as possible

- Transparency with regard to the functions and processing of personal data

- Enabling the data subject to monitor the data processing

- Enabling the controller to create and improve security features

- Services and applications should be encouraged to take into account the right to data protection when developing and designing such products, services, and applications and, with due regard to the state of the art, to make sure that controllers and processors are able to fulfill their data protection obligations.

- Storage time limitation

- Ensure that by default, personal data are not made accessible without the individual's intervention to an indefinite number of natural persons

- Ensure the ongoing confidentiality, integrity, availability, and resilience of processing systems and services

- Ensure the ability to restore the availability and access to personal data in a timely manner in the event of a physical or technical incident

- Include a process for regularly testing, assessing, and evaluating the effectiveness of technical and organizational measures for ensuring the security of the processing.

- Render the personal data unintelligible to any person who is not authorized to access it, leveraging cryptographic capabilities such as encryption.

So, what does all this mean? The system technology must provide state-of-the-art standard of care for the video streams and especially for the machine learning analytics results that are personally identifying. The data must be confidentiality protected when at rest and when in transit throughout the life cycle and processing path. In the next section, you will read how these systems are designed, and how the security features support these requirements.

Principle IMSS System Components

Following the general description of an IMSS, the principal components: a smart camera, network video analytics recorder, edge server, and operations data center server are described. Figure 2-6 illustrates the major processing devices in an end-to-end IMSS. Video is generated in cameras, transmitted over the ethernet to a networked video recorder, stored in an edge server, and transmitted upstream to an operations center, to a cloud server running video analytics as a service, and to remote viewers using client devices.

IMSS System View

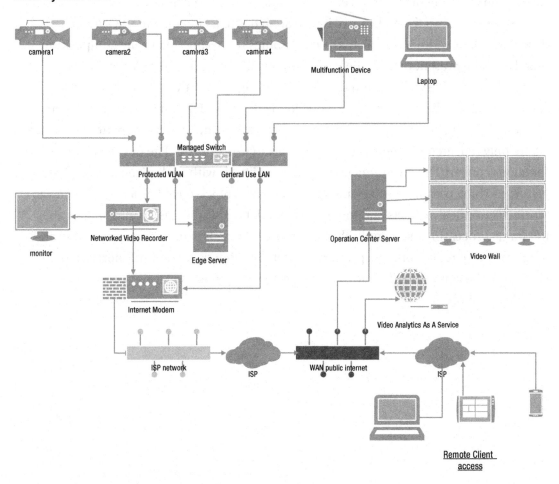

Figure 2-6. *IMSS topology*

IMSS System View

Cybersecurity is a key element in any IMSS, particularly when the system is connected to the public Internet for flexible access to the video streams. Not only is it important to provide confidentiality and privacy by encrypting the video transmitted via the ethernet but also security within the devices is critical for a fully robust security system.

Smart IP Camera

You learned about the generational progress of cameras earlier in this chapter. Now we will go into more detail about the emerging Video 3.0 smart cameras.

Figure 2-7 shows the addition of image analytics (earning the Smart Camera designation). In addition to the analytics, graphics rendering (including composition blend) may be present to label the video and overlay graphics such as a region of interest box. The basic IP camera functions from Figure 2-7 are the lens and image sensor, image synthesis, processing, and video encoding. The lens system focuses an image on the sensor through a color filter array. This produces a Bayer patterned image where only red, green, or blue is sensed in a given sensor pixel. The image synthesis functions convert The Bayer image to a full color image with each pixel having a red, green, and blue component. The image is then given block-based processing to dewarp (correct for optical artifacts and motion artifacts). Finally, there is a function that does full frame processing using multiple input frames: high dynamic range processing and temporal noise reduction. The primary output is encoded video over Ethernet (so the video must be compressed). The optional display output is used for installation and troubleshooting.

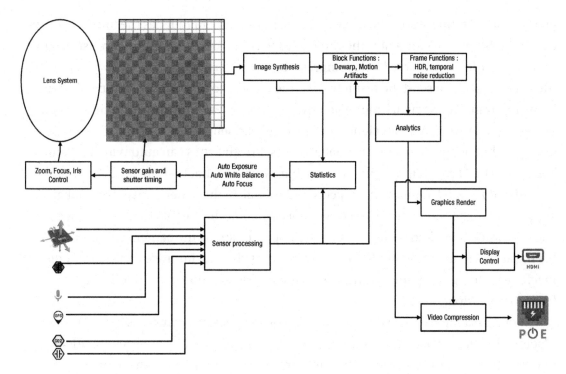

Figure 2-7. *Smart camera*

The sensor processing, statistics, exposure, white balance, focus, sensor control, and lens control functions are standard mandatory elements of a camera.

Once a video stream is compressed, it can be protected for the upstream link to an edge video recorder or server or the cloud with link protection under ONVIF standards.

Analytics performed in the camera are characterized by latency sensitivity constraints and by the value proposition of performing analytics on uncompressed video streams.

An example of an analytics function that requires low latency is license plate recognition. To recognize a license plate, the plate must first be detected (located in the frame), tracked until the size of the license plate fits the accuracy required for recognition, whereupon a hi-resolution image of just the plate is sent to the recognition application. The latency between the initial image capture, object detection, and the region of interest capture for recognition is critical because if it is too long, the region of interest capture will fail (because the object will already be gone). In this example, the loop time constraint is determined by the speed the object is moving, the largest distance from the camera that the object can be detected, and the point when the object is out of frame. Performing the function in the camera reduces the time response constraint because it eliminates the time delay to compress the video and transmit it to a video recorder or server to be decompressed, run through the analytics application, track the object, and send the result back to the camera to identify the region of interest in the raw frame at the right time. When the function is less constrained by time, it can be performed with a more efficient processor, further benefitting in accuracy because the algorithm operates on the raw image frames. ML analytics can automate the Pan-Tilt-Zoom (PTZ) capability of cameras, raising assurance that they are always pointed toward and zoomed in on critical objects and events. In the general case, any analytics application that is interacting in a closed loop with objects benefits from the reduced latency. A side benefit to performing analytics processing in the camera comes from having access to the pre-compressed video frames. This can improve the accuracy of machine learning compared to analysis after compression due to the additional noise from compression.

Another example of the value proposition of analytics in a camera is to use a Machine Learning algorithm to determine where to optimize the compression bitstream budget, increasing the visual quality of important objects, and reducing quality elsewhere to make the best use of ethernet bandwidth and stream storage footprint.

The basic level of security for the video stream and metadata from the camera is provided by encrypting and optionally cryptographic hashing of the content. As we will show in later chapters, link protection for the stream is valuable, but does not provide complete protection from all the threats to an IMSS camera.

Network Video Recorder with Analytics

Figure 2-8 is a very simple functional process flow model of an on-premises NVR that is not performing any security functions (shown to highlight the data path processing).

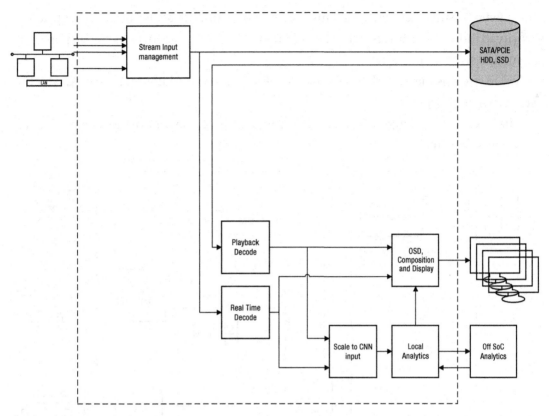

Figure 2-8. *On-premises NVR, no security features*

The boundary indicated by the dashed line is the boundary of the System on a Chip (SoC) CPU. The compressed video streams from the cameras enter through a stream management function via an Ethernet LAN connection. The streams are spooled to storage (generally a hard disk drive or solid state drive) and fed to a real time decode processing function. After the compressed streams are decoded (or decompressed), the image frames are scaled to the frame size of the neural network before performing analytics functions such as object detection and classification. The analytics function may be performed locally, with an external accelerator, or the processing may be split across both. The metadata from the analytics will be stored and used to generate graphics elements that are composited (overlayed) with the video stream as it is sent to the display for viewing. The graphic elements may range from a simple text overlay indicating the video source location to simple rectangular bounding boxes with a text field, to complex semitransparent object overlays to call attention to objects of interest. For simplicity, this example does not include storage or subsequent transmission of

25

the analytics results metadata. Systems that are doing that must also apply appropriate security to those data objects (which would meet the same objectives as the display output and stream output).

Video streams that have been stored can also be retrieved later for playback, which uses the same processes.

The process flow diagram in Figure 2-9 adds a remote user or upstream capability to the process flow in Figure 2-8.

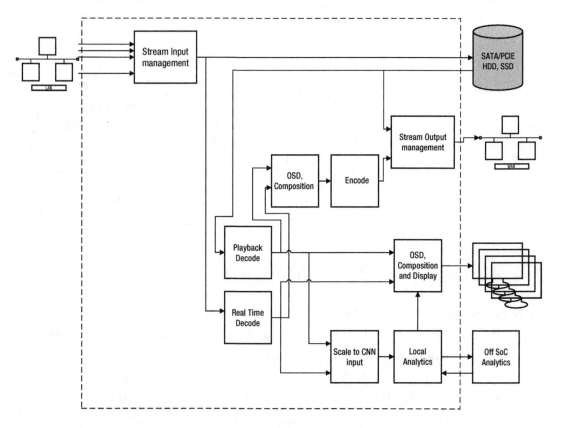

Figure 2-9. *On-premises NVR with remote user/upstream link*

Again, there are no security functions shown here to emphasize the data processing tasks. This adds stream output management process and an additional OSD composition task. Because the remote user connects to the NVR via a Wide Area Network (WAN) connection for viewing via a simple player application, the video stream must be encoded (or compressed). The raw stream will be composited with graphics derived from the analytics results as described previously. Raw video streams can also be sent from storage via WAN to a user or to an upstream video server, data center, or an operations center with no analytics analysis.

Figure 2-10 introduces the added functions in an NVR to include full confidentiality and integrity protections for the video streams and analytics data. This will be described in detail later in the context of a complete processing implementation and a complete security implementation.

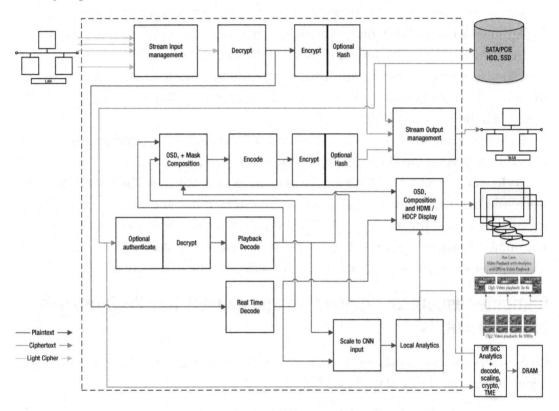

Figure 2-10. *NVR with security and privacy rights management*

For this example, the security functions are included. Unprotected or cleartext streams are shown in red and protected or ciphertext streams are shown in green. When the camera sends the streams to the video recorder, they are confidentiality protected by encrypting the streams in an SSL/TLS session. These must be decrypted for processing and for storage (after having been re-encrypted with a storage device key). Note that the encryption is done inside the SoC to protect the stream on the external datapath to the storage. If it is encrypted in the storage system, it will protect from theft of the disk but will not protect against an observer on the bus.

Real-time streams, having been decrypted, are ready for decoding before running analytics or displaying them. Streams from storage (secured with the storage key) must be decrypted before the playback decode task.

Local analytics has access to both real time and playback streams in plaintext. If the streams are to be processed in an off chip analytics accelerator, the streams must be encrypted to protect them on the public bus between the SoC and accelerator.

When streams have been composited with the graphics as described earlier, the display interface uses HDCP protection to prevent cloning or copying the streams being sent over the HDMI or DP interface to the local display.

Likewise, when the streams are upstreamed to another server or to a remote user, the stream is encrypted to protect the confidentiality and privacy of the information in the stream and the analytics results.

So in this example, video streams that are transported over interfaces that are physically accessible are always protected with encryption.

NVRs will consume from 8 streams to as many as 200+ streams. The amount of local storage depends on customer's design choices on storage cost and the amount of time required to retrieve streams for forensic investigation and sometimes as required by law. The number of streams processed by analytics, viewed, and upstreamed also depends on customer's design choices, optimized as described in the next section.

Compute resources – General to Specialized, Key Performance Indicators (KPIs)

Compute resources are assigned to the processes in the task graph of Figure 2-10, depending on the choice of workload for

- The number of video streams input to the platform

- The number of streams stored

- The number of live and recorded streams played back

- The number of streams processed with Machine Learning analytics

- The number of streams post-processed adding graphics elements representing the result of the analytics

- The number of streams viewed on local displays

- The number of streams upstreamed or viewed remotely on a client device via the Internet

Tradeoffs between cost, performance, and power are made to optimize a system for these three constraints to meet the preceding workload attributes. For example, analytics can be performed on a CPU at lower Bill Of Materials (BOM) cost, but higher cost efficiency measured in frames per second per watt. When a GPU is available, better performance at lower power is available at no cost if the GPU is otherwise lightly loaded. Higher performance and performance efficiency are realized with dedicated Machine Learning inferencing processors such as FPGAs and VPU accelerators. However, adding these accelerators will increase system cost and may increase overall system power use while still improving the performance per watt. The critical consideration for devices that are energy- or power supply-limited is that the only way to get more overall performance is through improvements in efficiency. For example, if the device is limited to 25 watts and you need 10 watts to process one video stream on a CPU, you will be limited to 2 video streams. However, if you can process a stream using a high efficiency dedicated Machine Learning accelerator for 2 watts per stream, you can process 12 video streams.

The security workload can also vary dramatically depending on how the protection for the video streams and analytics metadata is managed at the system level. Using link and storage protection requires multiple decrypt/encrypt operations, whereas encryption keys assigned to the streams rather than the links will eliminate the redundant operations required to change keys. More detail on this is discussed in Chapters 5 and 7.

Edge Server

Edge Servers will generally ingest up to several hundred streams. While the primary role of an edge server is storage, edge servers can also provide analytics processing and display functions. The task graph for an edge server will look like the video recorder task graph from Figure 2-10, but will balance the workload differently to optimize for the storage function.

Operations Data Center Server

Operational data centers will ingest up to thousands of streams and may display hundreds of video streams.

In the operational center, human operators have difficulty remaining attentive to video streams for more than 20 minutes,[7] and the detection accuracy decreases when the number of streams to be monitored increases, dropping to ~50% for nine streams.[8] Machine Learning analytics provides valuable workload reduction for the operators by analyzing the streams for events that require human attention and judgment, enabling the operators to focus attention on critical events.

Machine Learning analytics is applied in data centers for after-the-fact (forensic) analysis requiring complex analytics. Investigations are performed when a critical event becomes known, often weeks after it occurred. Analytics can help to quickly locate the content that leads to law enforcement actions.

Functions such as tracking a person or vehicle across a large area scene observed by many cameras are often performed in operations centers because the aggregation of a large number of video streams is mandatory.

Another important application suited to operational centers is situational awareness. For this capability, sensor fusion can be performed in conjunction with an ML application to combine input from multiple cameras, audio sensors, environmental sensors, and scene state data to provide a rich, big data estimate with improved accuracy compared to any sensor alone. High quality situational awareness shifts the response from forensics to real time response to critical events.

Security principles must be applied across the complete end-to-end system to address gaps, weaknesses, and vulnerabilities that compromise the overall system security, that is, the system is only as secure as its weakest link.

End-to-End Security

As shown in Figure 2-11, security is proportional to the value of the assets in the system, therefore a diligent analysis is required for tradeoffs and the associated complexity.

Figure 2-11. *Cost of security*

---

[7] Video Surveillance Techniques and Technologies – Google Books

[8] How many monitors should a CCTV operator view? – December 2004 – Leaderware – Hi-Tech Security Solutions (securitysa.com)

The exponential growth of devices (projected to reach 50 billion) is driving a demand for security from the cloud to the sensor device edge. Secure processing has become necessary, and the degree of security required will vary depending on customer needs. In a security spectrum, commercial customers today have less of a demand as compared to Defense/Government customers, which often have the highest security needs. Defense customers are often concerned with physical security threats to their systems. To obtain the highest levels of security today, customers often pay a large price that is often commensurate with the criticality of the information that is being protected.

IMSS's span this security continuum. Depending on the installation environment, and the risks related to system availability and accuracy, the required security level and the resulting implementation and maintenance costs vary accordingly.

Threats are constantly evolving and changing. Hackers and exploiters are no longer content with exploitations at the application or at the operating system (OS) level. They are working around the applications that would normally provide some indication that something is wrong. Attackers are digging their way into the boot code, communication channels, and compromising the integrity of the physical interfaces on the system. Once they obtain access, they cause physical changes that cause havoc on systems, or at minimum, cause unpredictable behavior that results in inadvertent release of information that can be used in the next level of exploitation. These threats are driving security and performance enhancements needed in both commercial and government ecosystems to stay ahead of the adversaries.

Solutions that provide security and enable trust have become increasingly necessary. It is increasingly important for customers to have systems that can reliably process what is expected, when it is expected, for as long as it is expected, and can discriminate against both malicious processes and malicious circuitry. Customers are driving demand for solutions that allow them to design trust into their systems, while providing additional security capabilities against exploitation.

The representative attack surfaces and the possible threat exposures are shown in Figure 2-12. The trends are indicating that the attacks are progressing down the stack from applications to operating system to hypervisors to firmware and eventually to hardware. The attack surfaces at different layers in the stack expose multiple threats. As an example, the booting of a device with unauthorized firmware will render the defenses above that layer in the stack weaker, resulting in a compromised system that's hard to recover.

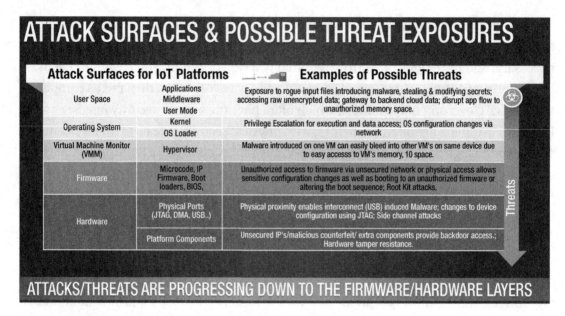

Figure 2-12. *Attack surfaces and evolving threat exposure*

Intel has spent a great deal of time and effort in designing computer systems that can be secure. That effort has brought changes to many design aspects of computer systems, including:

- How systems identify themselves on the network (an immutable and unchangeable ID)

- How systems do a secure boot

- How systems protect information on local storage devices

- How systems create and manage trusted run-time environments

- How systems protect access to security keys

- How systems encrypt and decrypt messages

- How systems perform Intra- and Inter-communication within a platform

- How systems manage authority certificates

- How systems manage communications channels

The changes in security and the evolving threats have resulted in the release of Intel Security Essentials as shown in Figure 2-13. Intel technology is mapped to the areas that Intel considers to be the four core security capabilities. All vendors must enable these core capabilities at different layers, and the capabilities must be enabled at the right layers by the right entities. The Intel mapped technologies include:

- **Platform Integrity** – Includes Intel˙ Boot Guard, Intel˙ PTT, discrete TPM support, and others.

- **Protected Data, Key, and ID** – Provides protected storage like Intel PTT, Discrete TPM, and total memory encryption (TME) that guards against frozen DRAM attacks.

- **Trusted Execution** – Protects the runtime environment and application memory with solutions like Software Guard Extensions, MKTME, and others.

- **Crypto Acceleration** – Includes particular crypto operations that perform AES encryptions/decryption and SHA for sign/verify operations, and Secure Key which includes a random number generator to create keys.

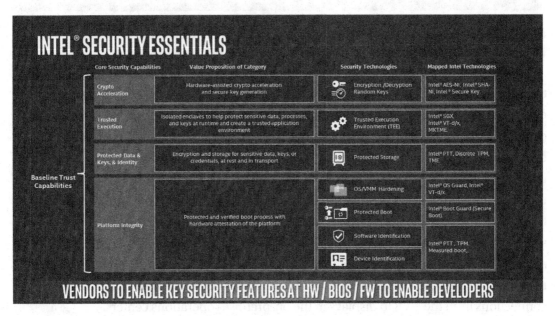

Figure 2-13. *Intel core security capabilities baseline for trusted systems*

Figure 2-14 shows a simplified surveillance use case with end-to-end flow of data from the edge devices to the cloud. The smart cameras (on the left) generate live video streams and send it to the network video recorder (in the middle), which could be analyzing some data from the video streams. The endpoints (on the right) receive the data and store it, display it, or upload it to the cloud.

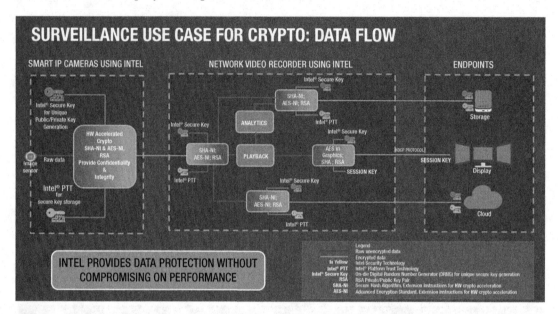

Figure 2-14. *Example of encryption in a surveillance use case*

In Figure 2-14, there are several areas where crypto capabilities are required to protect the data in transit. Encrypted data is shown in green; several areas may require data encryption while the data is in transit. In this simple surveillance system, Intel technology can protect the video streams and analytics data throughout the system. For example, data streams sent from the camera to the Network Video Recorder (NVR) can be protected using Secure Real Time Streaming Protocol streaming protocol under ONVIF or with a VPN tunnel to the NVR. This is especially important when using cameras on a publicly accessible transmission means like the Internet. In addition, protection can be applied to the data sent to storage (providing at-rest protection) by using storage encryption or per-stream encryption. When data is up-streamed to an operation center or a cloud, the video and metadata can be protected using HDCP encryption; this protection is included in HDMI connections from the NVR to displays in the on-premises operations centers.

In Chapter 7, we will see how the overall security of an IMSS can be improved over this basic level of security.

Cost Overheads for Security

Applying security in the data path has some performance implications due to latency from cryptographic operations such as encrypt/decrypt and sign/verify operations. The key generation may not be as impacted due to infrequent nature of such operations.

Intel® QuickAssist Technology (Intel® QAT) on server platforms accelerates and compresses cryptographic workloads by offloading the cryptographic operations to hardware capable of optimizing those functions. This makes it easier for developers to integrate built-in cryptographic accelerators into network and security applications.

- Symmetric cryptography functions include: Cipher operations (AES, DES, 3DES, ARC4); Wireless (Kasumi, Snow, 3G); Hash/Authenticate operations (SHA-1, MD5, SHA-2 [SHA-224, SHA-256, SHA-384, SHA-512]); Authentication (HMAC, AES-XCBC, AES-CCM); Random number generation.

- Public Key Functions include: RSA operation; Diffie-Hellman operation; Digital signature standard operation; Key derivation operation; Elliptic curve cryptography (ECDSA and ECDH) Random number generation and price number testing.

- Compression/Decompression include: DEFLATE (Lempel-Ziv 77)

Confidentiality, Integrity, Availability

These principles can be implemented using the AES-NI, SHA-NI, and DRNG CPU instructions at high performance. The protection at runtime for code and data can be achieved with Trusted Execution Environments such as virtual machines or with Software Guard Extensions (SGX). SGX technology can also be used to protect the Intellectual Property of the ML/DL models-related assets such as labels, features, models, training data, etc. Emerging memory encryption technologies provide protection for the workloads and data as they are written, stored, and read in DRAM. Relevant firmware over the air (FOTA) and software over the air (SOTA) updates can be deployed to improve the availability of the platform and handle the patching required to mitigate the security incidents.

Confidentiality, integrity, and availability are also critical for protecting the video streams and the analytics results. Privacy requirements will use the confidentiality benefits from the cryptographic accelerators, CPU instructions, and trusted execution capabilities. For usages in criminal prosecutions and in applications where the integrity of the video and metadata is critical, these capabilities also are mandatory.

Secure Data Storage

Intel Platform Trust Technology (PTT) or a discrete Trusted Platform Module (TPM) can be leveraged for storing the data and keys securely tethered to Silicon and paired with the platform. These keys are used to encrypt/decrypt the data stored on the mass storage volume.

Conclusion

In this chapter, we explored the historical transformations of IMSS technologies and introduced how Intel is changing the future by driving pertinent changes end-to-end from edge devices, on the network edge, and in the cloud. We also described an IMSS with a focus on E2E security and articulated the Intel security assets to leverage and build a robust IMSS system.

The IMSS domain doesn't exist in a vacuum, the next chapter provides a detailed discussion of the relevant technologies in a surveillance system.

- Basic Image Synthesis and Video Processing functions

- Breakdown is important to understand how they work and will be secured (what is the value they get out of it)

- Standard Computer Vision and Machine Learning functions

- Provide standard of care Cybersecurity (pragmatic, yet robust)

CHAPTER 3

Architecting and E2E IMSS Pipeline

What Does It Take?

Goal: Define and dissect the data pipeline with focus on key criteria and enable the reader to understand the mapping of this pipeline to Intel hardware and software blocks. With this knowledge, the reader will also be equipped with knowledge to optimize the partition and future-proof with security and manageability.

- Key considerations and elements in architecting a data pipeline

- Basic tasks of a E2E IMSS pipeline – Capture, Storage, and Display

- Evolution of IMSS Systems – Analog to Digital to Connected to Intelligent

- Sensing the World – Video and Beyond

- Making Sense of the World – Algorithms, Neural Networks, and Metadata

- Architecting IMSS Systems – IP Cameras, Network Video Recorders (NVRs), and Accelerators

The chapter will start by defining the purpose of a data pipeline, the key elements of the pipeline and the key criteria for specifying a data pipeline. The next section will describe the types of data comprising a data pipeline, key characteristics of the data types, and the relationship of the data types to each other. The final section will apply the data pipeline concept to the fundamental system architectures commonly used in the

The original version of this chapter was previously published without open access. A correction to this chapter is available at https://doi.org/10.1007/978-1-4842-8297-7_9

J. Booth et al., *Demystifying Intelligent Multimode Security Systems*,
https://doi.org/10.1007/978-1-4842-8297-7_3

IMSS space and demonstrate how IMSS systems are evolving. This builds the foundation for the subsequent chapter describing the attack models on IMSS systems and how to mitigate the attacks.

IMSS Data Pipeline Terminology

Abbr	Term	Definition
	Pipeline	A complete description of the data elements, processing steps, and resources required to implement an IMSS system
CCTV	Closed-Circuit Television	An analog security system built upon modifications of television standards
CIF, QCIF	(Quarter) Common Interchange Format	Early video standard for analog systems – CIF = 352x288 pixels, QCIF = 176x144 pixels
D1	Television Standard	NTSC Broadcast and DVD television standard of 720x480 pixels at 29.97 frames per second
IMSS	Digital Safety and Security	A system with the primary purpose to enhance the safety and security of information, assets, and/or personnel
	Video Frame	A two-dimensional array of pixels. Frames are typically described in terms of rows (lines) x columns (width). Hence a 1080x1920 frame has 1080 rows and 1920 columns of pixels. The frames may be either progressive (every line in the frame is captured in each frame) or interlaced (every other line is captured in each frame, requiring at least two frames to sample every line in the frame).
FPS	Frames Per Second	The temporal sampling rate of a frame capture oriented video stream is measured in frames per second, that is, number of frames captured per second
ML	Machine Learning	Any of several techniques whereby machines extract information from observing and hence analyzing/processing the real-world data

(continued)

Abbr	Term	Definition
CNN	Convolutional Neural Networks	A specific branch of Machine Learning based on algorithms relying on convolution, that is, multiplication and accumulation as a key operation
	Video	A time sequence of image data, typically image frames captured at rates sufficient for the humans to perceive motion. As used in this context, color images captured from visible light sensors
IP	Intellectual Property	Any knowledge regarding methods, data, processes, or other non-tangible items having value and owned by a legal entity. Often IP will have enforceable rights for use or prevention of use by others.
	Metadata	Information inferred from sensed data or other data sets
	Pixel	Picture Element, a single element of a picture describing the video at a single spatial location. Pixels are arranged in arrays of rows and columns to form a video frame. A pixel may have a single value if grey scale for monochrome frames or three values, for example, RGB, for color frames.
PII	Personally Identifiable Information	The most sensitive type of metadata, often subject to contractual, regulatory, and/or legal controls

Defining the Data Pipeline – Key Concepts

The fundamental purpose of an IMSS system is to sense information in the physical world and allow appropriate actions to be taken based on that information. Accomplishing this purpose is the role of the data pipeline. A typical IMSS system will span several physical locations and several processing steps. Consequently, the data pipeline will also span several physical locations and several logical processing steps or tasks operating on the sensed data.

Defining a data pipeline starts with understanding the key elements of the data pipeline. The elements can be classified into broad categories – the sensed data, the algorithms that transform data into information (metadata), the decisions, D, that are taken based on the metadata and the actions resulting from decisions. Definition of the data pipeline can then be approached as a set of interrelated questions about sensed data, algorithms, metadata, decisions, and actions. This fundamental data pipeline is shown schematically in Figure 3-1.

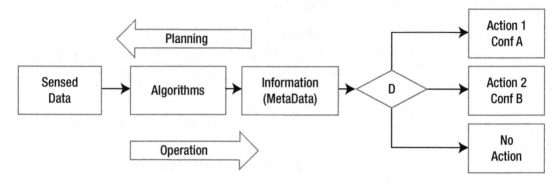

Figure 3-1. *Fundamental data pipeline features*

- What are the desired actions to be taken and at what confidence level?

- What information is needed to make the decisions that will lead to actions being taken?

- What is the sensed data that needs to be gathered from a scene to create that information?

- What are the algorithms required to transform sensed data to information and information into decisions?

A key aspect of the Data Pipeline, Figure 3-1, is that definition should proceed in the opposite direction of the final data flow. In the example shown, what are the desired actions and with what confidence level should each action be taken, with the null case of "No Action" being clearly understood. With this framework in mind, let us look at each of the key questions in more depth.

Desired Actions and Outcomes

The most critical step in the definition of a data pipeline is understanding what actions will be taken because of the system. The more specific and focused the desired actions can be defined, the more precisely the data pipeline can be defined. Ideally, a system has a single, well-defined action or set of actions as the desired outcome. These actions may range from issuing a ticket for traffic violations, to triggering alarms of intrusion in a restricted area, to identifying authorized personnel for a particular activity. By far the most common action is to take no action at all. It is critical to understand the array of events in the real world that will result in no action being taken, especially as these are usually far more numerous than events that will trigger an action. Failure to do so is the leading cause of false negatives, that is, failure to act when action should have been taken.

If you don't know where you are going, then any road will do.

It is common that a single system will have multiple possible actions as outcomes. Based on the same database of real-world information, that database may drive multiple actions (or non-actions). For example, a camera viewing a street scene in an urban area may capture information on the number of vehicles, the presence of pedestrians and the state of the roadway. A traffic bureau may use the data in real time to advise commuters on traffic routes; a developer may use demographic data collected over several weeks to determine if a store of a particular type should be opened in the area and the city repair department may use the information to monitor infrastructure status and schedule maintenance. These all have vastly different goals, but each can be defined in terms of several key criteria to determine the overall system needs.

Accuracy. The single criteria most influencing data pipeline design is accuracy, or the ability to reliably take an action. In principle, to achieve perfect accuracy would require infinite information, driven by the substantial number of unusual or outlier events. While it may seem paradoxical that there are many unusual events, this phenomenon is driven by the observation that to observe, hence comprehend, exceedingly rare events will require enormous amounts of observational data. Again, in principle to observe an event that occurs once in 500 years will require about 500 years of data!

The accuracy specified should be related to the consequence of error or taking the incorrect action. The consequence of taking incorrect action can be further segregated into false positives and false negatives. The consequences of these types of errors are very application dependent, and it is often possible to tune the system to be more tolerant for one type of error than the other.

Accuracy requirements will strongly impact system specifications for the data resolution at which the scene is sampled, the computational complexity requirements of the algorithms to analyze the video, and storage requirements, among others.

Frequency of Actions – Throughput. Another critical factor is determining how often an action needs to be taken. The frequency of taking an action may be either event driven (i.e., act on detection of event A) or may be periodic (take an action every hour). If the action is event driven, it may be necessary to specify the minimum times between successive events in which the system is expected to act or the time interval in which the multiple events must occur (send ticket only if light is red and vehicle is in intersection).

The frequency at which actions must be taken, the throughput, will drive the sample rate of the scene and hence the total amount of data collected. The throughput requirements of the system drive many system parameters such as the total storage required as well as communication bandwidth for local and wide area links.

Latency. A third critical factor in specifying the system goals for acting is the latency from the time the scene is sampled to the time an action is potentially taken. In the urban street scene example, the time span required to act may range from a few seconds to several months.

A system may also have multiple latencies associated with the entire architecture. There may be a latency defined for sensed data capture, a second latency for analytics, and a third for action to be taken. The data capture latency may be determined by the characteristics of the object being sensed – how fast it is moving, how long a traffic light is on, etc. The latency for analytics may be determined by the algorithmic complexity and computational power available. The latency for action may be determined by mechanical constraints of an actuator on factory floor, or reaction time of a human operator.

At the most abstract level, a data pipeline can be thought of as a balance of the factors discussed earlier. A simple example is shown in Figure 3-2 comparing the specifications of two systems on a limited number of attributes. (Note that latency is graphed as 1/Latency such that shorter latencies have higher values). In this case, two actions are considered, each with an associated Accuracy and Confidence Level. A single value for throughput and latency is specified for the systems. In the example shown, System 1 has been optimized for greater accuracy at the sacrifice of throughput and latency relative to System 2. Neither system is "better" than the other; each will be appropriate for a given application.

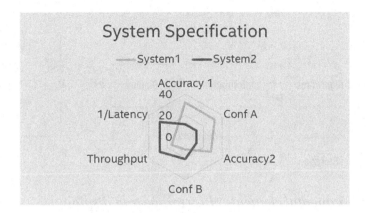

Figure 3-2. *Example system specifications*

At this point, the reader may well ask – why not just specify a "best" system which is the best of both worlds, that is the superset of System1 and System2? The answer is that such a system specification may well violate program constraints such as cost, power, schedule, resources, etc. The "best" system often ends up becoming a camel.

A camel is a horse designed by a committee.

Three Basic Tasks – Storage, Display, and Analytics

To this point, we have described the fundamental data pipeline elements – sensing data, algorithms for analytics, decisions and actions resulting from decisions. In addition to the fundamental elements, two additional elements are often present – storage and display, as in Figure 3-3.

Storage is often required to meet legal and insurance requirements that the data be archived as evidence and available for a specified period. The purpose is to allow retrospective access to the data for analysis of key events of interest and/or provide a legal source of record for evidence purposes. Two types of data are stored – the sensed data, for example, a video stream, and metadata. Metadata is information about the sensed data.

Display is required when the decision-making element is a human operator, D_O. The analytics and decision elements are taken over by the operator, D_O. The default mechanism for providing information to the operator is a visual display. In some installations, the display function may take the form of an array of two or more panels.

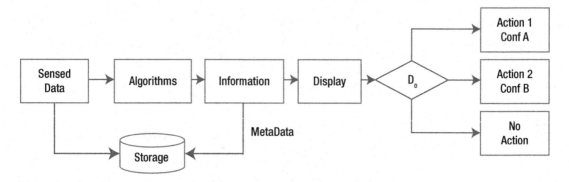

Figure 3-3. *Fundamental elements plus storage and display*

In applications where the decisions are taken by algorithms, the display function may be omitted. This situation will be examined in more detail in the section related to Machine Learning and neural networks.

Basic Datatypes and Relationships – Sensed Data, Algorithms, and Metadata

A Digital Surveillance system operates with diverse types of data, each of which has a specific purpose. When architecting a digital surveillance system, it is necessary to identify the basic data types in the data pipeline. These data types have quite distinctive characteristics and require different treatment in their processing, storage, and protection.

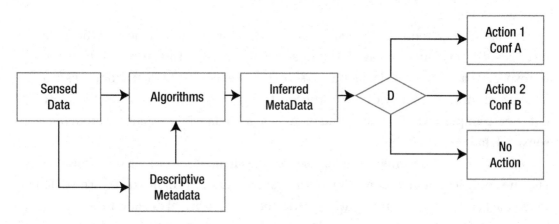

Figure 3-4. *Basic data types and relationships*

The basic data type of sensed data has already been introduced. The sensed data is the information captured about the real world through a sensor and the transforms of that data into a form suitable for analysis. Fundamentally, the information contained in the sensed data is defined at the moment the sensed data is captured. The subsequent transforms of the sensed data do not change the information content, only the representation of the information. The sensed data is typically the largest in terms of quantity. Video data sets can easily reach up to hundreds of Gigabytes (GB) in size. An uncompressed video stream can reach tens of Megabytes (MB) per second and even compressed video can reach several to tens of Megabits per second (Mbps). The sensed data will often contain sensitive information such as Personally Identifiable Information (PII) subject to legal or regulatory control.

The second data type consists of algorithms. While algorithms are normally considered processing elements, when stored or transmitted, the algorithms can be considered a particularly sensitive type of data. The instructions for algorithms are typically represented in computer code. The code is the data type that represents the knowledge of how to transform the sensed data into information. The information output by the algorithm is referred to as Inferred Metadata and will be discussed in detail in the concluding section. The size of the algorithmic data can vary substantially and is stable during the operation of the pipeline. The algorithmic code does not change, though which portions are executed may be dependent on the sensed data. Corruption or tampering of the algorithm may lead to "undefined results" and hence errors in the decision and action elements of the pipeline. Algorithms will often use information in the Descriptive Metadata as an input to properly interpret the structure and format of the sensed data. Additionally, the algorithm itself is often the result of significant investment in its development. The algorithms are often highly valued Intellectual Property (IP) and may comprise a substantial portion of an enterprise's net worth. Combined with the quality of the sensed data, the algorithm is critical in determining the accuracy and confidence level of the information used to take decisions and implement actions.

The final general data type consists of two subtypes: Descriptive Metadata – *information about* the sensed data and Inferred Metadata – *information derived, or inferred*, from the sensed data. Descriptive metadata describes how the sensed data was created, and key traits of the sensed data such as encoding methods. Examples of key traits of the sensed data include key elements such as location, time stamps, file sizes, codecs, and file names. Descriptive metadata enables use of the sensed data and provides context. Descriptive metadata is typically less than 1–2% the size of the sensed data. The descriptive metadata is often embedded into the same file or data structure as the sensed data for ease of reference. Descriptive metadata typically does not contain sensitive information per se, but, if corrupted or tampered with, can affect how the sensed data is interpreted, or if it is even usable.

Inferred metadata is information derived from the sensed data that summarizes or classifies the information content in a more concise form. Typical examples of inferred metadata are identifying objects in a scene such as pedestrian, a vehicle, or the state of a traffic light. Inferred metadata is the information that will be used for making decisions and taking actions. Consequently, the critical characteristics of inferred data are accuracy and confidence level. These are two of the fundamental criteria we defined for describing the data pipeline goals. Corruption or tampering of the inferred metadata, causing errors in accuracy or confidence level of the inferred metadata, will lead to errors in decisions and hence the actions taken. For this reason, the inferred metadata must be accorded the same level of protection as the sensed data. Additionally, the inferred metadata will often contain the same Personally Identifiable Information (PII) as the sensed data. Again, inferred metadata is subject to the same legal or regulatory control.

Fundamental Principle of Computation:
GIGO: Garbage In, Garbage Out

In summary, the three fundamental data types each have unique and critical characteristics and requirements. The interaction of these data types is critical to success of the data pipeline. Furthermore, protection of these elements is critical to the data pipeline operating securely and in a predictable manner.

Table 3-1. *Summary of Data Types and Characteristics*

ATTRIBUTE	SENSED DATA	DESCRIPTIVE METADATA	INFERRED METADATA	ALGORITHMS
SIZE	Large	Small	Small	Variable
THROUGHPUT (BW)	Large	Small	Small	Static
PURPOSE	Contains raw data from real world	Describes raw data	Inferences about real world that are actionable	Transforms raw data into Inferred Metadata

(*continued*)

Table 3-1. (*continued*)

ATTRIBUTE	SENSED DATA	DESCRIPTIVE METADATA	INFERRED METADATA	ALGORITHMS
PII	Yes- but often implicit	No	Yes – explicit	No
PROPRIETRARY ENTERPRISE IP	No	Format standards based, Content Yes	Yes	Yes
INPUT FROM	Sensor	Sensor system	Algorithms	Sensed Data and Descriptive Metadata
OUTPUT TO	Algorithms	Algorithms	Decision	Inferred Metadata

Evolution of IMSS Systems, or a Brief History of Crime

The primary purpose of this text is to describe the architecture and requirements of a modern IMSS system based on video analytics. For many readers, it will be helpful to place the modern system in context with its predecessors to understand the evolution and the motivation for the modern systems.

IMSS 1.0 In the Beginning, There Was Analog…

The very earliest systems were based on analog technology, essentially television on a private system. Prior to IMSS 1.0, security systems were based on either human observers or no surveillance at all. Human observers were able to monitor only one area at a time, and continuous coverage demanded multiple shifts. In addition, humans were subject to errors in recall, attention, etc. The expense of human security systems restricted their use to only high value situations and often only at specific locations such as checkpoints, lobbies, etc.

The analog system architecture is described in Figure 3-5. The system consists of:

- Capture: Video sensors, typically QCIF (176x144 pixels) or CIF (352x288 pixels)

- Camera Connection: Coaxial cable

- Storage – Magnetic tape, for example, VHS tape with one recorder per camera

- Inferred metadata (analysis) – Performed manually by human watching recorded scene

- Decision – Decisions made by human after watching video on a display

The IMSS 1.0 systems offered the advantage that multiple locations could be observed simultaneously for the cost of a camera and a recorder. Further, continuous coverage could be maintained at substantially lower cost than with human observers and a persistent record maintained by the videotape. Further, the recorded video could be used as evidence in legal and other proceedings, without relying on human memory or interpretation.

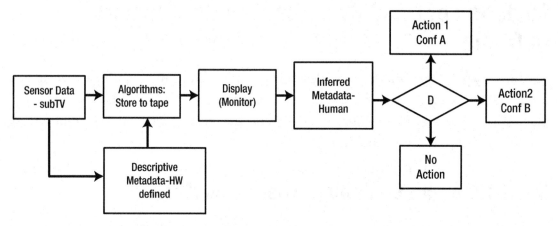

Figure 3-5. *IMSS 1.0 analog system*

IMSS 1.0 systems still suffered from significant drawbacks imposed by the technology. The VHS magnetic tapes possessed limited storage, approximately two to six hours of broadcast quality television. Extending the recording life required reducing the camera resolution from the D1 standard of 720x480 pixels to the CIF and even QCIF referred to previously. In addition, the frame rate was often reduced from the D1 standard 29.97 FPS to a lower value, again to extend recording time on the magnetic tape. Additionally, due to limitations on cable length, the VHS recorder had to be located near the cameras, so retrieval of any data meant traveling to the location being monitored. Finally, there was no real time response – unless the system was monitored by a human observer. The system was primarily retrospective.

IMSS 1.0 systems suffered from additional vulnerabilities and security risks. The limited camera resolution imposed by the storage technology made identification and classification of subjects difficult because of the potential low fidelity of video. The analytics functions were strongly dependent on the human operator, thus leading to inconsistencies in analysis. Tapes were often in unsecured locations and subject to theft or erasure by unskilled persons. While IMSS 10 systems had significant advantages over the previous human-based methods, the disadvantages were the impetus for IMSS 2.0 systems.

IMSS 2.0 …And Then There Was Digital…

The evolution to IMSS 2.0 was driven primarily by the conversion from an analog representation of the video data to a digital representation. A digital representation leveraged the wider computer technology base, enabling greater customization. Storage capacity was no longer dictated by analog television standards, but by the variety of storage capacities provided by the emerging computer industry. A second consequence of conversion to a digital representation was the emergence of video compression technology. Much of the information in a video frame is redundant, varying little from one frame to another.

The key innovation was to change how the information was encoded, going from an analog representation to a digital representation. In an analog representation, the video information is represented by a signal with all possible values between a specified lower bound and an upper bound. Analog encoding required very strict adherence to timing conventions for both the information in a line and the information in a frame, that is, a sequential number of lines that were displayed together. Figure 3-6 compares typical analog and digital video encoding techniques. The intensity of the video signal is represented by relative units designated as IRE (Derived from the initials of the Institute of Radio Engineers), which corresponded to specific values of voltage. Higher values of the IRE corresponded to brighter (whiter) tones and lower values to darker (blacker) tones. The precise correspondence depended on the exact analog system used, requiring substantial calibration to achieve correct results. Additionally, the timing is shown for two representative analog systems, NTSC (primarily US) and PAL (primarily European). The PAL system uses 625 lines of which 576 are used for visible video information; the NTSC system uses 525 lines of which 480 are used for video information. Add in different refresh rates (PAL ~ 50Hz and NTSC ~ 60HZ), and conversion from one system to the other was not for the faint of heart. In summary, the analog encoding system was extremely rigid in practice and limited one to a few standardized choices. The choices were largely dictated by the ultimate display technology to be used.

Conversely, digital encoding was much more flexible and conversion from one format to another (an operation known as transcoding) was considerably more straightforward. A digital frame was represented as an array of M x N pixels, as illustrated on the right-hand side of Figure 3-6. Each square in the array represents one pixel. Each pixel can be described by three numbers, in this example, three values of Red, Green, and Blue. It should be noted that RGB is not the only representation, and indeed, there are other representations which are of practical application. The three values of the pixel are represented by a binary format consisting of 1's and 0's. In this example, eight (8) binary values (bits) are used to represent each value of R, G, or B. This example can then represent 2^8 different values for each color, or 256 hues of a color. For all three colors, with eight bits each 256 * 256 * 256 = ~16.7M different colors are possible with a relatively compact representation. Finally, the waveform for the blue value is shown as a waveform with allowed values of either "0" or "1." The precise voltages corresponding to a "0" or "1" are entirely arbitrary, allowing great flexibility in system design.

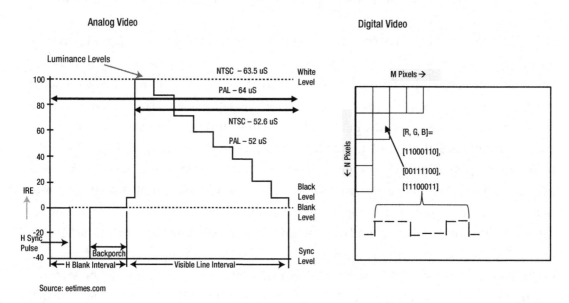

Figure 3-6. *Analog vs. digital video encoding*

The image pixel array size is a flexible parameter for system design and now decoupled from the display choice. Using digital signal processing techniques, the MxN pixel array can be scaled and cropped to fit a wide array of display formats.

While decoupling the sensor capture architecture from the display architecture is a major benefit of digital signal processing, far more important was the ability to apply digital signal processing techniques to the video signal. The ability to detect and remove redundant information to achieve video compression is the most critical feature impacting system architecture. The next section will describe the principles of video compression and the impact on storage, transmission, and display of the video.

Video compression technology used two techniques to retain and store only the critical information. The first technique took advantage of the operation of the human visual system. A well-known example is shown in Figure 3-7, which shows how the human eye perceives frequency vs. contrast, with higher contrast (greater difference between black and white) at the bottom of the graph. As the contrast decreases, the human visual system becomes less able to perceive information. In a digital representation, signal processing can be used to filter out information that humans cannot perceive, and so save storage. The mechanisms will be discussed in more detail in a later section.

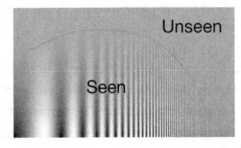

Figure 3-7. *Human visual system (Source: Understandinglowvision.com)*

The second technique relies on the observation that much of the data in two successive video frames is the same. In an analog system, this redundant data must be captured, stored, and recalled for each video frame, leading to a tremendous amount of redundant information.

Figure 3-8 illustrates a typical scene, here composed of a bicyclist traveling along a road with buildings and scenery in the background. Between video frames, the only object changing is the bicycle; all other objects are the same as in the previous frame. Digital signal processing allows the video system to identify which parts of the scene are constant, performing the mathematical equivalent of "Do not Resend this information."

Between these two techniques, it is typical to achieve a data reduction of 50X, that is fifty times less data to be transmitted and stored compared to the uncompressed video stream. As an example, suppose one was capturing a scene at a standard HD resolution of 1280x720 pixels @ 8 bits/pixel (if gray scale image) at a rate of 30 frames per second (fps). The load on the system network bandwidth and storage would be 1280x720x30 fps x 8 bits = 27MB per second. For color imagery, it will be three times this size. Conversely, with compression, the data is reduced to approximately 0.5 MB/s. The actual reduction seen is scene-dependent – scenes with few moving objects and/or less noise will compress better than scenes with the opposite traits.

Figure 3-8. *Redundant video frame information (road, buildings, mountains) and changing information (bicycle)*

As important as compression, the move to the digital domain also permitted encryption of the video data. Encryption is a reversible mathematical process for translating "plaintext," data anyone can read, into "ciphertext," data only those with the correct key and algorithm can read. Ciphers have been employed since antiquity to protect military, commercial, and even scientific secrets. Methods ranged from simple substitution codes to the process illustrated in Figure 3-9 using a common technique of public key/private key within the class of asymmetric cryptography. In the public key/private key example, the public key is published, and anyone can encrypt the data. However, only those with access to the private key can decrypt the data and read the ciphertext.

From a security perspective, the data is now much more secure from tampering and access by unauthorized parties. Only those with the correct key can read the video data. Of course, the data is only as secure as the key. If the key is compromised, then the data is now readable. In IMSS 2.0 systems, the encryption is applied primarily to data in storage, not during the transmission of the data or during the display of the data.

It is important to note that the encryption must be applied *after* the video compression; before encryption, all redundant data patterns are removed. This is necessary to prevent breaking the encryption by examining the cipher text for any patterns that correlate with the plaintext that was input. Encryption techniques depend on mathematical algorithms that map an input symbol to an output symbol based upon the key. In general, the more complex the algorithm, the more complex the key, the more difficult it is to break the code. For the majority of practical IMSS systems, the algorithm is known, documented, and implemented as a standard. This is a requirement for encryption systems such as the public key/private key flow illustrated in Figure 3-9, because the users must know the encryption algorithm. A second motivation is that the encryption throughput is often enhanced by a piece of dedicated hardware; hence the hardware must be designed to precisely execute the algorithm for both decryption and encryption. The result is that the security of the data is entirely dependent on the security of the key. For this reason, the more complex the key, the harder to guess the correct value. Initial deployments utilized 56-bit keys enabling 2^{56} different keys, or about 7.2×10^{16} combinations. Initially thought sufficient, such keys have now been broken with the inexorable advance of computational capabilities, hence are no longer considered secure. Commonly used modern encryption systems have a key minimum of 128 bits, allowing $2^{128} = 3.4 \times 10^{38}$ possible keys making brute force attempts at guessing a key impractical as of this writing. However, the advent of quantum computing foreshadows an evolution to 256-bit keys within the operational lifetime of many systems being designed and deployed today. Security breaches are now centered on securely creating, distributing, and storing the keys.

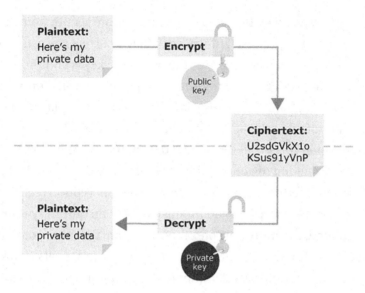

Figure 3-9. *Digital data enables encryption and decryption (Source: ico.org.uk)*

The introduction of digital technology enabled the critical capabilities of separating the video data format from the display technology, video compression, and encryption/decryption. The IMSS 2.0 resulting digital system architecture is described in the following figure. The system consists of:

- Capture: Video sensors, resolution up to HD now possible

- Camera Connection: EtherNet, usually Power over EtherNet (POE)

- Video data compression

- Encryption and Decryption of Video Data

- Storage – Rotating magnetic media, HDD, with multiple cameras per unit

- Inferred metadata (analysis) – Performed manually by human watching recorded scene

- D: Decisions made by a human after watching video on display

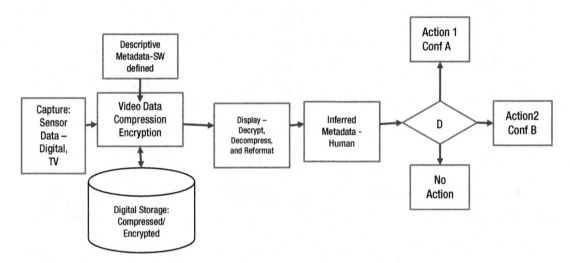

Figure 3-10. *IMSS 2.0 digital system architecture*

IMSS 2.0 systems offered qualitative improvements in system flexibility over the analog IMSS 1.0 systems in several key respects. The higher resolution sensors meant either a wider area of coverage at the same number of pixels on a target or a higher number of pixels on a target for the same coverage. The former required fewer cameras for a given installation; the latter improved image quality and the ability to identify objects more confidently. The ability to tune the video compression algorithm meant longer recording time could be achieved either increasing the video compression ratio for a given amount of storage or increasing the amount of storage purchased. Finally, the number of cameras per recording units may be varied by trading off total recording time and the video algorithm compression. Figure 3-11 schematically represents the flexibility of IMSS 2.0 systems architecture over IMSS 1.0 systems. The arrow indicates increasing values of a quantity. Key to this flexibility is that an objective may often be achieved in more than one way, for example, increase recording time by increasing video algorithm compression or storage.

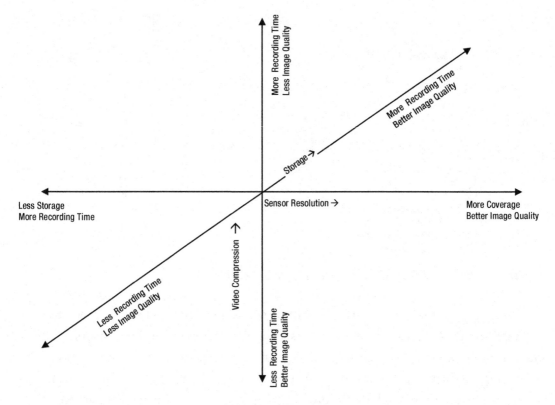

Figure 3-11. *IMSS 2.0 system architecture flexibility*

IMSS 2.0 systems did still retain significant drawbacks with IMSS 1.0 systems. Again, the digital recorder had to be located relatively near the cameras, so retrieval of any data meant traveling to the location being monitored. There was no real time response – unless the system was monitored by a human observer. The analytics functions were still strongly dependent on the human operator, thus leading to inconsistencies in analysis. The system was still primarily retrospective.

In terms of security risks, IMSS 2.0 systems did offer some advantages, but retained significant drawbacks. Analog tape systems required operators to periodically either manually replace or manually rewind the tapes. Consequently, analog video tapes could be viewed and erased by anyone with access to the storage/playback system. Digital storage enabled digital encryption and access methods to be employed. Passwords could be used to restrict viewing and erasing to only authorized personnel. It was also now possible to use automated programs to set the recording time and when previous data would be erased and recorded over. The result was a substantial increase in system availability and robustness. The systems were often installed in unsecured, remote locations and vulnerable to physical tampering or destruction. Techniques as simple as a spray can of paint or fogger could disable a system and evade detection until a human was sent on-site to investigate.

IMSS 3.0 …Better Together – Network Effects…

Many of the deficiencies of IMSS 2.0 systems related to the data being local and inaccessible to remote operators. In smaller systems or high value assets such as critical infrastructure, it is possible to co-locate the IMSS system and the operators, but is not broadly economically feasible. The rise of the Internet enabled adoption by IMSS systems of technology intended for a much broader set of applications. Leveraging the broad technology base enabled cost-effective implementations and integration into the broader IT infrastructure called the Internet.

The key difference between the IMSS 2.0 digital system and the IMSS 3.0 digital systems is extending digital encoding to comprehend the transport of the digital data. In IMSS 2.0 digital systems, the encryption was primarily used to protect stored data; compression was primarily used to make more efficient use of storage media. IMSS 2.0 systems were primarily implemented on dedicated infrastructure over local distances (<<1 km) with known and predictable data patterns. The move to an Internet-centered system architecture meant comprehending the transmission of video data over substantial distances with low latency and on a shared infrastructure. Key to the Internet-based system is error resilience, how to respond to lost or corrupted data.

Breaking Up Is Hard to Do…Packets Everywhere…

The Internet was designed to support a wide variety of applications, hence it was built on flexible structure. A complete description is beyond the scope of this tome, a simplified version will be presented to bring out basic concepts. Figure 3-12 shows four basic components, or layers, that provide the Internet with the necessary flexibility to support a broad range of applications.

Because the Internet is a shared resource, all the information is broken up into packets, or discrete chunks. A packet comprises discrete elements, each of which is used by a different layer of software to accomplish a specific portion of the data transport task. At the heart of the packet is the application data. The application data is determined by the application and could be anything of interest, video or audio or voice or database records. The size of the application data is in theory quite flexible, though in practice, one of a few standard sizes are chosen. This reflects the practice that packet processing is often accelerated by hardware with predefined characteristics such as buffer sizes and register allocations. As an example, for Ethernet protocols, a common packet size is 1500 bytes, a common lower bound is 576 bytes. Even with compression, a consequence is that for practical purposes, all video streams will require multiple packets to be transmitted.

The next element in the packet is the Transport Control Protocol, commonly referred to as the TCP. Transmission may fail in one of two ways – either data corruption or losing a packet in transit. The element contains information regarding detecting and, in some cases, correcting errors in the application data. The element also can determine if a packet is missing and request retransmission. The right-hand side of Figure 3-12 illustrates a case where three data packets are sent, D1 through D3, however, one packet has been lost (D2, as indicated by the dotted line). In this case, retransmission may be requested and data packet 2 resent. This element may also contain information regarding ordering of the data as packets may not be received in the order transmitted.

Conceptually, the IP layer contains information related to routing such as the destination address. The network uses this element to transport the packet from the point of origin, across the network to the destination. While traversing the network, the packet may traverse through several nodes, and individual packets may take unique routes through the network. There is not necessarily a single unique path through the network.

Finally, the link layer is related to the physical characteristic of the connection the device is connected to. Note that it is not required that the origin and destination devices have the same physical connection type. As an example, an originating device may have a copper wire EtherNet cable, which an intermediate device may convert to an optical fiber, and finally, the destination device may be Wi-Fi connected.

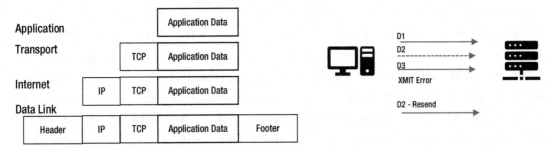

Figure 3-12. *Simplified Internet Packet description*

What is the impact of introducing networking on architecting a secure IMSS 3.0 system? The most critical impact is that the system elements can now be physically disaggregated from one another. There is no longer a requirement to have a sensor unit, such as a video camera, in close physical proximity to the recording unit. Similarly, there is no longer a requirement to have the display and operator in close physical proximity to the storage unit. Equally critical is that the shared, open network infrastructure now means data can be shared across a wide range of actors and geographies. The open, shared network infrastructure is both an advantage – you can share with anyone, anywhere, and a disadvantage – anyone, anywhere can potentially access your data as it travels across the network. In security terms, your attack surface has just greatly expanded.

Learning to Share...

In practice, there are two fundamental strategies to employ in designing an architecture. The first is to restrict oneself to only private Internet infrastructure. In the private infrastructure approach, a single entity owns all the elements of the systems – the sensors, the storage, the displays, and the operator terminals. In practice, the private infrastructure approach is only feasible when the substantial costs of construction, operation, and maintenance justify the value of the data being protected. Even then, private infrastructure severely limits the geographic span and access of the network in all but a very few instances. Conversely, encryption during transport now becomes critical to ensure secure use of the shared infrastructure.

Encryption during transport becomes a question then of what elements of the packet to encrypt. Figure 3-13 schematically illustrates how the elements of the packet are used as the packet traverses the network from origin to destination via one or more intermediate nodes. Dotted arrows indicate interaction between the nodes at each level. The criteria become: what information is being protected? The Application data itself? The source and destination? The data integrity – that is, correction for data corruption and or retransmission of lost packets? Intertwined with the data integrity question is that of authentication. Is the source trusted? Is the destination a trusted destination? Has an intermediate party tampered with the data and how to detect such tampering? The specific attacks, vulnerabilities, and countermeasures will be dealt with in detail in a later chapter. At this point, the intent is to raise the readers' awareness of the vulnerabilities and critical architectural decision points.

Several different protocols may be used at each layer of the system, and hence require modification of the packet structure. It is not unusual for the packet structure to be modified as the packet traverses the system. Some representative protocols are given in Table 3-2. As an example, consider an origin device connected with a Wi-Fi link to a router connected by Ethernet cable to a second router connected by Bluetooth to a destination device. Packets traversing this route would have the Physical/Datalink element modified from a Wi-Fi to Ethernet to Bluetooth structure; return packets from the destination to the origin device would follow the inverse transformation. Note that the protocols indicated by the dashed arrows in Figure 3-13 must match at each end of the arrow. Hence transport layer must match to transport layer, application layer to application layer, and so forth, even though the layers underneath are changing.

Table 3-2. *Representative Networking Protocols*

Layer	Example protocols
Application	HTTP, HTTPs, SSL, POP3, SMTP, MQTT, gRPC…
Transport	TCP, UDP
Network/Internet	IPv6, IPv4, DHCP,…
Physical/Datalink	Ethernet, Wi-Fi, Bluetooth, PPP, ADSL,…

Hook Me Up…Let's Get Together

IMSS 3.0 introduced critical networking capabilities, enabling the system to be physically distributed. The IMSS 3.0 resulting digital system architecture is described in Figure 3-14. The system consists of:

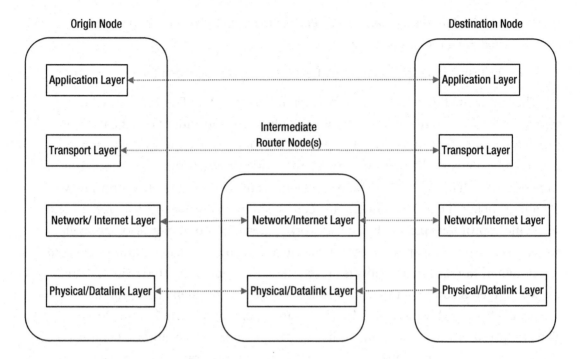

Figure 3-13. *Internet Protocol layers*

- Capture: Video sensors, resolution up to HD or even higher resolution is now possible

- Camera Connection: Ethernet, usually Power over Ethernet (POE)

- Video data compression between nodes

- Network Link at Specified Points

  - Encryption and Decryption of Sensor Data between nodes

  - Compression and Decompression of Sensor Data

- Storage – Rotating magnetic media, HDD, with multiple cameras per unit

  - Compressed and Encrypted sensor data

- Display Functionality – Decrypt, Decompress, and format to display one or more sensor data streams

- Inferred metadata (analysis) – Performed manually by human watching recorded scene

- Decisions made by a human after watching video on display

The key distinction of IMSS 3.0 IMSS systems, as shown in Figure 3-14, is the separation of the system elements made possible by the introduction of the network capability. Commonly, the network architecture is partitioned into a private network and a public network. The private network will aggregate data from multiple sensors, as shown on the left of Figure 3-14. Note, not all the sensors may natively support network capability, hence the public router may need to construct the appropriate packets and select the appropriate protocols. The network aggregation point may also optionally support storage of data or may simply pass the data through to a node further along in the system. If storage functionality is present then the node is referred to as an NVR, Network Video recorder. The second critical feature is a complementary router node connected to the public network, designated in the diagram as the "Public Router." The public router will accept data from the private router and/or storage, compress and encrypt the data, packetize the data to the appropriate granularity, and generate the addresses and protocols in each packet to ensure arrival at the destination node. Between the origin node (NVR) and the destination node (Operations Center) there may be one or more intermediate nodes on the public network. To construct secure systems, it is quite critical that the origin node have separate router functions for the private and public networks to provide isolation.

As noted in Figure 3-14, multiple NVR units may connect to a given destination node, here an operations center. The disaggregation allowed by multiple NVRs connecting to a single operation center increases the overall system efficiency and response time. Particularly expensive resources such as displays, human operators, and response systems need not be duplicated multiple times across the entire system. These resources can be concentrated in a single location and shared. Additionally, because the information from multiple locations is available at a single location, the operators can obtain a much more complete situational awareness. As an example, a traffic monitoring system can gather the sensor data from an entire city, rather than look at the traffic patterns in only a single neighborhood or a single street.

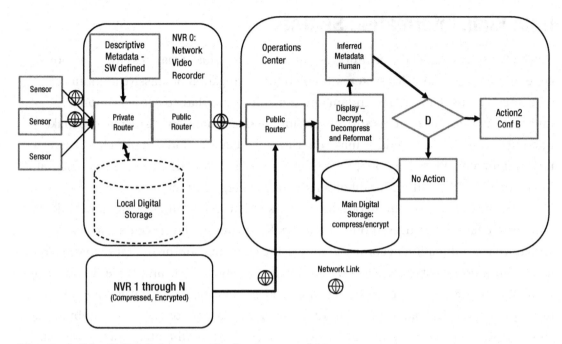

Figure 3-14. *IMSS 3.0 networked system architecture*

A key system architecture decision is the partitioning of storage between "local" storage near the sensor and "main" storage near the operators. The partitioning is driven by the balance of network bandwidth and latency available for the expected sensor data volume generated and the cost of providing local vs. main storage. The one extremum of the continuum is to have no local storage at all and send all the sensor data to the operations center for storage. The consequence is placing a heavy premium on both network bandwidth and latency, in the face of unpredictable loading of the public network. The other extremum is to have all sensor data stored at the NVR level in local storage and only forward sensor data to the destination node, operations center, as requested for analysis. The consequence is minimizing the network resources required for bandwidth; however, latency may become an issue depending on the public network loading. Additionally, with access to only a portion of the data, it may be difficult for the operations center to know which sensor data to request. The intricacies of network analysis are beyond the scope of this book, suffice to say on this point that application-dependent balance will need to be determined.

Data Rich, Information Sparse...

IMSS 3.0 systems, for all the advantages, retained one serious weakness from previous generations. While IMSS 3.0 systems enabled the aggregation of massive amounts of data, much of the data was redundant and difficult to correlate to extract actionable information. IMSS 3.0 systems still rely on human operators viewing displays to make inferences from the sensor data, make decisions, and take actions. In principle, there is no fundamental difference from previous generations, in practice, there is a considerable qualitative change. As the amount of sensor data aggregated increases, it becomes increasingly difficult for human operators to assimilate and synthesize the sensor data and form reliable inferences about a situation. Knowing which sensor data to access and in what combination becomes an increasing challenge for the operators requiring increasing amounts of expertise and training. In our city traffic example cited previously, imaging a moderate size city with a few hundred cameras on the traffic grid feeding a display system which can service tens of the sensor streams at once in any combination. How to select which sensor streams? How to select which combinations of the streams? The impact of variation in the human operators' skill on overall system performance is greatly magnified in these cases.

From a system security perspective, IMSS 3.0 systems also introduced a vulnerability in traversing public networks. Without a clear understanding of the potential attacks on packetized data, IMSS 3.0 systems were open to exploitation. Using encryption and secure protocols, it is feasible to construct robust systems resistant to attack. Doing so requires substantial knowledge of how networks work and how the packetized data is transformed during the transmission process. Use of the public network meant that attackers no longer required physical access to the data, but could remotely access the data over the public network. Attacks could come either while traversing the network or when the data was stored, either locally or at the main storage locations such as data centers. A practical consequence is to multiply the number of potential attackers to anyone with access to the public network – in effect, the global population. The number and types of attacks grew rapidly and were difficult for human defenders to monitor, identify, and react to in a timely fashion.

Addressing both the massive data available for analysis and the necessity to secure that data from increasingly sophisticated attackers forced the next step in IMSS system evolution.

IMSS 4.0…If I Only Had a Brain…

A well-developed tool kit for analyzing images was developed under the general heading of Computer Vision. Recently, there has been a resurgence in a related but distinct branch of analytics under the general heading of Artificial Intelligence (AI) or Machine Learning (ML). The field of Artificial Intelligence (AI) can be traced back at least to the 1950s, the origins often attributed to a 1956 conference at Dartmouth College. Since the inception of AI, the field has endured several periods swinging between irrational exuberance followed by disappointment with actual performance and a fallow period. The latest revival started in 2012 using machine learning (ML) techniques requiring intense computation using a technique called Convolutional Neural Networks (CNN). Figure 3-15 demonstrates the decline in the cost of computation, storage, and network speeds that enabled the introduction of Machine learning techniques. Compute is based on the fundamental operation of a CNN being matrix multiplication. In 2012, Moore's Law of computation finally intersected the CNN mathematical techniques to produce practical results. The CNN algorithms require Trillions of Operations per Second (TOPs) combined. The large databases, primarily video data, required memory enough to hold tens of millions of parameters and intermediate results during computation. The storage demands of the video data required low-cost storage; a single video camera could easily generate one Terabyte (1,000 Megabytes) of data per month. Transmitting the data to where it could be processed demanded connection speeds on the order of Mbits per seconds per camera. Architecting, developing, and installing the new systems at economically viable costs required coordinated scaling in compute, storage, and transmission.

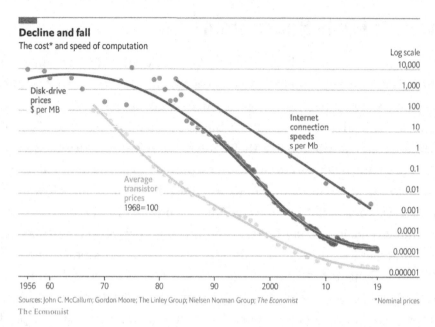

Figure 3-15. *Falling costs: compute, storage and networking (Source: The Economist, Sept 14th, 2019)*

When all elements were in place, it was possible for the next stage to appear – intelligent IMSS systems.

Classical CV Techniques – Algorithms First, Then Test against Data

Traditional Computer Vision (CV) consists of a developer selecting and connecting computational filters based on linear algebra with the goal of extracting key features of a scene, then correlating the key features with an object(s) so the system can recognize the object(s).[1] The key feature of traditional CV methodology is that the developer selects which filters to use and, hence, which features will be used to identify an object. This method works well when the object is well defined and the scene is well understood or controlled. However, as the number of objects increases or the scene conditions vary widely, it becomes increasingly difficult for the developer to predict the critical features that must be detected to identify an object.

---

[1] Image Processing: Principles and Applications | Wiley

Deep Learning – Data First, Then Create Algorithms

The terminology used in the AI field can often be confusing; for the purposes of this discussion, we will use the taxonomy described in Figure 3-16. AI shall refer to tasks that are related to the physical world, focused on the subset related to perceptual understanding. In this sense, AI is a subset of the broader field of data analytics, which may or may not refer to the real word. The next level is machine learning, a class of algorithms which relies on exposing a mathematical model to numerous examples of objects, the algorithms then "learning" how to identify objects from the examples. In effect, the mathematical approach is in direct contrast to the traditional CV approach, where a human programmer decides explicitly what features will identify an object.

The mathematical models are inspired by the neural networks found in nature, which are based on a hierarchical structure. The neurons are arranged in layers, each layer extracting more complex and more abstract information based on the processing performed by previous layers. Using the human visual system as an example, the first layer recognizes simple structures in the visual field: color blobs, corners, and how edges are oriented. The next layer will take this information, construct simple geometrical forms, and perform tracking of these forms. Finally, these geometric forms are assembled into more complex objects such as hands, automobiles, and strawberries based on attributes such as combinations of shapes, colors, textures, and so forth.

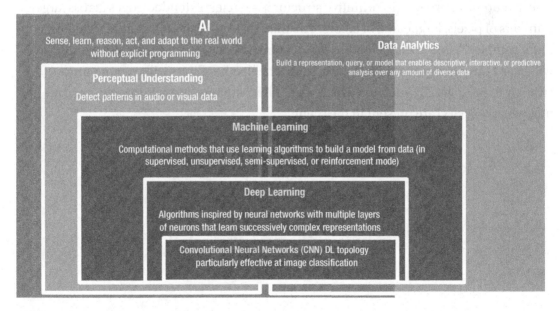

Figure 3-16. *AI taxonomy*

Deep learning and CNN are based on the hierarchical neural network approach, building from the simple to the complex. Rather than try to "guess" the right filters to apply to identify an object, the neural network first applies many filters to the image in the convolution stage. Based on the filters in the CNN, the network extracts features based on the response to the filters. In the full connected stage, the network analyzes the features in the object(s) with the goal of associating each input image with an output node for each type of object, the value at output node representing the probability that the image is the object associated with the output node.

Convolutional Neural Networks and Filters…Go Forth and Multiply…and Multiply

The convolution in CNN refers to a set of filters, the filters constructed on matrix multiplication. An incoming set of data is multiplied by parameters, designated as weights. The results are summed, and a filter is deemed "activated" if the sum exceeds a designated threshold. The filters are arranged in a hierarchy, with the results of previous filters feeding into later filters. An example of this hierarchical approach of the filters is shown in Figure 3-17 for the case of an automobile sitting on a field of grass. The very low-level features are drawn from a very local region of pixels recognizing simple attributes – colors, lines, edges. The next layer of mid-level features combines the low-level features to start to form primitive structures – circles, extended edges across larger numbers of pixels, larger area of colors. The third level of High-level features creates more complex, more abstract features associated with the car, the grass, etc. Some filters will have a strong response to a feature, say a wheel, other filters will respond more strongly to the grass. By knowing which set of filters are responding strongly, one can infer what object(s) are present in the scene.

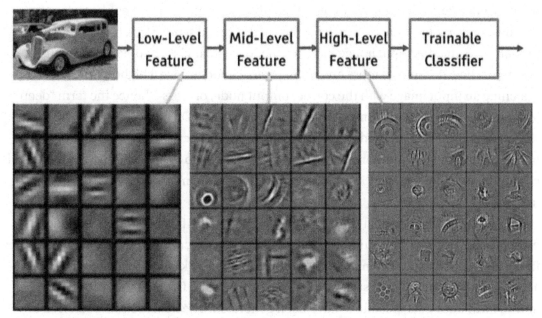

Feature visualization of convolutional net trained on ImageNet from [Zeiler & Fergus 2013]

Figure 3-17. *CNN feature visualization*

The term Neural Network is derived from how the mathematical filters are connected into a structure. There are two stages to the process of recognizing an object – feature extraction (convolutions) and classifiers (fully connected layers). The detailed mathematical descriptions are beyond the scope of this book; however, there are numerous treatments available in the literature for those wanting more detailed information.

A simplified example of a neural network and its operation is shown in Figure 3-18. The key difference between DL and traditional CV is that in deep learning, there is no attempt to preselect which filters or features are the key identifiers for a particular object. Instead, all the filters are applied to every object during the convolution phase to extract features. During the fully connected phase, the system "learns" which features characterize a particular object. The learning occurs at a series of nodes that analyze the strength of particular features in some combination. If the response of that combination of features is over some threshold, then the node is activated and considered a characteristic of that object. It is applying many filters and having to look at all the combinations of features that makes deep learning so computationally intense. In addition, the more combinations of features and combinations of combinations the network examines in the fully connected phase, the more likely key characteristics that describe an object are to be discovered. At the end, a score is given related to how probable it is that the input image matches that particular class or object at the output.

In practice, this means more and more layers of nodes have a higher probability of matching an input image with the correct output node, or class—hence the term "deep learning." In return for the computational resources used, DL is often much more robust than conventional CV methods and, hence, much more accurate across a broader range of objects and scene conditions. The developer will need to assess whether the increased computation and robustness is required vs. traditional CV methods for the particular use case.

The image data is input at the left of the diagram in the form of an image in the example shown. The first section is applying the filters described in Figure 3-17. Note the filters are applied in layers, analogous to the neural network layers in a biological brain. The output of filters in the first layer are fed to one or more filters in the second layer, and so forth until a set of features have been generated. The next section is referred to as the fully connected layers which assess the features that were created and the relative strengths of the features in various combinations. The output nodes at the right of the diagram represent the possible outcomes, referred to as "classes." The result is a score for each output node (class) estimating the strength of response of that particular output node to the input image. All output nodes will have some response to the input image, though it may be quite low. However, it is not unusual for more than one output node to have a significate response to a given image. Often the output score is misinterpreted to relate to the probability of a node being correct, it is only the score given by the network. Adding all the scores together will, in general, not add up to 1 or any other particular value. (An exception is when a normalization operation has been implemented, but that still does not give the probability.)

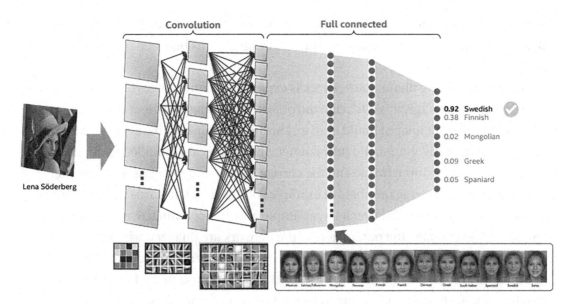

Figure 3-18. *Neural networks features and classifiers example*

This raises the question of how to interpret the outputs of the neural networks and how to define the classes that are the output nodes. How does the neural network know how to match an image input to output node, or class? To understand that, we need to explore the entire deep learning flow.

Teaching a Network to Learn…

Earlier it was stated that the difference between traditional computer vision techniques and machine learning techniques is the deep learning aspect. In deep learning it was stated that the data comes first, then the algorithm or filters – how is this accomplished? The deep learning workflow for neural networks is illustrated in Figure 3-19. The workflow is partitioned into two phases: training and inferencing. The previous section described how inferencing occurs. Data is presented to the network and after processing through successive layers of convolutions filters, each of the output nodes, or classes, is given a score. The algorithm that determines the score for the classes is created during the "training" phase of the process.

The training phase starts with the selection of a neural network model, the basic structure of filters and layers and how these filters and layers are connected. There are a wide variety of models in existence which represent trade-offs between computational complexity, accuracy, latency, and system constraints such as power and cost.

These aspects will be discussed in a later section. The selected mode is represented schematically by the circles (nodes) and arrows (connections between nodes) in the diagram.

During the training phase, the network is exposed to many images of a given object(s). For each image, it is told what the object in the image is—that is, which output node the input image should map to. During the training phase, the parameters of the CNN in the convolution and fully connected sections are modified to minimize the error between the input image and the correct output node or class. Because the network is exposed to large numbers of examples of the object, it learns which features are associated with the object over a large sample and, hence, which features tend to be persistent. Eventually, the parameters of the network are finalized when application requirements for number of classes (objects) to be recognized and accuracy are met. Once training is complete, the network can be deployed for use in the field, the step called inferencing or scoring. The green mound represents the decrease in error that occurs during training over multiple parameters. For purposes of illustration, the decrease over two parameters is shown.

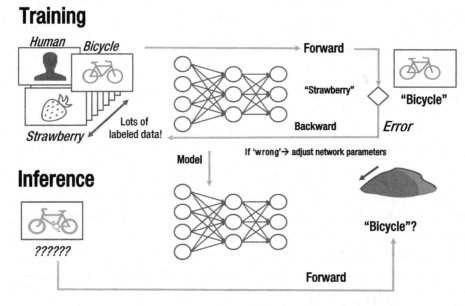

Figure 3-19. *Neural network: training and inferencing*

In the training phase, there must be a source of "ground truth," usually in the form of labeled data curated by humans. It is this labeled data that will determine what classes of objects the neural network model will respond to. In the example shown, images of Humans, Strawberries, and Bicycles are used, therefore, the only objects the neural network will be capable of recognizing are Humans, Strawberries, and Bicycles. A critical consequence is that this neural network will try to map ANY object into Humans, Strawberries, and Bicycles. Shown an image of a refrigerator, the model will give it a score in each of the Humans, Strawberries, and Bicycles classes, though probably a low score. For this reason, when evaluating the results of a neural network, it is critical to understand not only what the highest-ranking class is, but how strongly the object scored in that class.

During training, if an error is made in classification, then a correction is made to the parameters in the model. In Figure 3-19, the neural network has been presented with an image of a Bicycle and incorrectly mapped it the class of "Strawberry." The neural network model is now adjusted by altering parameters in the convolutions and fully connected sections until the correct predictions are made for that image. For pragmatic models with acceptable accuracy over a wide range of real-world conditions, the training data set is typically in the range of tens of thousands to hundreds of thousands of examples. The size of the training data required is a function of the number of classes to be recognized, the robustness to different observing conditions (lighting, angles of observation, presence of other objects), etc. Training a neural network is subject to the classic computer program GIGO, Garbage In, Garbage Out. Poor data labeling, poor quantity of data and poor definition of output classes will yield poor results.

Types of Neural Networks: Detection and Classification

There are numerous types of neural network models, two are especially common in IMSS video systems. In the training phase, we tell the CNN what objects are in the image—that is, which output node an input image should map to. Conversely, in the inference stage, we don't know what is in the scene. This means that the network must first determine if there is an object of interest in the scene (detection phase) and, if so, identify what the object is (classification phase). There are networks that are optimized for each task. In addition, it is possible to mix DL and conventional techniques (e.g., one could perform detection with traditional CV and classification with DL).

Detection is done at the video frame level. It consists of examining a video frame to detect how many objects are in it. A frame of video may contain 0, 1, 2, or many objects. The key metric for detection is frames per second (fps).

Classification is identifying the objects detected in a frame. Is it a car, a person, etc.? A classification may have multiple attributes (e.g., car—blue, sedan, Audi*), and a frame may give rise to 0, 1, 2, or many classification tasks. Classification is measured in inferences/second. Identifying one object equals one inference.

An example of a complete Deep Learning data flow is shown Figure 3-20 for a street scene. Starting in the upper left portion of the diagram, the model is trained on a large data set of street scenes. At this point, it is determined that the model will be trained to recognize automobiles and pedestrians. Each training sample requires tens of GOPs (One GOP = one Giga Operation = 1 billion operations), and training the model requires tens of thousands of examples, means the training is often performed on specialized systems in a data center or the equivalent. Once the model is trained, it is commonplace for mathematical optimizations to be performed to increase computational efficiency while preserving desirable traits. The common mathematical techniques involve removing nodes or filters that are not used in the final model or have only a minimal impact, combining filters based on mathematical transforms that are equivalent but less compute and reducing precision, for example, using 8-bit operations instead of 16-bit operations. Collectively, these constitute model compression.

As mentioned previously, it is common to train multiple models depending on the application, such as a detection and one or more classification models, as shown in Figure 3-20. The detection and classification models are then deployed to the location(s) where inferencing is to occur. There are two broad classes of system architecture in this respect. In the first class, all the data is sent to a central location for the inferencing to take place. The advantage is computing and storage resources and to be amortized; the disadvantage is that transporting the required amount of data to be analyzed may strain network BW. Conversely, in the second class of system architecture, the analysis is performed at or near the site at which the data is collected. The disadvantage is that compute resources may be more limited, but now only the results of inferencing need to be sent elsewhere, or in some cases, action can be taken locally. Hybrid systems are on a continuum between the two extremes cited.

Deep Learning Data Flow

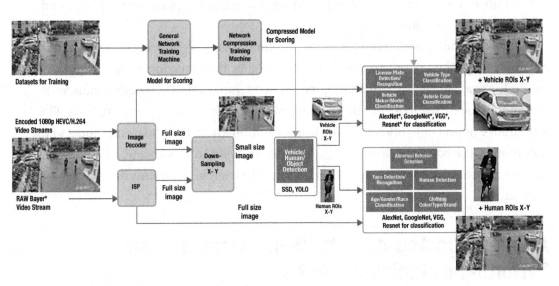

Figure 3-20. *Example of Deep Learning flow: street monitoring*

In either system architecture, the task is inferencing – ingesting data from the real world and extracting actionable information. Starting in the lower left-hand corner, the image is ingested into the system for analysis. If connected directly to a sensor, such as an image sensor, then the raw image will be processed through an Image Signal Processor to convert the raw sensor data into a format useful for the neural network to operate on. Conversely, the image may be coming from another device which has already converted the image to a standard format, compressed it, and encoded the video into a standard video format such as High Efficiency Video Coding (HEVC). Once the video data is ingested as either sensor data or as a video stream, the video data is usually resampled from the video resolution to the resolution required by the neural network model using well known scaling, cropping, and color space conversion techniques. The video stream is then sent one frame at a time to the first neural network where detection occurs. Typical families of neural network models used for detection are SSD (Single Shot Detection) and YOLO (You Only Look Once). Recall detection networks operate on video frames, their performance is measured in frames per second (fps). The output of the detection network is a series of Regions of Interest (ROIs) which contain a bounding box identifying the portion of the image in where an object of interest is located. Some classes of detection networks may also perform an initial classification of the object into broad classes such as car, pedestrian, bicycle. Again, recall classification networks operate on ROIs, not video frames, and are measured in inferences per second. The two metrics are often conflated and will lead to serious errors in system specification and sizing if not properly applied.

Following the detection function, it is common that more specialized classification networks may then operate on the ROI's identified by the detection network. In the example shown in Figure 3-20 subsequent networks specialized for pedestrians and automobiles are used to gather more fine-grained information about the objects. The automotive neural network may provide information about the make and model of the automobile, the color, the license plate, etc. The pedestrian classification network may provide information about the location of the pedestrian in the scene, demographic data, etc.

A Pragmatic Approach to Deep Learning …Key Performance Indicators (KPIs)

The previous sections described a high-level overview of how a deep learning system works at a conceptual level in terms of the neural network model workflow and basic concepts. We will now turn to pragmatic considerations in implementing a deep learning based for IMSS 4.0 systems. In architecting an IMSS 4.0 system, the critical concept is that the DL workflow has different KPIs and capabilities at different points in the system architecture.

The system architecture KPIs are driven by the relative number of units at each level in the system architecture, the power available, the location and size of the required data, and cost constraints. Table 3-3 gives typical system level KPIs for DL that are related to the system architecture structure. The actual values may vary for an application or use case. For purposes of taxonomy, the system architecture is partitioned into three general elements: Data center, Gateways, and Cameras/Edge devices. The boundaries between these elements are not rigid and are subject to adaptation depending on the specific industry.

Data centers refer to installations aggregating large compute resources in a controlled environment and may be either public (e.g., Cloud Service Providers) or private. Gateways are often located remotely, often in unsupervised locations with uncontrolled access. The primary purpose of a gateway is to access data from multiple sources, process some of the data locally and often store some of the data locally. If a data center is present, the gateway will often send processed data to the data center for further analysis. Multiple gateways will typically support a single processing element in a data center. Finally, a camera/edge device is responsible for sensing the data directly, performing any required signal processing to transform the data to a consumable format and forward the data to a gateway. It is not unusual that a single data center processor may be ingesting data originating from 100 to 5000 edge devices. Managing the data flow between the edge and the data center is a critical system architecture function.

The resources and capabilities of each of the elements varies substantially across the system architecture. The tasks allocated to the elements thus varies to reflect the differing capabilities and resources available. Using three elements as a starting point, it is possible to architect a variety of different Deep Learning based IMSS systems. The optimal system architecture for a given application will depend on the neural network(s) selected, the storage needed, the compute performance of the system components, cost and speed of networks, and program constraints (cost, schedule, pre-existing systems that must be supported). The relative values of these KPIs will determine the optimal partitioning of the workload among the three elements. The KPIs of each of these elements and the effect on system architecture will be investigated in some detail later in this chapter.

Table 3-3. *Typical Deep Learning-based System KPIs*

DL TASK -SYSTEM ARCHITECTURE LOCATION	DL TASK	POWER PER SOC	LATENCY	DATA, SIZE (O)	RELATIVE # UNITS	KEY SYSTEM-LEVEL DL KPI
DATA CENTER, CLOUD	Training Classification Complex DL Tasks	Unconstrained >100W	100's mS	Training Data, (TB)	1	Training Time, Throughput Perf/Sec
GATEWAY	Classification, Scene Analysis, Object Tracking in Area (Detection if Not Done at Camera)	Moderate 15–75W	Moderate (Several 10's mS)	Video Streams, (GB)	5–50	Video Steam Aggregation, Channel Density, Operation: 24X7X365
EDGE/CAMERA	Image Capture and Signal Processing, (Optional) Detection/ Classification	Constrained <5W	Critical, at Capture Frame Rate (1-10s mS)	Video Stream (MB)	20–100	Latency, Throughput, Perf/W Operation: 24X7X365

One Size Doesn't Fit All...

The constraints and KPIs are different at each point in the system architecture, hence it is difficult for a single type of processor architecture to satisfy all the demands. This will be reinforced when we examine the performance of different CNNs on different processor architectures. Different processor architectures are differently advantaged for different CNNs. There is no one-size-fits-all solution or one best processor architecture for the entire DL workflow.

IMSS 4.0: From Data to Information

IMSS 4.0 introduced the critical concept of Machine Learning enabling the mass transformation of data to information. Previously the transformation of data to information was gated by the ability of a human to view the data, assess the data, make inferences and act upon the data. IMSS 4.0 systems are distinguished by the ability of machine learning to transform data into information. The two immediate consequences are first, the system itself can make decisions within specified bounds, relieving humans of many of the rote tasks. As important, for those decisions reserved to humans, much of the data has been preprocessed to present only the most critical and relevant information for human consideration and judgment. The IMSS 4.0 resulting digital system architecture is described in Figure 3-21. The system consists of:

- Capture: Video sensors, resolution up to HD now possible

- Camera Connection: Ethernet, usually Power over Ethernet (POE)

- Video data compression between nodes

- Router: Network Link at Specified Points

  - Encryption and Decryption of Sensor Data between nodes

  - Compression and Decompression of Sensor Data

- Storage – Rotating magnetic media, HDD, with multiple cameras per unit

  - Compressed and Encrypted sensor data

- Display Functionality – Decrypt, Decompress and format to display one or more sensor data streams

- Inference: Inferred metadata (analysis) – Performed using inferencing capability at multiple locations in the system architecture

- *Routine* decisions, D_L, made by machine learning based on inference

- *Critical* decisions, D_H, made by a human based in inferenced data preprocessed by AI

The IMSS 4.0 system architecture allows for considerably more flexibility in where functions such as storage and video analytics are placed. With the addition of inferencing to video analytics, the element formerly designated NVR now becomes more powerful, able to take on decision making tasks in real time, superseding its formerly passive role as a recording device. In recognition of this extended functionality, this element is promoted to a Video Analytics Node (VAN). The decisions, D_L, and the corresponding responses, Action$_L$, will greatly simplify the overall system architecture constraints. The ability to act locally will substantially reduce both the network bandwidth to the operations center and the compute required at the operations center. In the overall IMSS 4.0 system architecture it is quite common to have a mixture of NVR and VAN elements in the overall system. The information sent from the VAN to the operations center can be any mix of metadata derived from inferencing and sensor data.

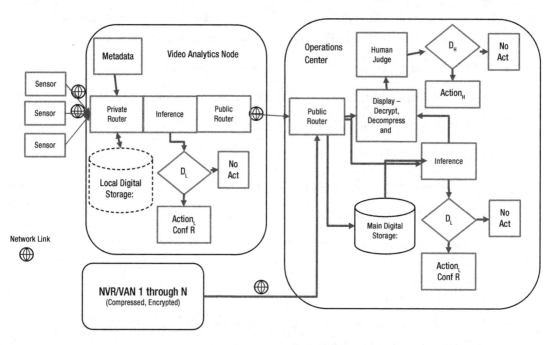

Figure 3-21. *IMSS 4.0 system architecture*

At the operations center, the data and metadata from multiple Video Analytics Nodes and NVRs may be combined. Like the VAN operation, a substantial portion of the aggregate data may be analyzed by Machine Learning algorithms, and decisions, D_L, and responses, Action$_L$, taken without human intervention. The scope of these Machine Learning decisions must be carefully considered and bounded as part of the overall system architecture design, development, and validation. The inferencing may operate either on real time information streaming into the operations center, on stored data or some combination of the two sources.

Those decisions and actions reserved for humans, D_H, and $Action_H$, can still benefit from the inferencing operations. The output of the inferencing operations may be presented to humans as part of the display element. Using inferencing in this manner will greatly reduce the cognitive load on human operators by presenting only the most relevant data for decisions requiring human judgment. Determining what information to display to the human operators, in what format, and the options permitted are a key step in the IMSS 4.0 system architecture. The tighter the constraints on real time response and accuracy, the more critical this often-overlooked design element becomes.

Information Rich, Target Rich...

Previously, it was highlighted that a drawback of IMSS 3.0 systems is that they were data rich, but information sparse. For adversaries to access significant information often means wading through mounds of data to extract the critical information. Hours, days, weeks, or months of video data amounting to Terabytes or more data would need to be exfiltrated, sifted through, and analyzed before useful information was available. The advent of machine learning changes this paradigm completely. The essence of machine learning is to distill the mass of data into easily accessible information, the information being substantially smaller in size. Consequently, in some sense, machine learning has created a target-rich environment for adversaries by concentrating the vast amount of data into a compact information representation.

Task Graph – Describing the Use Case/Workload – Overview

In the first section of the chapter, we discussed the evolution of IMSS systems from their analog starts to modern day systems based on digital architecture and artificial intelligence. In this section, we will detail the workflows found in the distinct phases of the IMSS system. The key concept is distinguishing the workflows performed, the sequence of tasks, from the underlying hardware architecture. A given workflow can be mapped to many different hardware architectures.

The workflows are commonly described as a graph, a series of tasks connected by arrows representing the transition from one task to another. The graph describing the workflow will be denoted as a **task graph**. Task graphs tend to be associated with specific locations or nodes in the system architecture. We will describe four distinct types of nodes in the system architecture, and the associated task graphs:

- Sensors, when based on video often referred to as Internet Protocol Cameras (IPC)

- Network Video Recorders (NVRs)

- Video Analytic nodes

- Video Analytic Accelerators, specialized devices that rely on a host

For purposes of clarity, the task graphs will be discussed in the context of a IMSS 4.0 type system. Once understood in this context, the reader will be able to easily extrapolate equivalent task graphs for prior generations, by removing functions present in IMSS 4.0 systems.

Sensors and Cameras – Sampling the Scene in Space, Time, and Spectra

In modern IMSS systems, the most common sensor is the video camera. By convention, a camera is a device that converts electromagnetic radiation into a two-dimensional array of pixels in a focal plane. The electromagnetic spectrum spans a considerable range as characterized by either wavelength or frequency (The two are related by the speed of light, c, such that every wavelength corresponds to a unique frequency. The wavelength will be influenced by the medium the radiation is travelling through). The most common camera is the video camera, which senses visible light in the electromagnetic spectrum, either intensity only (Black and White) or color modes. Video also implies that the scene is captured at some constant sampling rate.

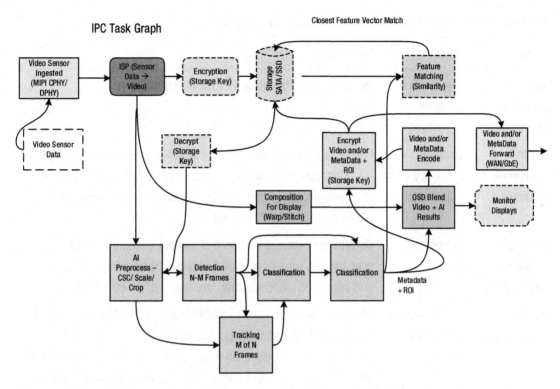

Figure 3-22. *Task graph for Internet Protocol Camera (IPC)*

Video sensors are characterized by a few key metrics described in Table 3-4.

Table 3-4. *Selected Sensor Characteristics and Metrics*

Metric	Units	Description
Spatial sampling – Resolution	Pixels, Rows X Columns	Describes how the image is spatially subsampled
Spectral Sampling – Bandpass	Quantum efficiency (%); V/light intensity	Can be given either as the total sensitivity over a spectral range (i.e., Quantum efficiency) or as a data set denoting sensitivity at each wavelength). Common spectral sampling schemes are RGB, CMY, Greyscale (B&W), Infrared (IR).
Temporal Sampling - Frame Rate	Frames per second	Determines how often a scene is sampled. Common sampling schemes are progressive (all pixels in a frame sampled at once) and interlaced (alternate rows are sampled on each frame.
Interface	Physical lanes (wires) and protocols	The most common sensor interfaces are MIPI CSI (Camera Serial Interface), LVDS (Low Voltage Differential Swing) and CMOS levels. Typically, multiple lanes are used, and a flexible framework allows the user to determine how the total data is divided across the multiple lanes.

These basic sensor characteristics determine many of the fundamental system parameters as regards data bandwidth and processing. Selecting the sampling parameters determines what types of information are gathered about the scene, and hence what information is available for analysis. The data generated by a sensor can be approximated as

Equation 1 Video Data Generated in 1 Second

$$Data_{1\,second} = Resolution \times Spectral\ Sampling\ Components \times Frame\ Rate$$

The implied data rates for common sensor formats and frame rates are shown in Table 3-5. Note the numerical values are approximate and reflect only the final image size. In practice, sensors will incorporate additional rows and columns for the purposes of removing noise and artifacts such as dark current. For a particular instantiation, refer to the sensor data sheet to understand the actual sensor readout specifications. The configurations given in Table 3-5 are not exhaustive and even within categories some variation exists. Note the two separate definitions for 4K resolution. The Data Rate from sensor is an estimate of the data traversing the path from the video sensor to the Image Signal Processor (ISP). At this point in the signal chain, the video data is raw and if intercepted, can easily be read and decoded by unauthorized actors.

Converting Sampled Data to Video

The spectral sampling metric describes how many spectral bands the sensor is trying to capture; for a typical video sensor, this is three bands – Red (R), Green(G), and Blue (B). Each pixel can capture only one band and hence information about the other two bands is lost. Part of the function of the ISP is to estimate the values of the missing bands, for example, if the Green bandpass is measured then the ISP will attempt to interpolate the values of Red and Blue at that pixel based on the values of Red and Blue for the surrounding pixels. The final column, Data Rate out of the ISP, estimates the data rate in Mbps after the color interpolation.

Table 3-5. *Common Sensor Formats and Data Rates*

Common Name	Pixels (Columns)	Pixels (rows)	Resolution (MPixels)	Frame rate (FPS)	Precision (bits/ pixels) 8b =SDR 10b = HDR	Data rate from sensor into ISP (Mbps)	Spectral Sampling	Data rate Out of ISP Sensor (Mbps)
VGA/SD	640	480	0.3	30	8	72	RGB	216
HD	1280	720	0.92	30	8	220	RGB	662
FHD	1920	1020	1.96	30	8	470	RGB	1,411
QHD	2560	1440	3.68	30	10	1,104	RGB	3,312
4K	3840	2160	8.29	30	10	2,487	RGB	7,461
4K	.4096	2160	8.85	30	10	2,655	RGB	7,965

A final observation in Table 3-5 concerns the precision, or number of bits used to represent a pixel value. A standard representation has been 8-bits, allowing for 256 distinct levels. The 8b representation has worked well for many sensor and display technologies over the history of video. However, with the advent of newer sensor and display technologies, it has become feasible to capture a wider dynamic range referred to as High Dynamic range (HDR) encoding. The trend is using 10b to 12b encoding for HDR systems.

Referring again to Figure 3-22, once the sensor data has been processed to form a complete image, several options are available for further action. The simplest is to perform any data composition onto the image such as date, time, location, and camera ID. The Composition for Display and OSD blocks perform this function.

The video data can then be encoded to reduce the data volume using video compression techniques. Common video compressors are h.264 and h.265. Video compressors operate by removing redundant spatial and temporal information. The compression rate achieved depends on the original resolution, complexity of the scene, and how fast things are changing in the scene. A low-resolution scene with no changes will compress much more than a high-resolution scene monitoring a busy highway with lots of change. Another often overlooked influence on the compression ratio is the amount of noise in the scene; an image captured at night will have much more noise than the same scene captured in daylight. Because compression relies on removing redundant information, it will not compress random or uncorrelated noise. A very rough heuristic for compression ratio based on initial resolution is given in Table 3-6. Depending on the codec used, settings, and content, the observed compression ratio can vary by up to a factor of three from the values shown. It is strongly recommended that architects should obtain and/or simulate video streams and codecs relevant to their applications to estimate pragmatic compression ratios.

Table 3-6. *Heuristics for Video Compression Ratio*

Resolution	Data Rate out of ISP (Mbps)	Bit Rate After Compression (Mbps)	Compression Ratio
VGA/SD (640x480)	216	0.5	~400:1
HD (1280 x 720)	662	1	~600:1
FHD (1920 x 1020)	1,411	5	~300:1
UHD (3840 x 2160)	7,461	20	~400:1

Transporting Data – Getting Safely from Point A to Point B

Once encoded, the video data should be encrypted to preserve privacy and confidentiality of the data. The encryption data rate is equal to the bit rate after compression as shown in Table 3-6. Finally, the data is prepared for transmission from the IPC to the world via a Wide Area Network (WAN) such as Ethernet or cellular data. The video compression step is critical to minimize bandwidth load on the WAN. It is not uncommon for the WAN to support hundreds to thousands of cameras; hence the aggregate bandwidth can accumulate rapidly.

The preceding system functions describe a traditional IPC such as might be used in an IMSS 3.0 system. An IMSS 4.0 system would include one or more of the AI-inferencing steps in Figure 3-22 to analyze the data:

- AI preprocessing/Color Space Conversion (CSC)/Crop

- Detection on selected frames

- Tracking of objects in selected Frames

- One or more classification operations

The advantage of performing these operations at the IPC stage is twofold: 1) reduce the amount of data sent over the WAN to a few KB/s and 2) to provide greater security for the data. No data need ever leave the device and the attack surface is much smaller. The disadvantage is fitting the analytic operations into the power and computational budget of the IPC device. The analytic blocks will be described in more detail in the next section.

NVR/Video Analytic Nodes – Making Sense of The World

The second major component of an IMSS system is the aggregation point for multiple video streams. Depending on the functionality, the aggregation point can be either a Network Video recorder (NVR) or a Video Analytics Node. The task graph for an NVR/Video Analytics node is shown in Figure 3-23.

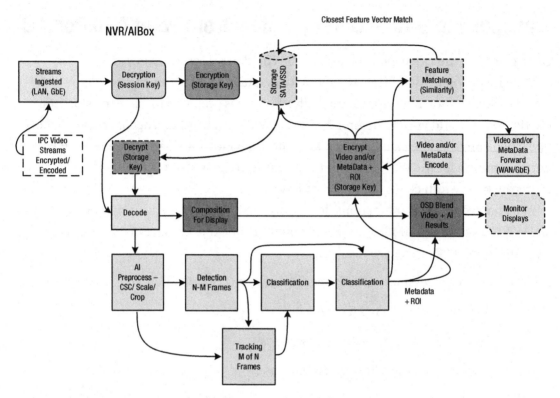

Figure 3-23. *Task graph for NVR/Video Analytics node*

Storing Data – Data at Rest

The initial elements of the task graph are common to the NVR and Video Analytics Node. Multiple video streams are ingested from either a Local Area Network (LAN) or a WAN. The streams from the IPC are assumed to be both encrypted and encoded for video compression. The encryption key used for transmission over the WAN/LAN is typically session dependent and hence ephemeral. The first step is to decrypt the video streams using the session key and then re-encrypt the video streams using a permanent key for storage. Depending on if the system is assigned a single tenant or multiple tenants will determine if a single storage key is used or multiple keys. Typically, all video streams that are ingested are stored. The storage period may range from a few hours up to 30 days (even month(s) depending upon the user requirements, often guided by law enforcement authorities), or in some cases, permanent storage. The number of video streams, bit rate per stream, and retention period will provide an estimate of the total storage required.

Equation 2 Storage

$$Storage_{GB} = Number\ of\ Video\ Streams\ X\ Bit\ Rate\left(Mbps\right)X\ Retention\ Period\left(s\right)$$

Recall the estimates made for bit rates per stream of selected camera resolutions earlier in Table 3-6. Based on these values, Table 3-7 shows a range of common storage requirements. Again, the actual storage requirements will depend on the details of the system configuration; however, these are representative of many configurations. It is apparent that the storage requirements can vary over several orders of magnitude. For systems with mixed cameras, a first approximation of total storage requirements can be had by summing the numbers and bit rates of the individual camera types.

Table 3-7. *Video Storage Heuristics*

Resolution	Number of Video Streams	Bit Rate After Compression (Mbps)	Decrypt/ Encrypt rate (Mbps)	Storage GB (1 Day Retention)	Storage GB (30 Day Retention)
VGA/SD (640x480)	16	0.5	8	0.69	21
HD (1280 x 720)	32	1	32	2.7	83
FHD (1920 x 1020)	64	5	320	28	829
UHD (3840 x 2160)	128	20	2,560	221	6,635

Table 3-7 also provides an estimate of the decryption and encryption rates required; note that this is the required rate for each function. Again, there is a large variation in the required rates. Implementations may vary from an algorithm run on a general-purpose CPU at the lower end to requiring dedicated hardware accelerators at the higher end.

Converting Reconstructed Data to Information – Inferencing and Classification

The key distinction between NVRs and Video Analytics Nodes is at the stage of converting the video data into information. There is not a bright line between the two and an optimal system design will use blend and balance the two methods in a complementary fashion. Recall from the earlier discussion that IMSS 3.0 and earlier systems rely on a human being to interpret the data. The distinguishing feature of an IMSS 4.0 system is that machine learning is added to support and enhance the interpretation by humans.

Humans Consumption – Display

An NVR relies on human interpretation of video streams for converting data to information. This method relies on the training and skill of the operator. The video data is typically presented to the human operator in the form of one or more displays on a monitor. Referring to Figure 3-23, the video streams may be either "real-time" from the ingested video streams or accessing stored video streams or a combination of the two. In either case, the first step is to decrypt the data with the appropriate key, and then to decode the data from the compressed format to a raw video stream suitable for display. This is the inverse of the process in Tables 3-5 and 3-6, described by Equations 1 and 2. Depending on the number of video streams, the original video stream resolution(s), and frame rate, there is a potential for exceptionally large data flows to be created. The video streams will typically need to be scaled to fit multiple streams on one or more monitors. Once the video streams are composed for display, the operator can then observe and interpret the video streams.

Recalling our earlier discussion of IMSS 2.0 systems, the operator approach still suffered from the drawbacks pointed out then.

> *There was no real time response – unless the system was monitored by a human observer. The analytics functions were still strongly dependent on the human operator, thus leading to inconsistencies in analysis. The system was still primarily retrospective.*

Despite these drawbacks, there are still compelling arguments for retaining human operators as the final arbiters and decision makers.

Machine Consumption – Algorithms, Databases, and Metadata

Video Analytics Nodes differ from NVRs in adding ML based on AI techniques to analyze and winnow the data, highlighting the important from the mundane. Again, referring to Figure 3-23, the analytics path can operate on either real time or stored video streams. The selection of video streams for analysis may range from a subset of the video streams analyzed periodically to the entire suite of video streams. Like the display function, it is often necessary to scale and or crop the video streams to match the input size requirements of a particular neural network. Input sizes may range from 224x224 pixels up to a full HD stream of 1920x1080p.

A selected set of Neural Networks is shown in Table 3-8 for common networks used for video analytics as of this writing. The network input size, compute requirements in GFLOPS (10^9 operations for each frame), and Millions of parameters (10^6 parameters per model) are shown. The reader should note that Neural Network models are rapidly evolving. It is not unusual that a network will go from discovery in an academic or industrial research setting to deployment in a matter of several months. As of this writing, hundreds of neural network models are in use ranging from public, general purpose models to models optimized for very specific tasks. There is a trade-off between model complexity (MParams), compute (GFLops), and accuracy, as illustrated in the following.

Table 3-8. *Selected Neural Network Models and Metrics as of the Time of Publication*

Neural Network Model	Type	Input Image Size	GFLOPs (Compute)	MParams	Accuracy[2]
Resnet-50	Classification	224x224x3	7	25	78
Squeezenet v1	Classification	227x227x3	1.79	1.25	58
MobileNetSSD	Classification	224x224	2.3	5.8	21
GoogleNet V4 (Inception V4)	Classification	299x299x3	24	43	80
EfficientDet-D2	Detection	768x768x3	11	8	43
YOLO v3	Detection	416x416x3	66	62	31
YOLO v5m	Detection	640x640	49	21.2	43
YOLO-tiny v2	Detection	416x416x3	7	16	22
Faster-rcnn-resnet101	Detection	1000x600x3	614	45	36

Referring to Figure 3-23, the first step is to scale and crop the incoming video frame to match the input size of the detection network. In selecting a detection network, the general heuristics are that accuracy improves with larger input sizes, more compute per video frame and more parameters; conversely throughput and latency decrease, power, and cost increase. Proper selection of the detection network will require balancing these factors for the application needs.

Recalling Figure 3-20, the output of the detection Neural Network model is a set of bounding boxes or Region of Interest (ROI) identifying the location of an object in the video frame and perhaps a first order identification such as car or person. There may be one, many, or no objects detected in a particular frame. In the example shown in Figure 3-20, the two classes of interest are cars and people. To gather more information about cars and people, specialized Neural Networks optimized for cars and people, respectively, are passed to the classifier networks. The input sizes of the classification networks are smaller than detection networks because the objects have been isolated

---

[2] Classification networks accuracy metric: MS-COCO dataset using mAP; detection ImageNet TOP1 score.

from the entire video frame. The objects detected by the detection network will have an arbitrary size depending on where they are in the video frame, their distance, the effective focal length of the camera lens and the resolution of the image sensor. This necessitates a second scaling operation between the output of the detection network and the input of the classification network.

Similarly, to the detection network, selection of the classification network requires balancing input size, compute, and the number of parameters against throughput, latency, power, and cost. Estimating the impact of a given network on accuracy can be performed independently of the system architecture; however, the throughput, latency cost, and power are strong functions of the underlying hardware and software selections comprising the system architecture.

The output of the classification neural networks will be a feature vector, typically 128 to 512 bytes in length. Each feature vector will correspond to a set of descriptors or attributes of the object. The feature vector is referred to as metadata. The feature vector and the ROI are returned as the result, giving both the object identification and the location of the object in the frame. With this information, it is possible to combine this with the video data, perhaps to draw a bounding box around the object using the ROI information and providing color coding or text annotation on the video frame (OSD Blend Video + AI Results block).

From this point, the data flow is like that described earlier for the NVR, except now it is feasible to construct a database of objects' identity, location, and times. The data can be used to flag events of interest to a human operator, relieving the operator of the tedium of monitoring routine events. In addition, the database can be queried to identify trends over time that would not otherwise be apparent. The guiding principle is that routine decisions, D_R, can be made by machines and critical decisions, D_C, can be retained for human operators.

Video Analytic Accelerators – Optimized Analytics

The final major component of an IMSS system is the introduction of specialized accelerators for the required processing. General purpose systems work well when the number of video streams is modest and or the compute per stream is modest. However, as Table 3-8 Selected Neural Network Models and Metrics indicates the compute load per Neural Network can be quite substantial.

The overall data flow is similar to that of the NVR/Video Analytics node with a few crucial differences. Figure 3-24 describes the Video Analytics Accelerators data flow for High Density Deep Learning (HDDL) segments. The primary difference is that the accelerator will be a specialized device optimized for the intense compute loads and memory bandwidths demanded by advanced Neural Networks applications. The dotted line demarcated the physical and logical boundary between the host system and the accelerator. In the example shown, the interface is a PCIe interface, common across a wide variety of computer systems.

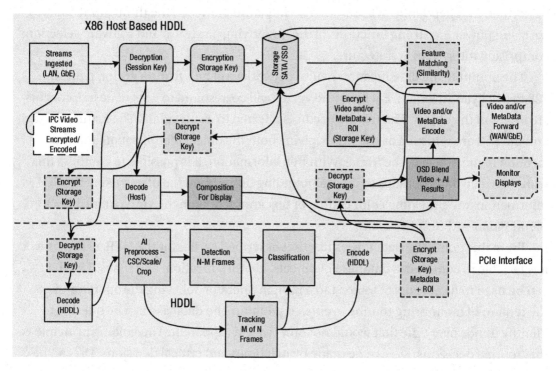

Figure 3-24. *Video analytics accelerator*

The introduction of the PCIe interface potentially exposes data transfers across the interface to interception and modification by adversaries. For this reason, it is necessary to ensure the data is encrypted and decrypted as part of traversing the PCIe (or equivalent) interconnect. Depending on if there is a single tenant or multiple tenants accessing the accelerator will determine if a single key is sufficient or if a multi-key schema is required. The second modification relates to minimizing the bandwidth traversing the PCIe interface. Referring to Tables 3-5 and 3-6 regarding compressed vs. uncompressed video, it is clearly advantageous in all but the most modest applications to compress the video before sending across the PCIe link. This will not only conserve bandwidth for other system activities but will also notably impact power consumption.

Within the accelerator, it is critical to ensure that there are features and capabilities to ensure that both the data and the Neural Network model are protected. The trained Neural Network model embodies substantial Intellectual Property value, in some cases representing much of a company's valuation.

Like the rapid evolution of Neural Networks themselves, the Neural Network Accelerators are rapidly evolving to service the computational, power, and cost requirements of applications. For inferencing tasks, the performance of an accelerator is up to 10x that of a general compute platform in terms of both absolute performance (FPS) and cost effectiveness (FPS/$).

Conclusions and Summary

At the beginning of this chapter, we set out to cover critical concepts aspects of the IMSS systems as a foundational framework for addressing security in IMSS systems. At that time, the goal was to address the following key topics:

- Key considerations and elements in architecting a data pipeline

- Basic tasks of an E2E IMSS pipeline – Capture, Storage, and Display

- Evolution of IMSS Systems – Analog to Digital to Connected to Intelligent

- Sensing the World – Video

- Making Sense of the World – Algorithms, Neural Networks, and Metadata

- Architecting IMSS Systems – IP Cameras, Network Video Recorders (NVRs), and Accelerators

In this chapter, we have discussed the basic IMSS systems and data paths. The key considerations regarding decision-making, accuracy, throughput, and latency were introduced. From these concepts, the fundamentals of capture, storage, and display were developed and related to how decisions are made, and action taken. A key concept was how data is transformed to information and information to action. The security risks at each of these stages were delineated.

The next stage was to apply these concepts to review the evolution of IMSS systems from the earliest analog systems to modern AI-based systems, showing how the basic concepts have evolved over that progression. At each stage, the security risks particular to the stage of evolution from IMSS 1.0 to IMSS 4.0 architectures were brought forward. Key architectural and feature changes were described and the impact on the overall system capabilities.

Key to recent advancements is the introduction of Machine Learning and AI in the form of Neural networks. These advancements both enable new and valuable features, but also introduce potential vulnerabilities, if not properly addressed.

Finally, basic elements of the IMSS system in terms of IP cameras, Network Video recorders/Video Analytics Nodes and Accelerators were described.

In the subsequent chapters, we will use this foundational understanding and framework to further explore the strengths, vulnerabilities, and strategies for robust implementation of security in the AI world. We will examine some representative systems

CHAPTER 4

Securing the IMSS Assets

This chapter provides an introductory understanding of assets, threat modeling, attacks, and mitigations. Let's start with a few definitions. Assets are the things that have value or present risk. Assets include personally identifying data like IDs, names, locations; confidential data like trade secrets or intellectual property; and cryptographic secrets like keys. Also the security processes like encryption and decryption processing, hashing, and signing and signature verification can be considered assets.

A threat is an agent or activity that is motivated to attack: to steal or tamper with an asset. And Mitigations are the defensive methods to prevent the attacks.

For more information, see the references.

Why Should You Think About Threats?

Threat modeling is a standard practice in security analysis for a number of reasons.

First, threat modeling is a method that provides insight into the assets that need to be protected and into the ways those assets can be compromised. The analysis provides insight into how you can deliver the best value to your customer and maximize your investment in mitigations. You can focus your resources on the most common, easiest attacks on the highest value assets and avoid spending resources on mitigations for threats that are costly to develop or execute. Some of these methods also make it easy to understand defense in depth which not only makes it more difficult to attack an asset, but also, defense in depth may be much easier and less expensive to implement compared to one really elaborate mitigation.

The second benefit of careful security threat modeling is you can prevent losses before they happen, which raises customer satisfaction and keeps customers coming back.

The original version of this chapter was previously published without open access. A correction to this chapter is available at https://doi.org/10.1007/978-1-4842-8297-7_9

© Intel 2023, corrected publication 2023
J. Booth et al., *Demystifying Intelligent Multimode Security Systems*,
https://doi.org/10.1007/978-1-4842-8297-7_4

Threat modeling requires thinking in militaristic terms, threats, attacks, defenses, and so on. While this may seem paranoid, it is a necessary mode of thinking for security analysis. One must change their mindset from how a system does work to how it can be fooled or get around mitigations in it to gain access to information or to make it stop working. In order to do that, one must think like an attacker. Secure design means thinking not only about making a system do what it is supposed to do but also designing a system that cannot do what it is not supposed to do.

Summary

Figure 4-1 illustrates the range of types of attacks, examples of typical system assets, technology that can mitigate the attacks, and the general types of adversaries at each level.

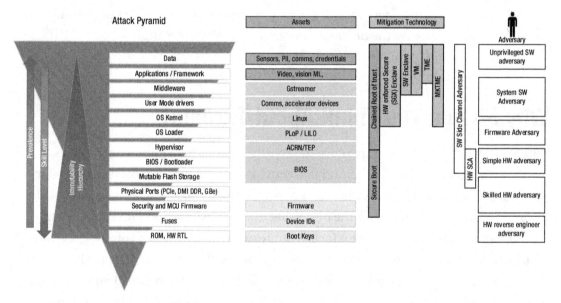

Figure 4-1. *Attacks, threats, and mitigations*

On the left-hand side of the figure, an inverted attack pyramid is shown. The general classes of assets in the white boxes are organized in a hierarchy where the easiest and most prevalent attacks are at the top and the most difficult and least common attacks are at the bottom. The hierarchy also represents the security hierarchy in terms of privilege. For example, if a hypervisor is attacked and compromised, that enables attacks on any higher assets, from the OS kernel to applications and data. As a general rule, when you progress down the asset stack, the assets are more immutable. Data and applications are easy to read or tamper with, but ROM and transistors are much more difficult to observe or change the state of. Some of that is inherent, and some is due to explicit design. The explicit design aspect is because of the hierarchy, that is, if those assets are compromised, anything else in the device or system can be compromised.

Threat Modeling

Threat modeling is performed by analyzing the assets and relevant threats in the context of the system environment, the value (or risk from) of the assets, and the cost and efficacy of the mitigations.

Threat Modeling Terminology

Abbr	Term	Definition
	Active Attack	An attack where the device, its inputs, or its environment are tampered with in order to make the device behave abnormally. Secrets are revealed by exploiting the abnormal behavior of the device. Active attacks are generally more detectable than passive attacks. (See Passive Attack and side channel attack)
APT	Advanced Persistent Threat	An advanced persistent threat is an attack in which an unauthorized person gains access to a network, or a malware component is inserted, and stays there undetected for a long period of time. The purpose of an APT attack is to steal data rather than to cause damage.

(continued)

Abbr	Term	Definition
	Asset	An asset is something that has intrinsic value to an enterprise or an individual. Also, an asset's value may be due to the liability or risk it carries for an enterprise or individual. Capabilities that protect functionality or valuable information are also considered security assets. Examples are: • Processing or Storage of data that reveals a person's identity (private data), for example, IDs numbers, names, sensor data, localization data, affiliations, etc. • Processing or Storage of Cryptographic secrets, for example, Keys, Hashes, constants. • Processing or Storage of confidential data, for example, protected audio or video content streams. • Cryptographic processing capabilities.
	Confidential Data	A person's or organization's information, which is expected to be private or disclosed only to selected individuals.
CC	Common Criteria	common criteria for Information Technology Security Evaluation.
	Cryptographic Key	A cryptographic key is a number used by a cryptographic algorithm to convert plain text into cipher text. If the algorithm is symmetric, the same key also converts from cipher text to plain text. There are many different types of keys (see Key Types). According to Kerckhoff's Principle, a cryptosystem should be secure even if everything about the system, except the key, is known.
	Foundational Asset	Device or System assets upon which the overall security architecture depends. The Root of Trust is *the* foundational element of security in a device. Other assets considered elements of the security foundation are platform Integrity; Secure IDs; cryptographic key generation and storage; Protected Data; cryptographic algorithms and the instructions and hardware used to compute them; Trusted Platform Modules, and Trusted Execution Technology.

(continued)

Abbr	Term	Definition
	Malware	**Malware** (a portmanteau for **malicious software**) is any software intentionally designed to cause damage to a computer, server, client, or computer network (by contrast, software that causes *unintentional* harm due to some deficiency is typically described as a software bug)
	Passive Attack	An attack where the crypto device is operated largely within specification. Secrets are revealed by observing physical properties of the device. (see active attack, side channel attack)
	Personally Identifiable Information	**"Personally identifiable information"** (PII), as used in US privacy law and information security, is information that can be used on its own or with other information to identify, contact, or locate a single person, or to identify an individual in context. The abbreviation PII is widely accepted in the US context, but the phrase it abbreviates has four common variants based on *personal/personally*, and *identifiable/identifying*. Not all are equivalent, and for legal purposes the effective definitions vary depending on the jurisdiction and the purposes for which the term is being used. (In other countries with privacy protection laws derived from the OECD privacy principles, the term used is more often "personal information," which may be somewhat broader: in Australia's *Privacy Act* 1988 [Cth] "personal information" also includes information from which the person's identity is "reasonably ascertainable," potentially covering some information not covered by PII.) *<http://en.wikipedia.org/wiki/Personally_identifiable_information>*
POSM	Power On State Machine	State machine (now either logic or FW) that controls the power on sequence
	Private Data	Information that can be used on its own or with other information to identify, contact, or locate a single person, or to identify an individual in context. *<http://en.wikipedia.org/wiki/Personally_identifiable_information>*

(continued)

Abbr	Term	Definition
	Root Key	A root key is a type of cryptographic key from which all other keys are derived or a key used to encrypt other cryptographic keys for storage.
	Rootkit	A **rootkit** is a stealthy type of software, often malicious, designed to hide the existence of certain processes or programs from normal methods of detection and enable continued privileged access to a computer.[1] The term *rootkit* is a concatenation of "root" (the traditional name of the privileged account on Unix operating systems) and the word "kit" (which refers to the software components that implement the tool). The term "rootkit" has negative connotations through its association with malware.[1]
		Rootkit installation can be automated, or an attacker can install it once they've obtained root or Administrator access. Obtaining this access is a result of direct attack on a system (i.e., exploiting a known vulnerability, password [either by cracking, privilege escalation, or social engineering]). Once installed, it becomes possible to hide the intrusion as well as to maintain privileged access. The key is the root/Administrator access. Full control over a system means that existing software can be modified, including software that might otherwise be used to detect or circumvent it.
		Pasted from <http://en.wikipedia.org/wiki/Rootkit>
RoT	Root of Trust	A Root of Trust is a source that can always be trusted in a device or in a system. In order to be trustworthy, the Root of Trust must be immutable. The Root of Trust must begin in the hardware for immutability. And even being in hardware, it must be carefully protected from being tampered with in any way.

(*continued*)

Abbr	Term	Definition
SCA	Side Channel Attack	In cryptography, a **side channel attack** is any attack based on information gained from the physical implementation of a cryptosystem, rather than brute force or theoretical weaknesses in the algorithms (compare cryptanalysis). For example, timing information, power consumption, electromagnetic leaks, or even sound can provide an extra source of information which can be exploited to break the system. Some side-channel attacks require technical knowledge of the internal operation of the system on which the cryptography is implemented, although others such as differential power analysis are effective as black-box attacks. Many powerful side channel attacks are based on statistical methods pioneered by Paul Kocher. *Pasted from <http://en.wikipedia.org/wiki/Side_ channel_attack>*
Stride	Spoofing, Tampering, Repudiation, Information Disclosure, Denial of Service, and Elevation of Privilege	Microsoft security threat modeling method • **Spoofing identity**. An example of identity spoofing is illegally accessing and then using another user's authentication information, such as username and password. • **Tampering with data**. Data tampering involves the malicious modification of data. Examples include unauthorized changes made to persistent data, such as that held in a database, and the alteration of data as it flows between two computers over an open network, such as the Internet. • **Repudiation**. Repudiation threats are associated with users who deny performing an action without other parties having any way to prove otherwise—for example, a user performs an illegal operation in a system that lacks the ability to trace the prohibited operations. **Nonrepudiation** refers to the ability of a system to counter repudiation threats. For example, a user who purchases an item might have to sign for the item upon receipt. The vendor can then use the signed receipt as evidence that the user did receive the package.

(continued)

Abbr	Term	Definition
		• **Information disclosure**. Information disclosure threats involve the exposure of information to individuals who are not supposed to have access to it—for example, the ability of users to read a file that they were not granted access to, or the ability of an intruder to read data in transit between two computers.
		• **Denial of service**. Denial of service (DoS) attacks deny service to valid users—for example, by making a Web server temporarily unavailable or unusable. You must protect against certain types of DoS threats simply to improve system availability and reliability.
		• **Elevation of privilege**. In this type of threat, an unprivileged user gains privileged access and thereby has sufficient access to compromise or destroy the entire system. Elevation of privilege threats include those situations in which an attacker has effectively penetrated all system defenses and become part of the trusted system itself, a dangerous situation indeed.
		*From <https://docs.microsoft.com/en-us/previous-versions/commerce-server/ee823878(v=cs.20)?ranMID=24542&ranEAID=XdSnOe3h3*k&ranSiteID=XdSnOe3h3.k-bc.qorAlSQUZhRf2UdCMFQ&tduid=(f31bb4549339eeddO06a8ba47b474f03)(256380)(2459594)(XdSnOe3h3.k-bc.qorAlSQUZhRf2UdCMFQ)()>*
	Spoofing	In the context of network security, a spoofing attack is a situation in which one person or program successfully masquerades as another by falsifying data, thereby gaining an illegitimate advantage. Wikipedia

(continued)

Abbr	Term	Definition
TCB	Trusted Computing Base	The **trusted computing base** (**TCB**) of a computer system is the set of all hardware, firmware, and/or software components that are critical to its security, in the sense that bugs or vulnerabilities occurring inside the TCB might jeopardize the security properties of the entire system. By contrast, parts of a computer system outside the TCB must not be able to misbehave in a way that would leak any more privileges than are granted to them in accordance with the security policy. From *<https://en.wikipedia.org/wiki/Trusted_computing_base>*
	Threat	An action which if successful would permit access to confidential information or permit a denial of service or escalation of service. Wiki: 1. In computer **security**, a **threat** is a possible danger that might exploit a **vulnerability** to breach **security** and thus cause possible harm. For more defs See also: `http://en.wikipedia.org/wiki/Threat_(computer)`
	Trojan	Malware that enters a device disguised or embedded in an apparently legitimate form. Trojans are most often SW but can also be embedded in component hardware as a malicious modification of logic. Once the trojan is executed it can take a wide range of actions.
	Trusted system	A system whose failure can break the security policy
	Trustworthy	A system or component that won't fail
TE or TXT	Trusted Execution Technology	Intel TXT is the name of a computer hardware technology whose primary goals are (a) Attestation – attest to the authenticity of a platform and its operating system (OS); (b) assure that an authentic OS starts in a trusted environment and thus can be considered a trusted OS; (c) provide the trusted OS with additional security capabilities not available to an unproven OS. Pasted from *<http://en.wikipedia.org/wiki/Trusted_Execution_Technology>*
	Vulnerability	A property of a system which, in conjunction with a threat, can lead to a security failure.

Threat Taxonomy

Threats to assets can be broken down into SW threats, HW threats, and special cases which involve both HW and SW.

Basic Types of Software Threats

Unprivileged SW threats come from low privilege shells, applications, or drivers (Ring3 or user mode). The privileges are granted by the system SW. The capabilities for unprivileged SW are the ability read or write mapped memory with privileges granted by system SW. User mode applications can also execute from with a secure enclave instance.

Remote threats come from access and control over various network fabrics used to communicate to other platforms, both locally or over the Internet. The remote agent can read messages on the network, forge, inject, intercept, delay, delete, reorder, deliver to the wrong party, and resend messages. It can also cause network endpoints to reveal session and long-lived state.

System Software has control over the operating system, virtual machine monitor, and system management. The System software can control scheduling execution; the execution mode (e.g., privileged mode, 32/64 bit compatibility, host/guest mode); read all architecturally visible memory (including page tables); write to all unprotected memory; read architectural registers and write unlocked ones; execute an enclave (even a malicious one); program HW devices (memory controllers, DMA engines); write page tables; control contents of caches; force reset and control power states; and control installation of patches and firmware.

Threats from firmware not only enable system SW threats, but they also enable control of boot code and system management mode. This can bypass secure boot checkpoints, control system state during power state changes, modify SMM RAM without detection, create virtual devices, modify system firmware (and make it persistent), and modify registers that are open to SMM privilege.

Basic Types of Hardware Threats

Threats to system hardware require physical access to the system. Here accessible busses can be monitored, and even read and written. This includes busses such as I2S and I2C for peripheral devices, non-volatile and DRAM memory, and interfaces to sensors and displays. System inputs such as USB, keyboards, and pointing devices can be monitored and controlled. Also, hardware debugger capabilities can be exploited to gain access to valuable assets if not properly protected, for example, TAP, ITP, and JTAG debug interfaces.

Some threat analysis methods (and the mitigations to the threats) consider the cost of discovering and carrying out the attack. For these threats, it is important not only to have physical possession of a system but also to have the proper equipment to monitor or control the interfaces or devices (which can be very expensive).

Hardware Reverse engineering threats involve expensive equipment and highly specialized skillsets. The cost generally limits these to nation states or criminal enterprises, and these are generally very expensive to mitigate.

Insider, Supply Chain, and Authorized Agent Threats

These threats come from agents with a high level of authorization and may also involve access to design, manufacturing, or distribution facilities and devices that have not completed all the manufacturing steps.

Note that remote attacks which gain access to systems via phishing, poor cybersecurity hygiene like default passwords, backdoors, or credential stuffing are often followed by exploiting a vulnerability to escalate privileges and then proceed to exfiltrate documents, install APT or RAT trojans, or mount lateral attacks on other devices in the system. These are generally exploiting a common weak point in any system: the humans that are trusted within a system. These attacks can be difficult to differentiate from valid administrative activity and often are not defended because a system trusts devices and agents inside an enterprise system.

Side Channel Attack Threats

Side channels attacks exploit information leakage, often from resources that are shared between processes that are expected to be isolated from each other. The leakage comes from the physical implementation of the system rather than the cryptographic algorithm or the protocol. These are second order effects and may require critical information about system leakage, but can also require only publicly disclosed information or even no information at all. Systems leak information through power consumption, timing, electromagnetic emission, or even acoustic information.

Figure 4-2 shows a taxonomy format for threats. The easiest (and most common) attacks are passive and active SW attacks. These can be performed without having physical access to a system and often are combined or sequenced to advance the attack.

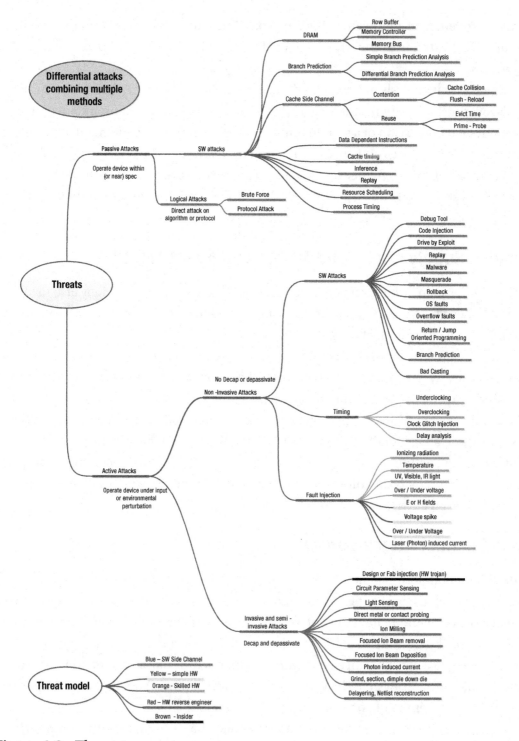

Figure 4-2. *Threat taxonomy*

The threats in Figure 4-2 may be combined with the observation methods in Figure 4-3 to reduce the time or effort of the attack. However, these generally require physical access and test equipment to perform.

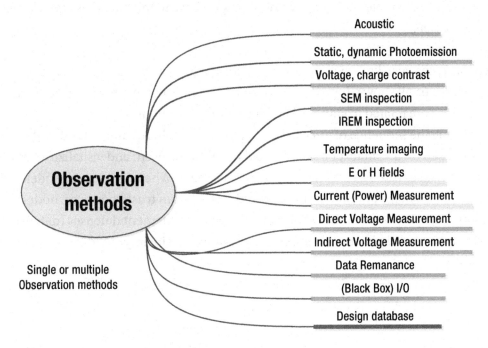

Figure 4-3. *Observation methods*

Threat Analysis Methods

This section describes the basic concept of threat analysis and two publicly available methods of analyzing threats.

Basic Concepts

The generalized methods of analyzing threats and mitigations to the threats start with identifying assets and stating objectives for protecting those assets. The mitigations should fully meet the objectives and ideally there are multiple layers of mitigations (defense in depth) which increases the difficulty of an attack.

Consideration of the consequences or risks of a successful attack is also valuable. Pragmatically, it would not make sense to add cost to a product to protect an asset with no value. Likewise, when attacks are very expensive and difficult, they also tend to be expensive and difficult to mitigate, so it only makes sense to mitigate these attacks for high value assets.

Threat Trees

Threat Trees (also known as attack trees) are a helpful way to analyze defense in depth. These will show where the attack starts and how it may progress through a system. These are related to standard fault tree formal methods.

Analyzing the sequence of attacks and the methods helps to understand preferred methods based on the attacker's skill set, tools that can be used, and visualize an attack path as it traverses through a device and across a system. When a system is modeled, a threat tree also helps to visualize unexpected attacks from trusted devices, nodes, and users. This also helps to show how several easy to implement defenses (defense in depth) may be provided better defense at less cost than a single-point defense.

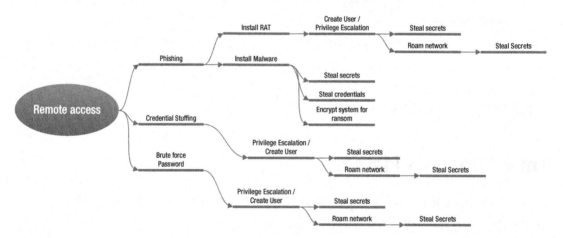

Figure 4-4. *Threat tree example*

Common Criteria for Information Technology Security Evaluation

The Common Criteria for Information Technology Security Evaluation (often shortened to Common Criteria) is a framework for vendors to specify and evaluate claims about security attributes of their products. See www.commoncriteriaportal.org/ for more detail. Common Criteria is much more than a threat analysis method, but the CC analysis method has useful characteristics that are described here.

Common criteria defines a quantitative method of evaluating the cost of identification and exploitation of an attack. Identification is the cost and difficulty incurred in the process of discovering a method of attack, and exploitation identifies the cost and difficulty of executing the attack. This is useful because attacks that are expensive and difficult to identify may represent a valid threat that needs to be mitigated if the exploitation is low cost and easy to perform. This is particularly true if the assets are high value and numerous. Cybersecurity calls this the smart cow problem – you only need one smart cow to figure out how to get out of the pen, after that, the dumb cattle can follow that example. Conversely, even if an attack is simple and Inexpensive to identify, if it is expensive or difficult to perform, it will be less likely to happen.

The evaluation criteria for identification are the equipment and tools needed; expertise; knowledge of the target; elapsed time; access to the target; and whether the attack investigation requires open targets where the mitigations may not be active. Exploitation uses the first five categories. Each category is assigned a standardized rating score from 0 to 8. The scores are summed for the cost of identification and cost of exploitation, and those two are summed again, and binned and rated as low to high cost.

Another benefit of the CC method is that standardizing the rating scores allows the ratings to be compared across components and systems from different manufacturers.

STRIDE

STRIDE[1] is an acronym for Spoofing, Tampering, Repudiation, Information disclosure, Denial of service, and Elevation of privilege.

Spoofing is an attack on the security principle of authenticity. Here the attacker attempts to appear to be someone else.

Tampering is an attack on data or system integrity. The attacker attempts to alter data, processes, or system state to bypass security functions or disrupt proper functionality of the system.

Repudiation refers to denying that an event occurred or that data was produced by a specific system or person. Conversely, non-repudiation assures that an event occurred or data was produced by a specific system or person. Altering logs, timestamps, location data, system IDs, and user IDs are examples of repudiation attacks.

---

[1]https://en.wikipedia.org/wiki/STRIDE_(security)

Information disclosure is an attack on the security principle of confidentiality or privacy. The target here is valuable information or other security assets that lead to valuable information like encryption keys.

Denial of service is an attack on the security principle of availability. Commonly, this attack will make a system unavailable by disrupting communication functions or overwhelming a system with activity. In some cases, a Denial-of-Service attack can cause permanent damage to a system, for example, by overheating the system.

Elevation of privilege is an attack on authorization. General users have limited rights in a system. But administrators have higher privileges of installing or deleting software; reading or writing anything in storage or DRAM; modifying system state; starting or stopping processes; changing logs; registering new users in a system; etc.

In the STRIDE analysis method, assets are examined under the STRIDE threats to understand the consequences of the attack and to define mitigations.

IMSS Assets
Value of Assets

An asset is something of value to an individual or enterprise or something that carries a risk if it becomes known. Functionality can also be considered an asset, not only from the availability perspective but also in the sense of proper execution of security protocol, cryptography, or components like machine learning applications that would result in economic damage, a compromise in safety, or loss of life if they fail.

In IMSS Systems, there are three basic classes of assets. These are classified by ownership of the asset into foundational, data, and application assets.

One measure of the security of an asset is its resistance to change. Although nothing is completely immutable, assets can be classified in terms of immutability. Often system security practices are designed to increase the immutability of assets and to detect when assets have been tampered with.

Figure 4-5 illustrates this relationship for the basic assets in a system.

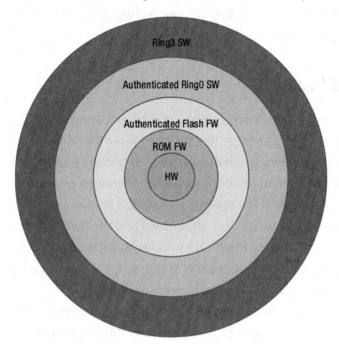

Figure 4-5. *Immutability ring diagram*

Semiconductor hardware represents the most immutable layer in a system, especially at the transistor and state machine levels. Transistors are the most reliable and robust elements, which is why the most robust security overall must be based on a hardware root of trust.

The next layer is processing that runs from code stored in Read only Memory (ROM). ROM is essentially hardwired transistor storage which cannot be changed without changing the semiconductor masks themselves. While this layer is also very robust, it is considered less so than pure HW due to the complexity of the processor that runs the code (the number of transistors involved) and due to the potential for exploitable vulnerabilities in the code.

Firmware that is executed from non-volatile memory (like Flash memory) is the next level of robustness. Flash memory (unless it is protected) can be modified easily by a user. When code stored in non-volatile memory gets copied to DRAM for execution, even if that code is protected, its immutability must be considered in terms of DRAM reliability and protection, not as the properties of the initial storage method. Because non-volatile memory is easily modified, achieving this level of robustness requires both protecting the ability to write to it, and strong cryptographic authentication to ensure it has not been tampered with.

Foundational Assets

Foundational Assets for a device or system are the basis upon which the overall security architecture depends. The hardware Root of Trust is *the* foundational element of security in a device; without a hardware root of trust and supporting foundational security capabilities, it is impossible to protect data and applications assets in an IMSS. Other assets considered elements of the security foundation are Secure IDs; cryptographic key generation and storage; cryptographic algorithms and the instructions and hardware used to compute them; Trusted Platform Modules; and Trusted Execution Technology. In addition, isolation technologies like HW architecture to support enclaves and virtual machines are important parts of an overall secure HW base.

At the platform level, foundational assets might be components like the power supply, sensors, non-volatile storage, discrete Trusted Platform Modules, DRAM, as well as the communications between these components.

Many software components can also be considered foundational assets. Firmware that is part of the secure boot chain of trust, Hypervisors, Operating Systems, Device Drivers are part of the security foundation that protect system data and applications assets. Also, firmware that has a role in security protocols such as security services for communication security, device configuration, key exchange, key generation, key storage, cryptographic services such as encryption, integrity checking, and authentication can be part of the overall trust chain in a system. Another critical security role is a maintenance role, which provides status and telemetry as well as manages secure, authenticated updates to system FW and SW. And finally, security services like packet inspection, intrusion detection, anomaly detection, alerts, automated responses would be part of the chain of trust for platforms.

At the system level, in addition to platforms like cameras and video recorders, the network links, network switches, gateways, ISP and public Internet, communications like Wi-Fi and cellular data carriers, and platforms in operations centers or cloud service providers may be critical in an end-to-end system.

The Internet is resilient to failure and inexpensive to use compared to private networks. However, from the security principle that higher complexity means less security (or complexity is the enemy of security), the Internet is arguably the most complex thing ever designed by humans. So, it is very important to consider that complexity when an end-to-end system uses the public Internet for communications. The basic Internet architecture was not designed with security in mind, it assumes all endpoints and transmission nodes are trustworthy. So, security is layered on top of a security-agnostic architecture. Because of this, it is essential to properly configure security for Internet protocols.

Foundational assets are intrinsic to the hardware and software of systems. Providers like component manufacturers, Original Design Manufacturers, Original Equipment Manufacturers, and OS and infrastructure software vendors must include and utilize foundational security assets to secure valuable assets in the systems: data assets and application assets. This is a system cost for those providers which provides a security benefit to protection of the end user and software providers' assets, which presents unique challenges to those parties that bear the cost. For more, see the section on Attackonomics.

Data Assets

Data assets in an IMSS are the inputs, event and sensor data; and the outputs, processed events and processed sensor data; plus the results of analytics inferences derived from the input data.

The IMSS inputs can be simple events like a door-opening indicator to more complex data from audio or still image or video systems. Output derived from these data range from basic understanding of characteristics of the data source to complex understanding requiring narrowly defined differentiating criteria all the way to high cognitive understanding such as situational awareness, which must process many different input data types and sources.

The value of the data assets depends on the cost of gathering and producing the data, and the benefit of the use of the data. In some cases, these data represent proprietary company data or trade secrets. Other types of data may be expensive to gather, such as Magnetic Resonance Imaging data.

The value of the output data is higher than the input data because of the additional knowledge provided by the analytics. Benefits of high accuracy, high throughput, and the amount of information that can be processed can save lives, provide improved outcomes, enable faster response, and more complete understanding based on more data than was possible until now.

These assets are generally the property of the system owner, but in some cases, laws confer ownership (or at least rights to determine use) to the subject that the data is gathered from and the system owner is a custodian of the data with legal responsibilities and limits for how it can be used or made public. This is particularly true for privacy-related data under the growing body of laws and regulations such as the EU General Data Protection Regulation and the California Consumer Privacy Act. These laws reflect how much people value their own privacy and want to control their personal data.

Application Assets

Application assets are the analytics applications themselves. Neural Networks are generally trained using an annotated set of training data, and there is a positive correlation between the amount of training data and the accuracy of the annotation with the accuracy of the inferencing results of the neural network.

In some cases, annotated data is the result of an existing data collection process. Take for example driver's licenses or national IDs, which associate personal information like names and addresses with biometric identification like a photograph. These databases may be made available to train neural networks for no cost to the model developer based on legally mandated uses of that database to benefit the public. In other cases, the cost of gathering a large number of sample data sets that have the required diversity to produce an accurate NN model can be very high. Larger data sets result in higher accuracy for the algorithms and collating and processing the data can take months. Furthermore, annotation often must be performed by humans. Imagine annotating an image of an automobile for five attributes, even for an expert this might take 20 seconds per image. For 100,000 images it takes more than 500 hours. Images from Magnetic Resonance Imaging take nearly seven minutes on average to judge, and must be done by a highly paid expert, so the cost of this database could be 400x the cost of a simple database requiring no particular expertise.

These data may also be subject to privacy laws and regulations and not only carry the cost of gathering and annotating the data but also the cost of getting permission to use the data from the subject.

Model training is an iterative process and there is no way to guarantee that the network will converge to a good solution, converge quickly, let alone converge at all. And there can be additional time required to profile and optimize the network to perform trade-off optimizations between accuracy, parameter finite register length representation, performance, power use, power efficiency, memory footprint, etc. In addition, developers may want to try several network topologies to find the optimal solution for performance and power. All of this can add up to 100s of hours of server time.

The neural network topology itself can also be a significant cost and a significant source of product differentiation. Many model topologies are public and free to use; however, some enterprises develop proprietary NN models to maximize against goals like the best accuracy or highest performance.

A complex application like situational awareness may comprise several neural networks plus a cognate function perhaps written with fuzzy logic that requires multiple areas of human expertise, adding yet more cost to the application.

These factors mean that the investment in machine learning algorithms can be big. And the hyped value of neural networks amplifies the perception of value. Chapter 5 provides more detail on machine learning security. In the next section we will see why that is important due to the economics of attacks, or *Attackonomics*.

Threats

Attackonomics

Attackonomics is the economics of the threat environment. The basic economic principle is the return on investment of an attack. If the attack becomes more expensive than the value of the asset, it doesn't make sense economically, so it won't happen. Correspondingly, high value assets will be threatened by more expensive attacks and therefore require more expensive mitigations to defend. To that desired outcome, well-implemented mitigations raise the expense of the attack to economic unfeasibility. The scale of an attack is another factor in the value derived from an attack. The economies of scale that keep costs low also make attacks scale easier. While there are billions of devices, those all use one of several CPU architectures and several OS implementations. In addition, while Open Source software is touted as being more secure because of wide use and multiple authors, it also is another source of vulnerability-based attack scalability due to a monoculture. Vulnerabilities in those few core components enable attacks that scale to billions of devices.

A recent case of vulnerabilities in Open Source SW serves as an example. Security researchers at Forescout analyzed Open Source TCP/IP stacks and in seven of those, identified 33 vulnerabilities, dubbed Amnesia-33.[2] An Internet scan identified 158 manufacturers using these seven stacks, and estimated that millions of devices may be affected.

The good news is that the vulnerabilities have been identified, and seven SW stacks need to be updated rather than 158. However, the bad news is the complexity, multiple responsible parties, and controllability of the updates mean that you can't count on actually updating the devices. The monoculture (in this case, seven cultures) scales the risks, but also scales the mitigations. The residual risk is a factor of the complexity of the updates and the timescale to update the devices.

Even in systems with full externalities, system manufacturers and system operators must consider the risk from disclosure of confidential or private information. The resultant loss of confidence and loss of reputation can have a devastating impact in the future, even if there is no direct revenue loss from a disclosure event. New ransomware business models[3] combining file encryption with disclosure of an enterprise's customer information are an example of that kind of risk.

There is also a perceptual problem with decisions on security and the risk of loss. Humans make poor judgments about risk that do not agree with objective measures. We tend to be risk averse when dealing with low probability losses and risk seeking when dealing with low probability gains. Why talk about that here? Because it is important to consider not only the quantitative probabilities when assessing the cost of mitigations, it is also important to understand how it will be perceived by non-expert decision makers. Methods to express decisions in ways to comprehend how people make decisions will lead to more effective cybersecurity policy.

The economics principle of externalities, which are common in Cybersecurity, are one of the most difficult conditions to address. Externalities occur when one party values an asset highly, but another party pays the cost for protecting that asset. For example, unless that asset is widely considered valuable, the cost of protecting that asset ends up falling solely on a small segment of the customer base who may not be able to afford the protection relative to the loss risk of the asset.

---

[2] SC Media, *Amnesia-33 Vulnerabilities affect 158 Vendors, millions of devices* (https://www.scmagazine.com/news/architecture/amnesia-33-vulnerabilities-affect-158-vendors-millions-of-devices)

[3] www.securityweek.com/fbi-warns-businesses-egregor-ransomware-attacks

There is another economy in security that is vital: white hat hackers. These may be members of an internal team in an enterprise, or members of a security services company, independent experts, or academics. The economy that motivates security services and independent experts is bug bounties. Criminal hackers must stay hidden, but all types of white hat hackers are also motivated by recognition. The goal of white hat attacks is to disclose the vulnerability to the enterprise or group responsible privately, giving them time to mitigate the vulnerability before it becomes public. These do not generally represent threats; however, publishing vulnerabilities is often accompanied by a proof-of-concept attack which can be weaponized by an attacker. So, the proof of concept is relevant in attackonomics because it reduces the cost of developing an attack. It is also relevant because the mitigation is often a software update, and systems that have not installed the update will be vulnerable. The economics and complexity of keeping a system up-to-date is part of the economics of attacks. That is, having an automated system that maintains the software stack lowers the cost of that activity.

Current Threats

According to the Security Industries Association 2020 Security Megatrends Report, the top megatrend in physical security systems is the impact of cybersecurity.

Cybersecurity threats are increasingly sophisticated and complex. A useful example is the Mirai (*future* in Japanese) Malware. Mirai started its evolution as part of a scheme by three college students to gain an advantage in the online computer game Minecraft. Mirai is a self-replicating worm that crawled the Internet looking for IoT devices that were using the default manufacturers' default login credentials. The infections initially doubled every 76 minutes. Realizing the power of this attack tool, the students started a new business model, botnets for hire. At its peak, the botnet had enslaved more than 600,000 devices worldwide, most of which were surveillance cameras, video recorders, and network routers, all of which are standard components in IMSS. As the attacks progressed from August to October 2016, the malware was iterated 24 times, making it more virulent. This botnet was used in four successive Distributed Denial of Service (dDoS) attacks that broke records. On September 16, 2016, the French hosting provider OVH suffered a 1.1 Tera bit per second (Tbs) dDoS attack from 145,000 devices. Up to that point, large dDoS attacks were in the range of 50 Megabits per second, so this was > 200 times as powerful. A few days later, a Mirai-based dDoS revenge attack was launched at the Krebs on Security website (hosted by Akamai), which peaked at 623 Giga bits per second, knocking the website offline for four days. Then, on October 21, most of Eastern United States was interrupted by the largest ever attack on Dyn, an Internet backbone DNS provider. This interrupted services in the United States and Europe for major sites like Amazon, Netflix, Paypal, and Reddit. Following the Dyn dDoS in November 2016, the entire country of Liberia was taken offline.

The Mirai source code was posted in September 2016, which opened the tool to a wide malware developer community to create their own attack variants and botnets. The DYN attack was significant because the code used to dDoS Dyn was a new evolution from the original source. By February 2017, more than 15,000 attacks were launched using dozens of variants of Mirai.

And Mirai is still being evolved to exploit new infection methods. Starting from default passwords as the entrance method, the tools were enhanced to add more default credentials, expand the portfolio of CPUs, add more attackable ports, and add more exploits like firmware and common use open source middleware vulnerabilities. Evolutionary Malware based on Mirai have been documented (Okiru, Satori, Matsuta and Pure Matsuta, and many more).

This illustrates several aspects of threats to IMSS systems. Poorly secured IoT devices will be exploited for nefarious means, threats evolve rapidly, and there is a market for developing and a market for exploiting vulnerable devices. It also illustrates the attackonomics aspect of monocultures in exploits of commonly used open source middleware like Simple Object Access Protocol (SOAP).

Vulnerabilities

There are several general types of vulnerabilities that can be exploited in IMSS systems.

The first and, in some analyses, the most common vulnerability is humans.

We can be fooled into revealing login credentials with social engineering or to download malware through Phishing emails, allowing attackers to remotely login to systems. Also, passwords are ubiquitous so people often will reuse passwords or use minor variants of passwords. When a website is hacked and improperly protected passwords are posted for sale on the dark web, not only can hackers purchase these to impersonate access to that website, but these also serve to prime credential stuffing tools to quickly crack passwords on other websites. Employing two-factor authentication also mitigates against leaked, stolen, and guessed credentials. Fast Identity Online (FIDO)[4] authentication devices can provide a robust authentication method that is more secure than email or SMS two-factor authentication.

Because humans must at times have access to security and privacy assets, they must understand and participate in implementing the cybersecurity of IMSS. Training personnel to recognize social engineering and Phishing attacks, adopting email authentication, isolating or sandboxing emails, using two factor authentication, and using password lockers with automatic password generators will help mitigate these human-oriented attacks. Note that several of these mitigations (email authentication, sandboxing emails, using password lockers) improve security by removing the human from the trust boundary.

The second class of vulnerabilities are failures of basic system hygiene principles.

The first task is to implement the **manufacturers' security hardening recommendations**. If they don't have a recommendation, you should select another manufacturer.

Systems should never be provisioned by the manufacturer with **missing, hardcoded, or fixed default login credentials** (i.e., the vulnerability that Mirai initially exploited). Passwords for systems delivered to end customers should be unique for each device and complex enough that they are difficult to guess or brute-force attack. Hidden backdoors, either for future envisioned convenience or just neglecting to remove test access, must also be deleted from all login authentication protocols. It might seem OK because they are not published, but there are numerous examples of hidden backdoors being discovered and exploited. Also, passwords should be well protected in storage and memory in the system.

In IMSS, there may be tens of thousands of devices under central management. While it is convenient to use a common password, it enables a Break Once, Repeat Everywhere (BORE) attack. A device management framework should eliminate the need for common passwords.

See the section on FIDO Onboarding for information on a secure way to perform this on initial power-on.

Administrative log files should be secure for forensic purposes. It shouldn't be easy for a hacker who poses as an administrator (escalates privileges) to cover their tracks by altering the log. Blockchain technology can ensure that log files can't be altered with

---

[4]https://fidoalliance.org/

no trace. This will not prevent nefarious activity, but it will allow system administrators to see what was done to the system to repair it, and they may be used for legal action against the hacker.

Security vulnerabilities can creep into systems at the **boundaries of secure processes**. For example, in a system with ethernet link encryption and storage volume encryption, data must be decrypted and re-encrypted. Plaintext data may be exposed to SW, the OS kernel, or exposed in memory during the transcription process. Processing in isolated environments such as virtual machines, or end-to-end security protocols will eliminate the exploitable gaps.

Adopt **Zero trust**[5] system design principles. Know what is on your network. While it is a good practice to physically isolate (airgap) the IP network used for physical security, it is more expensive, so some customers may not want to pay for the additional equipment (or naïvely believe their enterprise networks are secure). And some physical security systems are too geographically dispersed for a private network to be affordable, opting to use the public Internet instead. All devices have security weaknesses, plus devices may have latent interfaces like Wi-Fi, Bluetooth, or Zigbee that inadvertently bridge two networks resulting in a lateral attack on a physically isolated network. Endpoint devices like monitoring stations or the laptops, tablets, and cell phones providing remote monitoring capabilities may have both private network and public Internet access, serving as a bridge for attacks from the public Internet. Also, know who is on your network. IP addresses can be whitelisted for an extra layer of security. And the philosophy behind zero trust is based on the security principle of least privilege. That is, never automatically trust people or devices, only trust people and devices that you have authenticated, that you need to trust, and only for the time and to the level necessary. In addition, in consideration that the devices and personnel may not be trustworthy, provide defense in depth by encrypting all communications, irrespective of the expected isolation level of the network. See more details in the next section. Not only should you catalog the primary and secondary assets in the system but also you must measure them and monitor the integrity of those assets. Finally, the overall asset catalog, device catalog, authorized user catalog, activity logs, network traffic, asset access, requests for asset access, and asset data processing should be monitored, and abnormal behavior flagged.

---

[5] NIST.SP.800-207 Zero Trust Architecture (https://csrc.nist.gov/publications/detail/sp/800-207/final)

The multiple domains and the amount of information to be processed lends itself to a machine learning approach, which will be described in the Machine Learning Security Chapter.

Protect applications and data in storage and in transit. Applications should be deployed to be installed securely, allowing the installer to authenticate the application to make sure that it came from a reputable source (the one you expected), that the signature is current (has not been revoked), and that there were no transmission errors or tampering along the way. When stored, the storage media should also be protected with encryption and hashed to make it difficult to read or alter the drive contents. When read off the media at load time, the application should be integrity checked before allowing it to be executed. Additional runtime security isolation can be applied by using virtualization, isolating the applications from other applications running in the system, and for type 1 virtual machines, isolating them from the OS as well. In some platforms, high security trusted execution capabilities are available for applications such as Intel Software Guard Extension or Intel Trusted Domain. These capabilities add a HW enforcement layer for additional immutability and isolation.

An application developer may not want to rely on the system administrator to protect applications in storage. This is particularly true for high investment, high value applications such as machine learning. Applications can have a self-decrypting capability tied to license checks that enforces secure storage without relying on storage volume encryption. If storage volume encryption is also turned on, it then functions as a defense in depth, requiring two encryption protocols to be defeated to gain access to the application.

Data should likewise be protected in storage and in transit using encryption and integrity-checking protocols. Fully applying encryption and integrity not only protects the data but also if digital signatures are also applied (for example, having a camera sign the video stream), it also can allow assurance for forensic and legal use, and provides non-repudiation, preventing sources from denying where the content came from. ONVIF allows Secure Real Time Streaming Protocol (S-RTSP) which uses AES and AES-GCM cryptography to protect data transmitted over ethernet links. Proprietary and open source storage volume encryption protects the data while stored. And Digital Rights Management (DRM) methods can be used to protect streams across all transmission and Storage networks and devices.

Note that the application and data are often owned by different parties. While it is necessary for the applications to have access to the data in order to process it, the authentication and cryptographic keys belong to different parties and, therefore, must be delivered, maintained, and protected separately (i.e., isolated). Verifying that an application is not exfiltrating data that it shouldn't is difficult for system integrators and end users, particularly if the application includes performance telemetry that is returned to the application developer. Any telemetry returned to the application developer or any other party such as a cloud service provider, must be optional and under user control. This highlights the necessity of a trust relationship between the end user who owns the data and the application provider.

Universal Plug and Play and Port Forwarding is a simple way to allow access to security cameras and routers via the public Internet. Universal Plug and Play (UPnP) automates port forwarding and can also enable Network Address Translation (NAT) traversal. End users may not even be aware of UPnP being enabled by default, hence the don't shut it off and are not aware their systems are exposed and easily exploitable on the public Internet. This amounts to an open Internet interface and has been used in many attacks, including the Mirai and Persirai[6] botnets. Automatic onboarding tools (described in the next section), Virtual Private Networks, and Virtual Local Area Networks are more secure alternatives to UPnP and Port forwarding.

Auxiliary device interfaces like debug and USB ports may be present in devices that can be used in a physical attack to insert malware into a system. In the best case, physical ports that do not have strong security incorporated by default should be removed and the corresponding SW and drivers removed as well. If the ports are mandatory, they should not be enabled by default and should be covered with an access limit panel.

Remote access **Backdoors** must be removed from the SW. History has shown that backdoors left in systems will be discovered and exploited even if they are undisclosed.

Performance Profiling can be legitimate and useful for product improvement, but careful consideration must be applied to ensure that only the disclosed performance data is sent back to the manufacturer using a secure method, the profiling data channel cannot be hijacked, and the data gathered does not leak any personal information on individuals. <how to ensure this?>

Use automated tools to maintain secure systems with **updates**. The simpler and quicker you can provide SW updates to systems, the more secure they will be. IMSS can be complex and updates will need to be tested before broadly deploying them to avoid outages due to unforeseen interactions from SW updates. Updates should be tested as soon as they are available in a lab environment or in a limited low-risk deployment

---

[6]`www.trendmicro.com/en_us/research/17/e/persirai-new-internet-things-iot-botnet-targets-ip-cameras.html`

and manufacturers should be consulted right away if there are problems. If your manufacturer does not have a published update process and support hotline, you may consider another manufacturer.

Manufacturers must be responsive and responsible to provide updates that fix SW vulnerabilities. Updates must be fully validated and authenticated to ensure they can be verified from a trustworthy source and they are untampered.

The third class of vulnerabilities is in the firmware and software components.

The two most common software vulnerabilities cited in the IVPM Directory of Video Surveillance Cybersecurity Vulnerabilities and Exploits[7] are overflow and injection vulnerabilities.

Using **Open Source software** is a common cost-saving practice and also a good security practice in IMSS. Open Source software is often used for the OS kernel and drivers and middleware components. Just keep in mind, even though open source software have lots of inspection, all software have vulnerabilities. Also, malware has been discovered in Open Source SW many times. So, it is important to treat open source SW like custom-developed SW; analyze it for vulnerabilities and malware and monitor the source for sightings. Manufacturers must include the Open Source components into their vulnerability disclosure process. Also note that the monoculture of open source software scales the number of systems that may be attacked and therefore multiplies the risk. Prompt response to sightings is even more important for Open Source software.

The solution for SW vulnerabilities it to establish a Security Development Lifecycle that uses training in writing secure software, code inspections, and tools that test for vulnerabilities and enforce it.

Malware

Cited as the #1 threat by ENISA,[8] malware is the most common way that software controls are defeated. Malware is entered into a system via a vulnerability like the ones from the previous section. Furthermore, malware is becoming increasingly prevalent and harmful by continuously evolving new features and distribution methods. Malware takes several forms and can have a large number of consequences.

---

[7] https://ipvm.com/reports/security-exploits
[8] https://securityboulevard.com/2020/11/enisa-top-15-threats-spam-phishing-and-malware/

Malware (a portmanteau of MALicious softWARE) is software designed to do damage to computers or networks, to provide malicious people access to confidential or private data, or to control computers or networks to extract valuable work from them.

Computer Viruses[9] and Computer Worms[10] spread by replicating themselves on adjacent systems or crawling from one system to another. Similarly, a Remote Access Trojan (RAT) or Trojan Horse[11] enters a system hidden inside another SW package or delivered through email phishing attacks, online forms, or document macros. A deep analysis of malware methods is out of the scope of this document, but it is important to understand that the consequences of malware in IMSS result in systems accessed to cause damage, extract information, or to use the systems for unintended purposes such as to form botnets.

Damage to computers can result from malware that erases files or encrypts files to make them unreadable. In less common cases, malware can cause systems to overheat or wear out prematurely by overworking them.

Gaining remote access to a computer can happen due to phishing emails, document macros, or stolen, stuffed, or guessed credentials. Once an attacker has gained access to a system, the attacker can load Advanced Persistent Threats, backdoor access credentials, and search for valuable confidential data. Attackers can also take advantage of implicit trust in local systems to traverse internal networks to penetrate other computers and storage devices for additional valuable assets. Often traversal attacks can enable access to personal devices like cellphones or tablets that are trusted in a local network. Or the attack could originate with the mobile device and traverse to a trusted corporate network. In the case of IMSS, the video feeds may be sensitive themselves carrying sensitive physical security information, privacy-related information or proprietary company secrets. Highly valuable data such as financial data, enterprise assets like intellectual property and trade secrets, and government sensitive classified information can be revealed, often without the data owner being aware until much later. The data can be sold on the dark web, used for ransom, leaked for revenge, or used to enable business use of technology without the cost of development. And nation states may use the data for strategic value in negotiations or warfare.

---

[9] https://en.wikipedia.org/wiki/Computer_virus
[10] https://en.wikipedia.org/wiki/Computer_worm
[11] https://en.wikipedia.org/wiki/Trojan_horse_(computing)

Malware can provide a means of taking control over a computer to use its compute resources. Cryptomining is a quite common example of this. Because cryptocurrency uses a distributed transaction validation method that pays the validators, cryptominers use the compute power (ultimately the electrical power) to extract payment for the attacker. Other uses of compute resources are sending spam email, delivering malware, command and control relays for obfuscation,

Many of these attacks are more successful when the attacker can hide their presence. Once the computer owner becomes aware the access may be revoked and the attacker may even be identified. Once compromised, a system also may lie in wait until a command and control server instructs them to perform some function. These collections of computers are called botnets.

Botnets date back to 2001,[12] though IMSS devices were largely ignored by botnets until the Mirai botnet of 2016. Botnets have evolved from function-specific, malware-specific collections of computers into a botnet for hire economy through the dark web. Botnets represent a unique risk because of their ability to act collectively in coordinated large scale attacks as well as to hide the attackers.

Trends and Emerging Threats

The general driver of emerging threats is the attackonomics of cybersecurity. The money gained from cyberattacks is easy money and the chances of getting caught are low.

Attackonomics has encouraged the growth of a marketplace for easy-to-use, weaponized malware and systems of botnets, network infrastructure, and Command and Control servers for hire. Unregulated digital currency and the dark Internet provides a layer of anonymity and an active marketplace for both the tools and the stolen data. And the developers adopt the arms dealer philosophy that they aren't responsible for nefarious uses, they are simply supplying a market demand.

Malware, like biological viruses, is constantly evolving to adopt new ways of penetrating systems, more devices in a system, new replication methods, and evolution to avoid detection. Market forces are making the attack methods that cost just pocket money, return thousands for every dollar invested, are usable by an eleven-year-old, and can attack any system to get whatever asset that will generate untraceable cash for the attacker.

---

[12] https://en.wikipedia.org/wiki/Botnet#Historical_list_of_botnets

Attacks are becoming more carefully targeted and planned to gain access to highly valuable data such as financial data, intellectual property, trade secrets, classified data, and ransomable data. Along with the increased sophistication of the attacks comes greater ability to evade and defeat defenses.

These same market forces have created an active data marketplace. Lists of login credentials, vulnerable devices, banking information, and identity information can be purchased for pocket money. And these data fuel the cycle of exploitation. Corporate espionage as a service[13] is also available today on the dark web, enabling individuals or corporations to easily obtain the intellectual property or strategic information of a competitor, shielded by the anonymity of the dark web. These services include hacking tools, backdoors, credentials, and tailored malware.

As you will read about in the next chapter, Machine Learning is also being weaponized. ML applications can multiply the speed and destructive power of an attack, or help malware evade detection. Generative adversarial attacks are developed by pitting one machine learning application against another to produce a false positive or false negative result.

The Internet and networks connected to the Internet are increasingly populated with inexpensive devices whose security ranges from no security at all to default pro-forma security with slapped-together open-source SW with no identifiable supplier and no commitment to provide security updates. These devices can be the easiest entry point to a network, traversing it to load malware or locate high value assets. Devices on internal networks must not automatically trust connections from local devices for this reason, instead applying zero trust policies to stay secure. IMSS increasingly have the ability for users to view data on personal devices such as cellphones and tablets. These devices may not have the same level of security control as an IT professionally maintained device in an enterprise system. These personal devices can also be a weak entry point into an otherwise secure system.

Cloud Computing, including video analytics as a service, is changing the cybersecurity environment both by presenting a concentrated captive data store, that is, a target-rich environment, and by providing another means of leveraging implicit trust in the cloud services provider (CSP) as well as obfuscating the responsible party of attacks. The cloud also encourages partnerships between CSPs and security software providers to raise the bar. And the cloud is a proving ground for zero trust policies and protocols.

---

[13] https://threatpost.com/espionage-as-a-service-dark-web/145464/

On the positive side, laws and regulations are beginning to address cybersecurity. History has shown that regulations and holding parties responsible, including assessing penalties, can result in good solutions. This is particularly true when economic externalities are operative in a market.

So, what can you do about these problems? The next section outlines Intel technologies that system providers, software providers, and system integrators can use to help mitigate many of these types of threats.

Designing a Secure Platform Using Intel Technologies

During the design stage of a product, it is essential to understand the detailed capabilities of the selected HW, FW, and SW that's targeted. The journey starts with leveraging a Root of Trust, a device identity, provisioning, implementing a chain of trust via secure boot, securing the keys and data, protecting the code/data at runtime, and concluding with a defense in depth strategy.

Root of Trust (RoT)

In simple terms, a RoT is often used to build a foundation in a platform on which the properties of security and trust can be implemented in the different layers. The RoT is expected to be immutable on highly trusted systems and in this case implemented in HW or ROM code. In less trustworthy systems, the RoT is also implemented in FW and SW, and this renders the resulting system vulnerable to RoT tampering and a complete system compromise. A FW/SW Root of Trust can be strengthened by programming the RoT key hash of the OEM or ODM into the Field Programmable Fuses (FPF) of the Silicon. As an example, Intel Silicon provides FPF storage for programming the hash of the public key associated with the private key used to sign the boot and subsequently the OS images.

Secure IDs

The security posture of a device requires an immutable identity that can be cryptographically verified. The same identity can be used by the device to get admitted into the network and for the purposes of local or remote attestation. Some examples of this ID are supported by discrete TPM or PTT or a key programmed into the Silicon. For constrained IOT devices, another viable option is Device Identity Composition Engine (DICE),[14] which enables a layered identity and attestation scheme.

Provisioning the Device – FIDO Onboarding

One of the major threats exploited by hackers are the default passwords left un-provisioned on a device. The Onboarding standard being specified by FIDO alliance[15] is a secure, robust way to provision the credentials and persona into an IoT device. In some cases, the OS build can also be downloaded, authenticated, and stored on the platform's hard disk/storage.

Secure Boot – Chain of Trust

Also known as transitive trust is essential to ensure that the entire process and ingredients including boot, OS, and applications are verified before trusting to complete the platform bring-up. Secure boot is a mechanism to ensure that any/all FW and SW ingredients executing on the platform are authenticated, tethering back to the root of trust. Secure boot can include verified boot and measured boot where verified boot is a process of authenticating the ingredients and enforcing a predefined policy if there is a mismatch. Measured boot, on the other hand, stores the authenticated hash values into a secure storage such as TPM or PTT for a subsequent local or remote attestation. The following stack flow diagram shows how the transitive trust works to protect the boot process all the way from hardware to the applications running in a VM. The lowest layer to be the HW layer, and above that is the firmware layer which includes the modules required to handle the HW IP blocks and Digital Rights Management. Above that is the boot loader/UEFI used to initialize the CPU and chipset. The optional hypervisor supports the Virtual Machine Manager (VMM) functionality. The upper layers include

---

[14] https://trustedcomputinggroup.org/work-groups/dice-architectures/
[15] https://fidoalliance.org/intro-to-fido-device-onboard/

the OS ingredients for kernel and User mode. Above that layer are the middleware/ frameworks and applications. This diagram (Figure 4-6) also illustrates the security goal that trust begins at the lowest layers and must be extended into the layers above – and that doing so requires conscious techniques to get it right. If/when those techniques fail, the stack recovers by falling back to lower layers.

The stack includes booting into application TEEs and the need to distinguish security-sensitive function and workloads that should be separated from "traditional" function and workloads. We can refer to the TEE and lower layers as the trusted computing base upon which the rest of the stack depends.

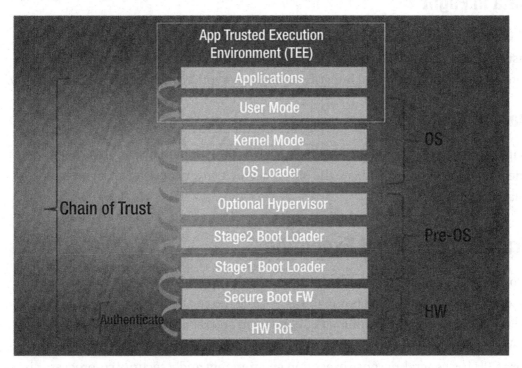

Figure 4-6. *Boot flow with the chain of trust and signing*

Securing Keys and Data

During and after the boot phases of the device, there is a need to store the keys in a vault type of storage with access controls and TPM is a notable example where the keys can be generated and wrapped. The wrapped keys can be used with handles to perform operations including sign/verify, encrypt/decrypt, etc.

Cryptographic Keys

Cryptographic Keys are an essential part of enforcing the confidentiality in a system during the encryption and decryption operations. A key disclosure to unauthorized entities will result in the decryption of data and making it available in clear text for analysis and compromising the assets. Therefore, protecting the keys must be the highest priority and can be achieved at various levels in the platform, but utilizing the standards-based technologies such as discrete TPM or Intel PTT are strongly recommended.

Data in Flight

This problem is well-known, and one can use either TPM or PTT or Intel CPU instructions for SHA, AES, and Random Number generation. The data is protected at egress for confidentiality and integrity through encryption and sign/verify, respectively.

Data at Rest

Data at rest or when stored on a medium such as flash or hard disk or RAM needs adequate protections to mitigate the offline secret recovery or reverse engineering-related attacks.

Trusted or Isolated Execution

Providing a protected runtime environment for the application's code and data is essential to protect the secrets and the assets that the code/data handles. In general, a Trusted Execution Environment (TEE) refers to an execution environment that is isolated from the normal general purpose execution environment. For example, the core CPU is a general-purpose execution environment and a security co-processor is an isolated environment. Trusted execution environments may include HW/SW/FW that establishes an isolated environment. By carefully controlling the infrastructure that produces the HW/FW/SW that implements the TEE, the TEE can have strong guarantees regarding safe and reliable execution of TEE workloads. Typically, workloads that involve use of cryptographic keys the confidentiality and integrity protection of data as it is transformed to and from cipher text are performed using a TEE.

There are several TEE technologies available across a variety of architectures. Intel® Software Guard Extensions (SGX) allows multiple instances of trusted execution environments for different applications and tenants. Intel® TXT allows trusted execution using CPU cache lines as RAM to minimize dependencies on external resources. It can be used for general purpose TEE operations when cache coherency isn't needed. Intel® Virtualization Technology (VT) suite offers another form of TEE where a trusted hypervisor creates execution environments with distinct thread, memory, interrupt, and IO contexts. Virtualization allows full OS and application images to run which may be counterproductive to security due to increased attack surface of a large OS and application framework. Therefore, it may yet be appropriate to employ some other TEE capabilities in concert with virtualization.

Defense in Depth

Implementing strong security properties such as Confidentiality, Integrity, and availability at all layers in the platform stack ensures that the breaches are contained to a particular layer and any vertical expansion is limited. This strategy also enables a structured recovery where in the compromised or corrupted FW/SW components at layer can be recovered by the layer immediately below in the stack.

OpenVINO Security Add-on

The OpenVINO Security Add-on is an open source security capability for OpenVINO analytics model developers to help defend against copying, cloning, and reverse engineering their valuable intellectual property. This capability is detailed in Chapter 5, section 5.3.1.

Secure Development Lifecycle (SDL)

SDL is a set of industry standard processes that is usually tuned to the internal development processes.[16] SDL should be applied to all the components within a platform including hardware, firmware, and software. SDL is essential to implement a security-minded development and validation disciplines within a company. The main goal of SDL follows defensive approach to prevent certain issues from occurring late in the development/validation phases by identifying triggers and mitigating them at different milestones throughout the product's lifecycle. In the past, secure coding used

---

[16] https://newsroom.intel.com/wp-content/uploads/sites/11/2020/10/sdl-2020-whitepaper.pdf

to be the focus, but secure design and the implementation of DevSecOps where security principles are embedded in every phase of the product has become the norm. Refer to Figure 4-7 for an example of SDL phases and note that it starts with planning of product, architecting, high-level and low-level design, implementation/coding, functional/ security validation, and deployment/maintenance.

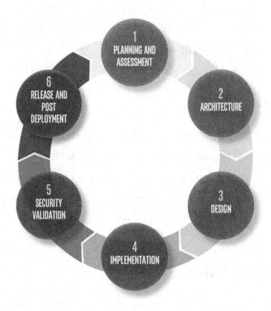

Figure 4-7. *Phases of SDL process*

Support and Response

It is essential to have a Product Security Incident Response Team (PSIRT) to intercept the vulnerabilities in the products, issue common vulnerability exposures (CVE), develop mitigations and distribute the patches/updates. These updates either developed internally or acquired from external source should then be deployed by the customers either through any of the following infrastructures including firmware over the air (FOTA) or software over the air (SOTA) or application over the air (AOTA).

Summary

Securing the assets pertinent to IMSS starts with threat modeling which involves understanding the threat taxonomy and selecting the right method. Subsequently, the assets must be identified along with the value and associated priority with the assets classified into foundational, data, and application. Designing a secure platform involves leveraging multiple technologies, including the available Root of Trust, immutable device ids, and secure key storage. Using these technologies, a secure boot chain of trust could be implemented to protect the boot integrity of the IMSS system. Provisioning is an important step in the lifecycle of an IMSS system where the right cryptographic credentials are programmed into the system. Once a system is correctly provisioned, securely booted, the runtime protection of the code/data can be securely implemented. Defense in depth strategies should be designed in to prevent, detect, correct, and recover from the emerging security threats including zero-day vulnerability exploits. An example technology, the OpenVINO Security Add-on is briefly explained to articulate the architecture that helps protect the Machine Learning IP assets. Encompassing all the preceding is the necessity for a structured and comprehensive Secure Development Lifecycle process and an incident response/support system to identify, report, and release patches to address security vulnerabilities.

In the next chapter, we will learn more about Machine Learning policies and standards and about protection solutions specific to machine learning.

CHAPTER 5

Machine Learning Security and Trustworthiness

> *"A robot may not harm humanity, or, by inaction, allow humanity to come to harm."*
>
> —*Zeroth Law of Robotics, Isaac Azimov*

Machine Learning (ML) is the innovation powerhouse for Intelligent Multimodal Security Systems (IMSS). Along with obvious benefits, ML brings unique risks that require thorough assessment. ML system security builds on "traditional" cybersecurity controls and spreads to cover the expanded attack surfaces for the new ML assets. Moreover, the problem of ML trustworthiness stands in the way of taking full advantage of ML advancements. This chapter introduces the challenges and risks of ML, highlights key trends in the global ML policies, and best practices, summarizes key standardization activities, and provides a detailed description of assets and threats. Putting the above into perspective, we present a practical framework for addressing ML-based IMSS security and trustworthiness and discuss relevant implementation options.

From myths and legends to modern day fiction, the idea of artificial intelligence (AI) has always fascinated people. The 1950s mark the symbolic birth of AI with the workshop held in Dartmouth.[1] It took another 50 years for the industry to reach the point predicted by Moore's law to provide enough computing power to enable complex neural

---

[1] https://250.dartmouth.edu/highlights/artificial-intelligence-ai-coined-dartmouth

---

The original version of this chapter was previously published without open access. A correction to this chapter is available at https://doi.org/10.1007/978-1-4842-8297-7_9

© Intel 2023, corrected publication 2023
J. Booth et al., *Demystifying Intelligent Multimode Security Systems*,
https://doi.org/10.1007/978-1-4842-8297-7_5

net computation algorithms capable of approaching human accuracy for limited tasks. At the same time, the exponential growth of data triggered the demand for technologies that can better utilize data for making business decisions. This became the catalyst for Machine Learning (ML), the applied field of AI focused on building applications that can learn from data, make predictions based on the data, and improve the accuracy of decision over time without explicitly changing the applications.

ML-based innovation rapidly grows and has a potential to generate immense economic value giving rise to an entirely new set of services. Several analysts, including Garner's Hype Cycle,[2] and Advanced AI and Analytics IDC, forecast that connected IOT devices, are expected to generate about 80ZB of Data in 2025.[3] Accumulation of enormous data paves the path for faster adoption of ML technologies across a broader spectrum of market segments. It has been widely publicized that more and more businesses across the world are increasing investments into ML research and solutions. Today we witness active engagement and adoption of ML to gain a competitive edge across a variety of market segments, e.g. retail, healthcare, industrial and many others. Organizations adjust and transform business processes to enable ML-based operations. The rapid adoption acts as a stimulus for further development of ML technologies, such as Tiny ML,[4] Quantum ML,[5] and Auto ML.[6] The latter comes with the promise to democratize ML for broad adoption, making it accessible for the organizations who don't have technical expertise to create ML-based solutions.

As any rapid technological innovation ML not only offers business and customer benefits but also introduces security risks due to the lack of security considerations during the early phases of ML solutions development. This includes a new class of risks that are unique to ML and require mitigations beyond what traditional cybersecurity practices. While the industry embarks on AI-powered digital transformations, those security risks may not only become a hurdle for adoption and scale of ML solutions but also can lead to significant negative consequences for enterprises (brand, compliance, financial loss), individuals (physical and safety risks) and nation's security (functioning of critical infrastructure).

---

[2] www.gartner.com/smarterwithgartner/5-trends-appear-on-the-gartner-hype-cycle-for-emerging-technologies-2019/

[3] www.idc.com/getdoc.jsp?containerId=prUS45213219

[4] https://venturebeat.com/2020/01/11/why-tinyml-is-a-giant-opportunity/

[5] www.tensorflow.org/quantum/concepts

[6] https://searchenterpriseai.techtarget.com/definition/automated-machine-learning-AutoML

The intense demand for real-time analysis and handling of a large volume of complex, sensitive data drives the need for ML processing at the edge; closer to the data origin at smart endpoints. Computing at the edge presents unique challenges and requirements for the ML solution. Proliferation of the ML at the edge triggered security concerns in society that resulted in several policy initiative emerging across governments, the private sector, trade organizations, and alliances.

Usage of Machine Learning in IMSS

A fast adoption of cameras across the industry resulted in a drastic increase in the amount of video data available for operation and analysis. Over the last decade, the rapid proliferation of technology-enabled high-quality video streaming solutions at affordable cost, are widely used in consumer, commercial, and industrial settings. According to the IDC report,[7] we expected solid growth for the video surveillance camera market as smart camera systems and analytical software enable new use cases. In 2020, despite the COVID-19, 82% of 22.6ZB of data created by IoT devices is from surveillance systems and this trend will continue to increase. More video data presents greater opportunities to analyze it, monitor risks, predict events, and recommend corrective actions. However, video data is mostly unstructured, and therefore traditional algorithms are not able to perform the predictive tasks on this type of data. AI/ML unleashes the power of unstructured data processing, making it usable for numerous new and exciting use cases beyond traditional video surveillance.

Using machine vision and object recognition makes checkout-free frictionless shopping possible. Amazon Go utilizes video observation and smart shelving in more than 20 new stores in the United States and recently introduced a new store in the United Kingdom to enable customers to autonomously walk through the store and select items for purchase. Upon finishing, purchases in the shopping bag will be processed and an electronic receipt will be sent to the customer when they leave the store. Amazon Go[8] uses the same types of technologies that are found in self-driving cars, such as

[7] www.idc.com/getdoc.jsp?containerId=US46847520&pageType=PRINTFRIENDLY#US46847520-F-0002

[8] www.amazon.com/b?ie=UTF8&node=16008589011

computer vision, sensor fusion, and deep learning. The combination of the AI, computer vision, and sensor data ensure that customers are only charged for the products that they finally picked, detecting when products are taken or returned to the shelves. It is recognized that the COVID-19 pandemic drastically changed social behaviors, including shopping experiences. Approaches based on AI and computer vision for frictionless retail shopping have obvious benefits in an age of social distancing, limiting human interaction, but they also speed retail transactions and help brick-and-mortar businesses be more competitive with online shopping.

Another exciting use case involves video data analytics to detect and correct problems in supply and distribution channels. Machine vision solutions coordinated with back-end systems track the inventory as it moves through the supply-chain, monitoring the quality and timeliness.

Manufacturing is also benefiting from machine vision and, specifically, computer vision. It has been used for inventory control, spectral image analysis of chemicals, maintenance and repair operations, and intelligent robotics. To address the performance issues with manufacturing equipment, local or cloud analytics perform equipment telemetry and predict when failures might arise. Cameras are now being embedded not only into the assembly line but also into labor management (time reporting, etc.) as well as warehousing and distribution.

Video surveillance technologies can be a great benefit for the healthcare domain. Thermal imaging combined with the appropriate analytics assesses the health of people entering and leaving controlled areas. Patient tracking in hospitals lets healthcare providers reach patients and improve efficiency in healthcare facilities. Video analysis is also being used as a diagnostic tool, a use case that has become far more popular in recent years. By combining video with analytics tools, healthcare providers can rely on artificial intelligence to aid their diagnostic capabilities. Advanced medical imaging can analyze and transform images and model possible situations. One of the well-known solutions in this space was brought to market by SkinVision,[9] which enables one to find skin cancer early by taking photos of skin with a phone and getting to a doctor at the right time. AI-powered medical imaging is also widely used in diagnosing COVID-19 cases and identifying patients who require ventilator support. Intel® AI Builders member

---

[9] www.skinvision.com/

Huiying Medical[10] has developed a medical imaging diagnostic solution that uses CT chest scans to assist with the early detection of coronavirus infections that complement standard lab testing with 96% accuracy.

These use cases have evolved even further to utilize multiple sensors such as vision, audio, and smell as Multisensory Surveillance solutions. Figure 5-1 Multisensory Surveillance Solution Evolution[11] demonstrates the 2017–2019 timeline.

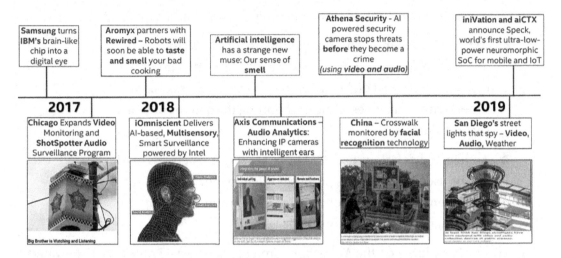

***Figure 5-1.** Multisensory surveillance solution evolution*

The COVID-19 pandemic introduced further demand for thermal cameras and solutions that aggregate video and thermal sensors. Thermal body temperature solutions are supposed to detect changes in human skin temperatures, identify individuals that may have a virus, detect face masks, and provide organizations with an additional layer of protection to their facility from increased exposure to the coronavirus.

Challenges and Risks

Traditional programming methods for multisensor fusion struggle with ambiguous and conflicting inputs. AI and ML solutions are providing more robust solutions for these difficult problems. There is no shortage of headlines about the unintended

---

[10] www.intel.com/content/www/us/en/artificial-intelligence/posts/huiying-medical-covid19.html

[11] https://intel.northernlight.com/document.php?docid=IL20190913030000020&datasource =INTELPRM&trans=view&caller=all_results_widget&context=quicksearch

consequences of new AI/ML adoption when AI/ ML systems are tricked, misled, circumvented, and therefore fail. However, many vendors are still largely unaware of the risks they are taking when they are adopting cutting-edge AI/ML technologies.

First, let's view the AI/ML and Security intersection. There are three major perspectives to explore when considering how AI is impacting security:

1. AI Systems Protection. This requires securing the AI System's assets, including training data, training pipelines, and models.

2. AI for Cybersecurity. This implies the use of AI/ML tools and techniques to autonomously identify and/or respond to cyber threats based on behavior analysis and automation of cybersecurity practices while augmenting the actions of human security analysts.

3. Anticipated nefarious use of AI by attackers. The benefits of AI can be used for malicious purposes. Identifying these attacks and defending against them will be an important addition to traditional cybersecurity practices.

In this book, we focus on the AI systems' protection aspects. Protecting AI-Powered Systems presents new attack surfaces and thus increases security risks. Leaders who plan to use advanced AI and ML analytics, must understand the regulatory guidelines, comprehend the risks, and take appropriate measures to address the risks, some of which were documented when Mckinsey conducted extensive research on artificial intelligence risks.[12] According to the study, AI/ML systems involve a very broad range of stakeholders and include not only the organizations, consumers, or individuals but also human society at large and the environment. The following Figure 5-2 is the summary of the multifaceted risks for individuals, organizations and society highlighted in Mckinsey research.

---

[12] www.mckinsey.com/business-functions/mckinsey-analytics/our-insights/confronting-the-risks-of-artificial-intelligence

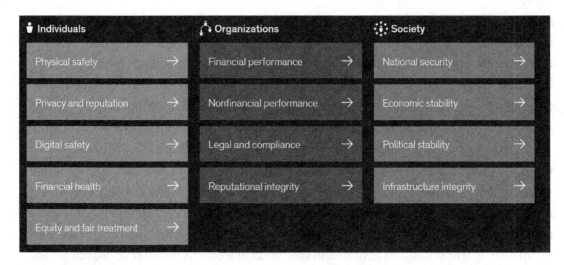

Figure 5-2. *Unintended consequences of AI (Mckinsey)*

These risks span across the entire life cycle of AI/ML solutions and arise from the data used to train the AI/ML system, as well as from the design and operation of the systems. Organizations that plan to adopt the AI/ML technology should implement specific AI risk management practices. These practices leverage existing industry-recommended principles such as ISO 31000:2018 Risk Management Guidelines[13] and emerging ones that intend to address the complexity of the supply chain of AI/ML systems and challenges of Data collection for large volumes of AI training and inferencing data, including texts, images, videos, audio, geo-local data, and other data modalities

The enormous growth of data introduces the challenges for proper data management. According to IDC,[14] IoT devices will generate up to 79.4 ZB of data by 2025. The consumption of this massive data is a complex problem, as the data needs to be triaged for sensitive information and conform to the privacy regulations, such as the pivotal European Union's General Data Protection Regulation (GDPR) and several US state-level initiatives, including the California Consumer Privacy Act (CCPA). Failure to follow privacy guidelines introduces huge reputation risks as well as financial penalties. When Hackers attacked cloud-based enterprise security startup Verkada's video surveillance cameras, they gained access to over 50,000 of the IoT devices and

---

[13] www.iso.org/obp/ui/#iso:std:iso:31000:ed-2:v1:en

[14] www.idc.com/research/viewtoc.jsp?containerId=US46718220

customers' associated video archives. The victims of this attack include such Verkada customers as a Tesla suppliers, Cloudflare, Equinox, various hospital networks, police departments, correctional facilities, and schools. This attack raised an intense dispute in society about how businesses, health care, and public safety workers monitor and treat people, as well as how they gather, store, and use data. In addition, many Verkada customers were concerned about Verkada's employees' access, raising privacy concerns.

Gartner Research published a recommendation[15] highlighting the risk of data manipulation, "Machine learning presents a new attack surface and increases security risks through the possibility of data manipulation." Solution developers and adopters must anticipate and prepare to mitigate potential risks of data corruption, model theft, and adversarial samples. Another scenario to consider is when the decision produced by ML will be translated and actuated in the physical world. A popular approach for data processing and decision-making systems is reinforcement learning. Reinforcement learning is a form of machine learning where the acting AI interacts with its environment and tries to maximize the reward that is determined by a function that, if determined correctly, should incorporate all goals (Sutton and Barto, 2017). This approach expands the perimeter of the system; along with inferencing, it includes online training susceptible to data manipulation that causes model drift. Thus, it substantially increases the surface of failure.

Data is a crucial component to developing every AI, therefore limiting access to sensitive data is the basis for building trustworthy AI/ML. As for any compute solution, AI/ML will be prone to security risks. If security measures are insufficient, it will be possible to plant an attack that forges the results and impacts recommendations, or decisions made by solution.

AI/ML models represent the core of the solution, and their implementation can introduce problems when they deliver biased results, become unstable, or produce results that are explainable or traceable. In 2019, Apple Card was investigated after gender discrimination complaints. When the husband and wife applied for Apple Card and compared their spending limits, they found out that the husband got 20 times more credit limit than his wife.[16] Safety represents one of the most critical risks connected

---

[15] www.gartner.com/en/documents/3899783/anticipate-data-manipulation-security-risks-to-ai-pipeli

[16] https://twitter.com/dhh/status/1192540900393705474?ref_src=twsrc%5Etfw%7Ctwcamp% 5Etweetembed%7Ctwterm%5E1192540900393705474%7Ctwgr%5E%7Ctwcon%5Es1_c10&ref_url= https%3A%2F%2Fthenextweb.com%2Fnews%2Fapple-cards-algorithm-under-investigation-for-sexist-credit-checks

with AI. The death of Elaine Herzberg was the first recorded case of a pedestrian fatality involving Uber's self-driving car, when the machine learning system failed to account for jaywalking[17] and the vehicle operator was distracted, failing to monitor the AD system. As a result, not only did Uber cease its testing program in Arizona but also caused its rival, Google's Waymo, to increase safety requirements.

Risks with AI models misbehaving become more prominent with large scale AI/ML deployments, where service providers aggregate a big number of pre-trained models from a diverse set of community developers. From this new service perspective, model theft attacks (in this case of intended misuse) are the most vital problem to be solved from a business standpoint. There were several cases when researchers demonstrated methods of "recreating" model IP. Two researchers, Aaron Gokaslan and Vanya Cohen,[18] managed to replicate the OpenAI model that intends to automatically generate text. Initially, OpenAI did not completely disclose the underlying model due to concerns about malicious applications of the technology. Another interesting example is the study[19] that describes the successful model theft attack on an intelligent IoT medical platform. Attacks like these demonstrate that intellectual property such as the trained AI models using private and sensitive information can be stolen and, as a result, the business could sustain both brand damage and investment losses due to weak AI/ML system protections.

For AI/ML supply chain vendors who build and deploy solutions, it is critical to comprehend the full range of risks of intelligent solutions introduced by specific AI/ML technologies that can lead not only to theft of the models and of the input training data sets but also incorrect results.

Policy and Standards

In this section, we will highlight the major trends, rapidly evolving worldwide policies and standards for IMSS. As mentioned earlier, IMSS is an essential segment of evolving IOT edge usages. Various forms of sensor-driven data processing, including computer vision and other forms of video data use cases contribute to the growth of IoT devices,

---

[17] Collision Between Vehicle Controlled by Developmental Automated Driving System and Pedestrian, Tempe, Arizona, March 18, 2018 (ntsb.gov)

[18] https://blog.usejournal.com/opengpt-2-we-replicated-gpt-2-because-you-can-too-45e34e6d36dc

[19] www.hindawi.com/journals/wcmc/2020/8859489/

edge infrastructure, and solutions. The widespread adoption of IoT/Edge devices, including the IoT deployment in high-risk environments, the expansion of the attack surface made IoT and Edge attractive targets for malicious actors that resulted in a surge of high-visibility attacks such as DDoS Mirai,[20] Strontium APT,[21] Mozi,[22] and many more. It started from poorly secured/configured IoT devices, Botnets, and evolved to high-profile distributed Denial of Services attacks, the most prominent one was Mirai in 2016 which targeted a wider range of IoT Devices. Botnets built from the Mirai codebase (e.g., Mozi) continue to disrupt in the IoT arena,[23] with cyberattacks taking advantage of loopholes in IoT device security to plant widespread attacks. Experts forecast[24] that even more nefarious threats will result from the surge of the attack volume and sophistication. Ransomware, physical attacks, sensitive data leakage, and attacks on privacy are some of the new attacks that emerged on the IoT horizon (Figure 5-3 IoT Threat Landscape).

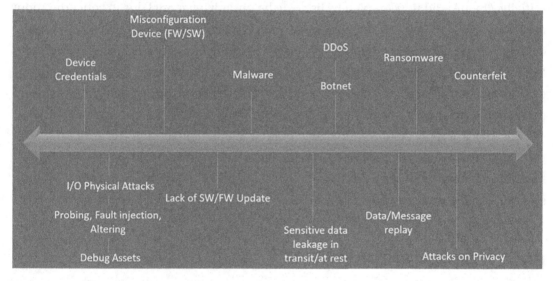

Figure 5-3. *IoT Threat landscape*

---

[20] https://en.wikipedia.org/wiki/Mirai_(malware)

[21] https://cyware.com/news/strontium-apt-group-compromises-iot-devices-to-infiltrate-enterprise-networks-8c7a9f9f

[22] www.microsoft.com/security/blog/2021/08/19/how-to-proactively-defend-against-mozi-iot-botnet/

[23] https://intel471.com/blog/iot-cybersecurity-threats-mirai-botnet

[24] www.iotsecurityfoundation.org/the-iot-ransomware-threat-is-more-serious-than-you-think/

These trends incentivize policymakers to propose a specific regulatory framework to address raising security and privacy concerns resulting in global industry-wide collaboration on the definition of IoT/Edge security frameworks.

Another major factor that contributes to global policy and standards activities is AI/ML technologies. For many decades, AI was limited in adoption; however, with the rise of ML that widened and enhanced the applicability of AI/ML technology, we see AI/ML solutions in almost every market – physical security, healthcare, industrial, retail, financial services, smart city, energy, utility transportation, agriculture, and many more.

The breadth of AI/ML technologies is expanding to leverage complex heterogeneous multi-party compute and at the same time, as it is for many innovative technologies, it is revealing personal, societal, and economic risks that can be exploited by malicious players. Over the past several years, several companies and institutions produced guidelines that proposed principles for artificial intelligence. Harvard's Berkman Klein Center conducted the analysis[25] of 35 documents on Principles worldwide and in January 2020 published the paper "Principled Artificial Intelligence: Mapping Consensus in Ethical and Rights-based Approaches to Principles for AI." This study systemized and visualized the key convergence trends covering segments such as government (US National Science & Technology Council, China, UK, Germany, G20, EU Commission, OECD), Private Sector and trade organizations (prominent players such as Microsoft, Google, Tencent, IBM, ITI, Telefonica), and think tanks such as academics, alliances, and civil society (e.g., IEEE, AI Industry Alliances, Academic institutions). Figure 5-4 Harvard AI Guidelines Analysis, illustrates in the following the study represented in a wheel shape where documents are represented by spokes with the highlighted scale of themes coverage. This project outlines very important trends. First, there is a strong convergence across the wide variety of industry efforts. Second, researchers identified eight common key themes for AI Principles:

1. Privacy

2. Accountability

3. Safety and Security

4. Transparency and Explainability

5. Fairness and Non-discrimination

---

[25] https://cyber.harvard.edu/publication/2020/principled-ai

6. Human Control of Technology

7. Professional Responsibility

8. Promotion of Human Values

The major conclusion is that these highlighted principles lay the foundation for measurable AI practices for both policymakers and technical professionals. The significance of this study is in the demonstration of the industry's demand and readiness to embrace the complex challenging problems of AI. Understanding the industry momentum around AI is critical for the IMSS developers.

Currently industry is embracing the journey from the general declaration of AI principles to implementable practices. IDC,[26] Gartner[27] analysts predict that companies will redesign their AI/ML systems to address explainability, fairness and operationalize the AI development pipeline to meet regulation requirements. Legislators worldwide move to adopt regulation by design. Regulation is a major way in which the government influences the market; however, traditionally, the market doesn't like these interventions.

It is critical to make sure that regulation is efficient and doesn't impede business. AI/ML adopters face a dilemma. Evolving regulatory frameworks might significantly impact the business ability to adopt and scale the technology. At the same time, regulation is at the conceptualization stage when technology is still maturing, the industry is still accumulating the knowledge of impacts and finally, new laws and best practices are still evolving. When would be the right time for IMSS technology developers and adopters to mediate? The specific action at this stage is to comprehend the policy and regulatory factors and focus on concrete actions that they can undertake to ensure the IMSS doesn't violate any existing and emerging laws and regulations.

---

[26] www.idc.com/getdoc.jsp?containerId=US47913321

[27] www.gartner.com/en/information-technology/insights/top-technology-trends

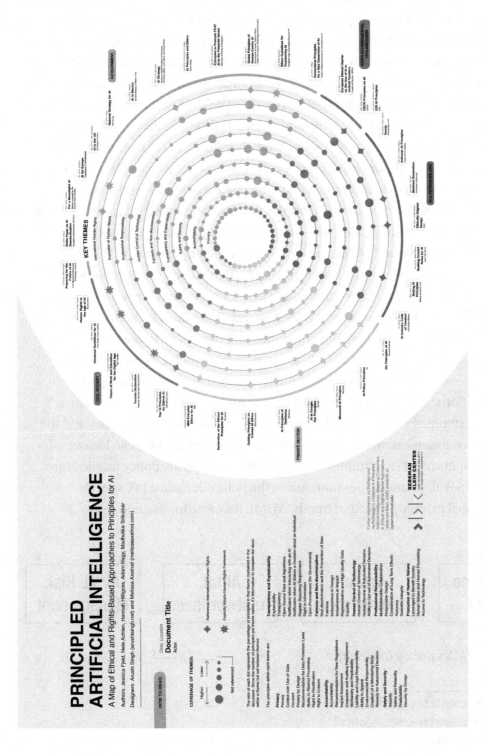

Figure 5-4. *Harvard AI guidelines analysis[28]*

[28]https://cyber.harvard.edu/publication/2020/principled-ai

To address effective AI/ML system governance goals, regulators and lawmakers rely on standards organizations to support policymakers' goals, besides regulation presents limited opportunities for experts to engage and provide feedback. Two major international standards bodies that are currently developing AI standards, International Standards Organization (ISO)/International Electrotechnical Commission (IEC) and the Institute of Electrical and Electronics Engineers (IEEE). JTC1 (joint ISO/IEC committee, established in 1987) SC42[29] subcommittee serves as the focal point for AI standardization development and has already published ten standards and more than 20 are in development. A diverse stakeholder ecosystem calls for close industry collaboration across domains (e.g., IoT), considering the usage of AI/ML technologies in the context of market and computation approaches of AI Systems. This is a very complex problem: the standardization approach cannot be conducted in a single area, and it requires interoperability approaches that go beyond current solutions. SC42 established a liaison collaboration with SC38[30] (Cloud Computing and Distributed Platforms is a standardization subcommittee) and SC27[31] (Information security, cybersecurity, and privacy protection is a standardization subcommittee). SC27 developed several widely adopted standards for security controls, services, cryptography, security evaluation/testing, and privacy technologies. Given the wide range of issues brought up by AI/ML, it is important to highlight the importance of trustworthiness, security, and privacy within the context of AI usage. Along with international efforts, it is important to consider the efforts of national bodies, such as the National Institute of Standards and Technology (NIST) in the United States, and the European Telecommunications Standards Institute (ETSI) in the European Union.

The developers of IMSS solutions should consider composite policy implications. Figure 5-5 IMSS Policy Landscape summarizes the policy domains: IoT specific regulation, global privacy protection trends, AI/ML trustworthiness, and risk management.

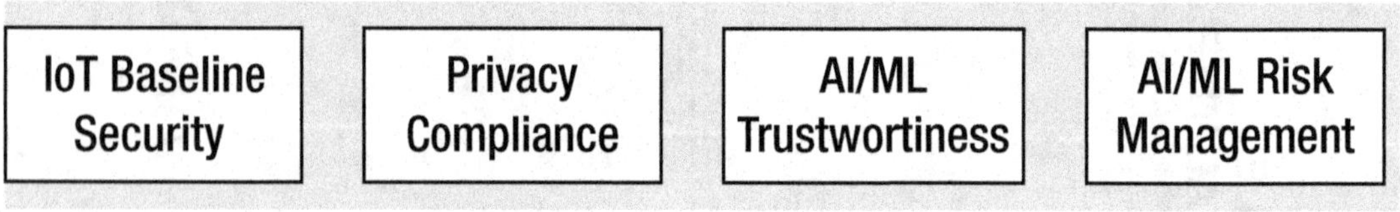

IoT Baseline Security	Privacy Compliance	AI/ML Trustwortiness	AI/ML Risk Management

Figure 5-5. *IMSS policy landscape*

---

[29] www.iso.org/committee/6794475.html

[30] www.iso.org/committee/601355.html

[31] www.iso.org/committee/45306.html

An independent expert group that advises the European Commission recommends banning the usage of AI in some "unacceptable" scenarios, for example, facial recognition and job application as they present great potential risk to society and individuals.

Regulatory Landscape

As it was mentioned, governments around the world launched national AI legislation activities (for example, European Union (EU), China, the United Kingdom, Canada).

The EU is the most prominent, advanced, risk-based approach to AI systems. In 2021 the European Commission (EC) introduced the first ever complex regulatory framework on AI, "Proposal for a Regulation laying down harmonized rules on artificial intelligence."[32] In 2021, Cyberspace Administration of China (CAC) passed the "Internet Information Service Algorithm Recommendation Management Regulations" that regulates the implementation and use of recommendation algorithms. There is direct implication for the AI/ML empowered IMSS; it tackles the problems of the transparency of algorithms function, discriminatory data practices, opaque recommendation models, and labor violations.

Both the EU and Chinese legislations will have a deep impact both on the global economy and lawmaking. If the EU passes the AI law, this will become mandatory for anyone who wants to operate in the EU market as well as based on learnings from the General Data Protection Act (GDPR), it will be leveraged by other nations for their legislative strategy. In the United States, there are several AI regulatory activities across agencies; to name a few – Department of Commerce (DoC), Federal Trade Commission (FTC), and the Federal Drug Administration (FDA). State lawmakers also are considering the benefits and challenges of AI.

A harmonized approach will be critical for AI/ML systems adoption and scale. Regulatory frameworks need to evolve to provide clear guidelines for AI solution adopters to avoid misinterpretation and reduce the compliance cost. At the same time, there is strong concern about the regulatory intervention to the technology space that can hamper innovation. It is critical for technologists to comprehend the legislative approaches and contribute through standards, best practices to avoid overregulation and achieve a balanced risk-based framework.

---

[32] https://eur-lex.europa.eu/legal-content/EN/TXT/?uri=CELEX%3A52021PC0206

IoT Security Baseline

The IoT regulatory and policy landscape are rapidly evolving. There is a growing number of state and federal legislation, best practices, and standards that span numerous market segments and countries include the EU, the United Kingdom, Japan, Brazil, Australia, and many others. For the United States, the IoT Cybersecurity Improvement Act of 2020 was pivotal because it defines that all IoT devices used by government agencies have to comply with US NIST-(National Institute of Standards and Technology)defined standards. This is not only a critical step for the security of solutions used by the US government, but it is expected that this security guideline will define the requirements for the broad segments of consumer and commercial IoT vendors and devices.

In 2016, NIST established the cybersecurity IoT program with the mission to "cultivate trust in the IoT and foster an environment that enables innovation on a global scale through standards, guidance, and related tools."[33] This program drove several key initiatives (Figure 5-6 NIST CYBERSECURITY FOR IOT PROGRAM (Source: NIST). NIST 8259 Series guides for manufacturers and supporting parties creating IoT devices and products. SP 800-213 is intended for Federated Agencies looking to deploy IoT devices in their systems. Consumer IoT Products are addressing Executive Order 14028.

Figure 5-6. *NIST cybersecurity for IOT program (Source: NIST)*

NIST recommendations are results of collaborative industry-wide effort that was conducted by partnering with industry experts and in the spirit of facilitating the harmonized approach.

---

[33] www.nist.gov/itl/applied-cybersecurity/nist-cybersecurity-iot-program

Collection of NISTIR 8259 reports (see Figure 5-7 NIST 8259 Series Roadmap and Federal Profile (as of January 2021) provides guidance for IOT device manufacturers on how to design, develop, and maintain IoT devices with foundational security.

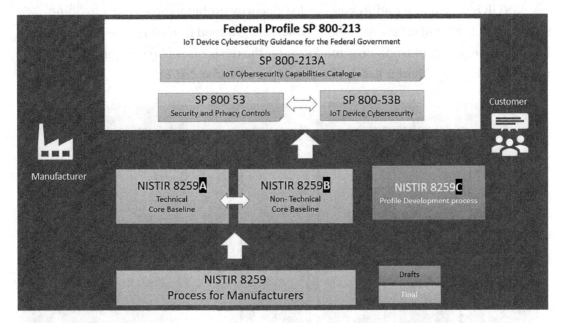

Figure 5-7. *NIST 8259 series roadmap and federal profile (as of January 2021)*

Three final documents have already been released:

- NISTIR 8259: Recommendations for IoT Device Manufacturers: Foundational Activities[34]

- NISTIR 8259A: Core Device Cybersecurity Capability Baseline[35]

- NISTIR 8259B: IoT Non-Technical Supporting Capability Core Baseline[36]

These recommendations and baseline help enhance cybersecurity for all new IoT devices. One of the major complexities is the range of the IoT device compute power with a large portion of the IoT market consisting of low or medium-complexity devices so called constrained devices. This complexity makes NIST recommendation even more

[34] https://csrc.nist.gov/publications/detail/nistir/8259/final
[35] https://csrc.nist.gov/publications/detail/nistir/8259a/final
[36] https://csrc.nist.gov/publications/detail/nistir/8259b/final

important as it defines the baseline that is applicable across all IoT devices and that is recognized globally. A consensus baseline grounded in international standards with broad support across the industry will help enable interoperable IoT security policies worldwide.

NISTIR 8259 guidance addresses our IoT Security problem directly by providing steps that manufacturers should follow, which are grouped into two phases; pre-market, before the device is sold, and post-market, after the device is sold (see Figure 5-8 NIST recommended activities for IoT device developers, Source: NIST).

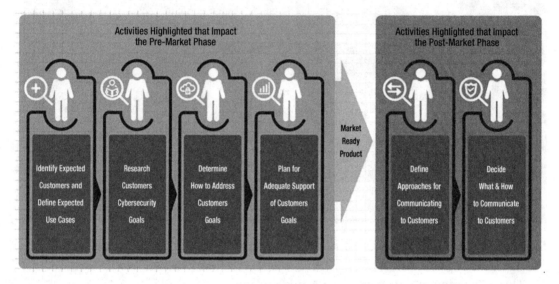

Figure 5-8. *NIST recommended activities for IoT device developers. Source: NIST*[37]

NISTIR 8259A publication outlines six technical capabilities, cross-referenced with applicable industry and federal standards, as a default for minimally securable IoT devices.

- Device identification: The IoT device can be uniquely identified logically and physically.

- Device configuration: The configuration of the IoT device's software can be changed, and such changes can be performed by authorized entities only.

- Data protection: The IoT device can protect the data it stores and transmits from unauthorized access and modification.

---

[37] https://nvlpubs.nist.gov/nistpubs/ir/2020/NIST.IR.8259.pdf

- Logical access to interfaces: The IoT device can restrict logical access to its local and network interfaces, and the protocols and services used by those interfaces, to authorized entities only.

- Software update: The IoT device's software can be updated by authorized entities only using a secure and configurable mechanism.

- Cybersecurity state awareness: The IoT device can report on its cybersecurity state and make that information accessible to authorized entities only.

NISTIR 8259B complements 8259A with guidance on nontechnical processes that manufacturers should implement that support IoT device cybersecurity, such as documenting updates, information collection and dissemination practices, and training for customers on how to implement them.

Together NISTIRs 8259 A and 8259B are a complementary pair, providing balance of technical and non-technical requirements, and giving comprehensive guidance for manufacturers executing the six activities outlined in NISTIR 8259 (see Figure 5-9 NISTIR 8259 IoT Security Technical and Non-Technical Baseline (Source NIST)

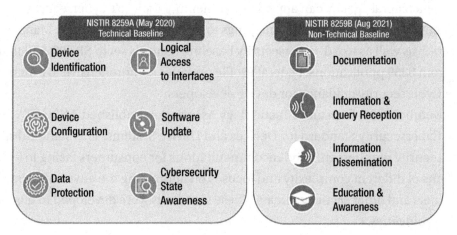

Figure 5-9. *NISTIR 8259 IoT security technical and non-technical baseline (Source NIST[38])*

---

[38] www.nist.gov/itl/applied-cybersecurity/nist-cybersecurity-iot-program/nistir-8259-series

The draft NISTIR 8259C "Creating a Profile Using the IoT Core Baseline and Non-Technical Baseline"[39] describes a process that can be leveraged by organizations to build IoT cybersecurity requirements set for particular market ecosystems, customers, applications, and/or environments. It starts with the core baselines provided in NISTIR 8259A and B and explains how to integrate those baselines with vertical or application-specific requirements to develop a profile suitable for specific IoT device usages This can be used for customer's vertical segment requirements, industry standards, or regulatory guidance.

SP 800-213, IoT Device Cybersecurity Guidance for the Federal Government: Establishing IoT Device Cybersecurity Requirements,[40] accumulated 8259 learnings and provides guidance for federal organizations in defining their IoT cybersecurity requirements. It demonstrates the results of applying the NISTIR 8259C process in a federal government customer space, where the requirements of the FISMA (Federal Information Security Management Act of 2002) and the SP 800-53[41] security and privacy controls catalog are the essential guidance. SP 800-213 includes SP 800-213A, the IoT Device Cybersecurity Requirements Catalog, a set of technical and non-technical cybersecurity controls defining IoT device capabilities and supporting non-technical actions that a federal agency can apply in documenting their IoT cybersecurity requirements. The catalog includes mappings to SP 800-53 and NIST Risk Management Framework[42] as well as to IoT cybersecurity baseline controls set in SP 800-53B that's derived from 8259 publications. Federal Profile provides comprehensive IoT market segment Cybersecurity guidance for device developers.

In November 2020, Consumer Technology Association published ANSI/CTA 2088[43] Baseline Cybersecurity Standard for Devices and Device Systems. This standard specifies baseline security requirements and recommendations for consumers facing IoT devices and systems of different complexity and focuses on addressing the adversarial impacts of the botnets and other security threats. These standards were developed in alignment with NIST guidelines.

---

[39] https://csrc.nist.gov/publications/detail/nistir/8259c/draft
[40] www.nist.gov/itl/applied-cybersecurity/nist-cybersecurity-iot-program/sp-800-213-series
[41] https://csrc.nist.gov/publications/detail/sp/800-53/rev-5/final
[42] https://csrc.nist.gov/projects/risk-management
[43] https://standards.cta.tech/apps/group_public/project/details.php?project_id=594

On the European arena, it is important to learn about European Union Agency for Cybersecurity (ENISA) Baseline Security Recommendations for IoT,[44] and European Standards Organization ETSI 303-645 standard for the Cyber Security for Consumer Internet of Things: Baseline Requirements.[45] ENISA's recommendation was developed in 2017 with the goals to specify the security requirements of IoT, map critical assets and relevant threats, assess attacks, and identify practices and security approaches to protect IoT systems in the context of Critical Information Infrastructure. This document has good foundational information on cybersecurity for the IoT systems consumers and provides an elaborated list of security measures and good practices, to mitigate the threats, vulnerabilities, and risks identified in the study that affect IoT devices and environments. This recommendation could be applied to the different IoT segments and environments and deployments in a horizontal manner as a baseline, in contrast to the vertical-specific recommendation.

ETSI 303-645 is a standard specifically designed for consumer IoT devices, including smart cameras and other smart household devices. It contains a set of security and privacy requirements and recommendations that manufacturers should follow to build secure products. These requirements are split into the following 13 categories:

1.   No universal default passwords.

2.   Implement a means to manage reports of vulnerabilities.

3.   Keep software updated.

4.   Securely store sensitive security parameters.

5.   Communicate securely.

6.   Minimize exposed attack surfaces.

7.   Ensure software integrity.

8.   Ensure that personal data is secure.

9.   Make systems resilient to outages.

10.   Examine system telemetry data.

---

[44] www.enisa.europa.eu/publications/baseline-security-recommendations-for-iot
[45] www.etsi.org/deliver/etsi_en/303600_303699/303645/02.01.00_30/
en_303645v020100v.pdf

11. Make it easy for users to delete personal data.

12. Make installation and maintenance of devices easy.

13. Validate input data.

In addition, ETSI EN 303 645 standard provides recommendations for data protection requirements to help manufacturers protect users' personal data.

With a plethora of emerging IOT Cybersecurity recommendations and standards, it is important to have a harmonized approach that is intended for the broad IoT industry, providers, manufacturers, consumers, and regulators. This is a consistent message from NIST and ENISA. Over 20 other industry groups and technology organizations came together to develop a global, industry-driven consensus on IoT security baselines convened by the Council to Secure the Digital Economy (CSDE)[46] and contributed to the NISTIR 8259 series. The International Standards Organization (ISO) expert group is working on defining the IoT security and privacy device baseline requirements standard (ISO/IEC 27402[47]) that aims to address this important problem of the connected IoT world.

The US Food and Drug Administration (FDA) regulates the use of AI in covered healthcare products and plays an important role in ensuring the safety and effectiveness of those products. In January 2021, FDA introduced the Artificial Intelligence/ Machine Learning (AI/ML)-based Software as a Medical Device (SaMD) Action Plan.[48] SaMD covers a wide range of AI-enabled products such as applications that run on smartphones, but also software that can detect and analyze stroke based on CT images of the brain or diagnose fractures based on X-ray imaging. FDA plan considers the entire lifecycle of a device, promotes transparency, real-world performance monitoring, and methodologies to assess algorithmic bias. Racial, ethnic, and gender bias is one of the key problems for the healthcare industry, that is even more critical for AI efficiency and safety.

It is important to consider that these standards apply to a wide range of IoT device types. Minimum compliance may be adequate for many devices, but IoT devices that protect valuable Machine Learning models theft and from tampering that will damage trust will require the highest levels of security.

---

[46] https://securingdigitaleconomy.org/

[47] www.iso.org/standard/80136.html

[48] www.fda.gov/media/145022/download

Privacy Compliance

Privacy considerations are critical for AI/ML solutions. IMSS that support ML-based solutions must comply with generic privacy regulations and practices. While there are many local and national privacy regulations, the most dominant regulation in privacy is the European Union's General Data Protection Regulation (GDPR). It defines the most widely used and enforced regulatory definition for privacy.

In April 2020, the United States Federal Trade Commission (FTC) published guidance[49] on using Artificial Intelligence and Algorithms. Later, in January 2021, the FTC took extraordinary law enforcement measures[50] after finding that artificial intelligence company Everalbum, the maker of the "Ever" photo, had deceived customers about its data collection and use practices. FTC ordered Everalbum to delete or destroy any ML models or algorithms developed in whole or in part using biometric information it unlawfully collected from users, along with the biometric data itself.

In addition to these, there are market segment-specific regulations, such as Health Insurance Portability and Accountability (HIPAA) for health care. Consumer Technology Association (CTA) has also developed voluntary privacy principles[51] for health data not covered by HIPAA (Health Insurance Portability and Accountability Act of 1996).

US privacy law proposals increasingly focused on AI accountability and discrimination, and continue to evolve. Keeping personal health information private and protected is a core component of trust. This is critical for AI/ML usage for health care where personal health information is the raw data for most AI systems. Consumers expect that personal data will be protected and want an assurance that organizations will keep their information confidential.

One of the privacy compliance implications is that the model/workload needs to have the ability to be revoked, for example, re-evaluate the right to use at any given time, based on noticing criteria have changed or (at least) operator direction. Depending on the platform application, this may require restarting the platform or the main application on the platform (e.g., the application may require continuous service, such as electric power).

---

[49] www.ftc.gov/news-events/blogs/business-blog/2020/04/using-artificial-intelligence-algorithms

[50] www.ftc.gov/enforcement/cases-proceedings/1923172/everalbum-inc-matter

[51] www.cta.tech/cta/media/Membership/PDFs/CTA-Guiding-Principles-for-the-Privacy-of-Personal-Health-and-Wellness-Information.pdf

A model licensing implementation which causes the model to be verified once and then operates continuously (potentially forever) would not be able to comply with an order to remove the model based on this kind of criteria.

Personal data in the healthcare systems can be divided into two categories. The first category is data collected by health plans and health providers, which is directly protected by HIPAA. The second category comprises such health information which has been collected by individuals or wellness data they have generated using health applications. While this second category is not protected by HIPAA, this protection is critical to ensure consumers trust the service providers and use the applications and services.

By providing information on how personal health information is used, shared, stored, and managed, organizations can promote the consumer trust necessary to encourage AI use.

HIPAA details some requirements for the secure storage of data and notification in the event of a security breach, but some organizations who provide AI-based services may not be covered by HIPAA. For example, an article in USA Today[52] demonstrated that data profiles from health tracking devices are shared with employee companies, as well as with healthcare providers who manage corporate wellness programs. As a result, Personal Identifiable Information (PII) data could later be used to identify who they are and link their identities to detailed medical profiles that can be bought by companies, researchers, or anyone else. Consumers may not be aware of the scope of HIPAA coverage and, as a result, don't realize that the information, they share is not protected by healthcare regulations (note, it doesn't exclude coverage by other regulations). It is expected that manufacturers and sellers of AI solutions will likely be subject to future regulations if they are not already covered by HIPAA.

Additionally, there are often regional privacy regulations that apply to IMSS. OEMs, consultants, system integrators, and system operators should monitor and seek legal advice on applicable local regulations. It is recommended that developers should consider data security whenever information is collected and stored. Organizations should assess their risk of breach and take steps to minimize the risk of exposure.

---

[52] www.usatoday.com/story/opinion/2019/01/28/health-privacy-laws-artificial-intelligence-hipaa-needs-update-column/2695386002/

GDPR and Emerging EU AI Regulation

European Union GDPR[53] (General Data Protection Regulation) is a prominent data privacy and security law with significant implications for businesses both in the EU and globally. AI is not explicitly outlined in the GDPR guidelines, but many provisions in GDPR directly apply to AI. According to the study conducted by the European Union Panel for the Future of Science and Technology,[54] AI system developers should consider the values and principles of the GDPR and "adopt a responsible and risk-oriented approach." However, given the complexity of the AI and ambiguities present in the GDPR, it is not straightforward for the AI system ecosystem to translate it into practices. This paper indicates that further development is required to generate appropriate responses, based on shared values for stakeholders (industry and society) and effective technologies. According to the study, consistent application of data protection principles, when combined with the ability to efficiently use AI technology, can contribute to the scalability of AI applications, by generating trust and preventing risks.

In essence, AI breaks the traditional data processing assumptions reflected in GDPR. This conflict between AI and GDPR is specific to the field of data processing, but not new given the known dichotomy between innovative technologies and regulation and requires both sides to absorb and adopt. Several publications that discuss the intersection of GDPR and AI, outlining that GDPR provides limited guidance on how to achieve data protection. In 2019, Andre Tang published "Making AI GDPR compliant"[55] addressing the challenges with GDPR compliance for AI solutions. Among highlighted conflicts (see Figure 5-10 AI and GDPR conflicts and possible remediations. Source ISACA) is the accuracy of automated decision-making, the right for erasure, data minimization, and the transparency principle. Some of the recommendations make sense to implement and we see the industry already moving in that direction (for example, federated Learning and Transfer Learning), others such as "rights to erasure" would be challenging to implement if we think about broad-scale deployment of models developed based on the personal data. Data minimization should not exclude the use of personal data for machine learning purposes. GDPR should not prevent the creation of training sets and the building of AI models whenever data protection rights compliance is addressed.

---

[53] https://gdpr.eu/what-is-gdpr/
[54] www.europarl.europa.eu/RegData/etudes/STUD/2020/641530/EPRS_STU(2020)641530_EN.pdf
[55] www.isaca.org/resources/isaca-journal/issues/2019/volume-5/making-ai-gdpr-compliant

AI vs. GDPR	Proposed Suggestions
Accuracy of automated decision-making	• Obtain human intervention and do not rely solely on a machine. • Use data accuracy analysis technology; monitor the AI agent performance and use ML to increase the accuracy. • Conduct a DPIA and trustworthy AI assessment. • Conduct rigorous testing, e.g., penetration tests and cybersecurity control assessments. • Implement traceability, auditability and transparent communication on system capabilities.
The right to erasure	• Utilize easy removal of information, such as Google's option of automatic deletion of their search and location history.
Data minimization	• Pseudonymize data. • Use data distortion processing technology; keep the property of data for statistics use in AI. • Apply federated ML and transfer learning when there is a need to collect personal data.
Transparency principle	• Use metadata management tools: data governance to authorize specific person accessing the specified DLT. • Have a specific privacy notice and explicit consent. • Use a differential privacy model; delete personally identifiable information without modifying the meaning of datasets.

Figure 5-10. *AI and GDPR conflicts and possible remediations. Source ISACA*

AI/ML Trustworthiness

Trustworthiness Journey

Trustworthiness has emerged as a fundamental security concept addressing AI systems being worthy of physical, cyber, and social trust. In 1999, the Trust in Cyberspace National Academies report[56] introduced the foundations of trustworthy computing. In 2002, Bill Gates wrote the famous "Trustworthy Computing" memo[57] where he raised the importance of trustworthy software and hardware products and identified four pillars to trustworthiness: security, privacy, reliability, and business integrity.

Since then, several programs researched the concept of trust, for example, Secure and Trustworthy Cyberspace Program (2011).[58] The practice of trustworthy computing adopted in standardization practices by Institute of Electrical and Electronics Engineers (IEEE) and The International Electrotechnical Commission (IEC)/The International Organization for Standardization (ISO) and defined as following:

---

[56] https://cacm.acm.org/magazines/2021/10/255716-trustworthy-ai/fulltext#R41

[57] Bill Gates: Trustworthy Computing | WIRED

[58] Secure and Trustworthy Cyberspace (SaTC) (nsf21500) | NSF - National Science Foundation

- "Trustworthiness of a computer system such that reliance can be justifiably placed on the service it delivers."[59]

- "Trustworthiness is a quality of being dependable and reliable"[60]

- "Trustworthiness is the ability to meet stakeholders' expectations in a verifiable way."[61, 62]

Today trustworthy computing remains one of the key topics in the development and operation of complex computing systems. The growing complexity of the edge to cloud compute ecosystem, the scale and widespread use of edge computing devices, makes the problem of trustworthy computing implementation even more difficult. This is especially true for the innovative AI/ML systems.

Figure 5-11 represents the timeline of the key European Union (EU) policy activities for the AI, starting with 2018 call to the EU Strategy for AI, following by Ethical Guidelines for Trustworthy AI in 2019, Assessment list of Trustworthy AI (ALTAI) in 2020 and finally the key initiative in AI space, the EU Regulation on Fostering a European Approach to AI (also known as EU AI ACT). The term "Trustworthy AI" was introduced by the High-Level Expert Group on Artificial Intelligence (AI HLEG).[63] This body was set up by the European Commission to develop a comprehensive EU AI strategy that "centers on excellence and trust, aiming to boost research and industrial capacity and ensure fundamental rights of the new technology."[64] In 2019, HLEG published Ethics the Guidelines for Trustworthy AI that captured a set of key requirements that AI systems should meet in order to be trustworthy[65]:

1. Human Agency and Oversight: fundamental rights, human agency, and human oversight

2. Technical Robustness and Safety: resilience to attack and security, fall back plan and general safety, accuracy, reliability, and reproducibility

---

[59] IEEE Std 982.1-2005 IEEE Standard Dictionary of Measures of the Software Aspects of Dependability

[60] www.iso.org/obp/ui/#iso:std:iso:19626:-1:ed-1:v1:en:term:3.27

[61] www.iso.org/obp/ui/#iso:std:iso-iec:tr:24028:ed-1:v1:en:term:3.42

[62] www.iso.org/obp/ui/#iso:std:iso-iec:30145:-2:ed-1:v1:en:term:3.9

[63] https://digital-strategy.ec.europa.eu/en/library/assessment-list-trustworthy-artificial-intelligence-altai-self-assessment

[64] A European approach to artificial intelligence | Shaping Europe's digital future (europa.eu)

[65] Ethics guidelines for trustworthy AI | Shaping Europe's digital future (europa.eu)

3. Privacy and Data Governance: respect for privacy, quality and integrity of data, access to data

4. Transparency: traceability, explainability, communication

5. Diversity, Non-discrimination, and Fairness: avoidance of unfair bias, accessibility, and universal design

6. Societal and Environmental Well-being: sustainability and environmental friendliness, social impact, society, and democracy

7. Accountability: auditability, minimization and reporting of negative impact, trade-offs, and redress

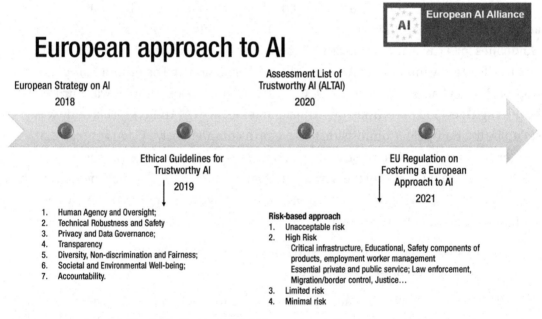

Figure 5-11. *Timeline of EU AI Guidelines*

In 2020, HLEG further translated the Ethical guideline into a practical tool and presented an Assessment List of Trustworthy AI[66] (ALTAI), as well as a prototype web-based tool version.[67] ALTAI's goal is to enable the evaluation process for Trustworthy AI

---

[66] Assessment List for Trustworthy Artificial Intelligence (ALTAI) for self-assessment | Shaping Europe's digital future (europa.eu)

[67] Home page - ALTAI (insight-centre.org)

self-evaluation. AI system developers and adopters can leverage relevant from ALTAI or augment to reflect their needs, based on the market sector they operate in. This helps to operationalize the Trustworthy AI and risks that AI systems might generate. Per HLEG and ALTAI, trustworthiness is key to enabling "responsible competitiveness," by providing the "foundation upon which all those using or affected by AI systems can trust that their design, development and use are lawful, ethical and robust." ALTAI's goal is to enable the evaluation process for Trustworthy AI self-evaluation. Figure 5-12 Interactive ALTAI tool for self-assessment illustrates some questions for the Privacy and Data Governance section, and Figure 5-13 ALTAI self-assessment scoring results demonstrate the sample outcome of the tool that also provides the recommendations for each of the assessment categories.

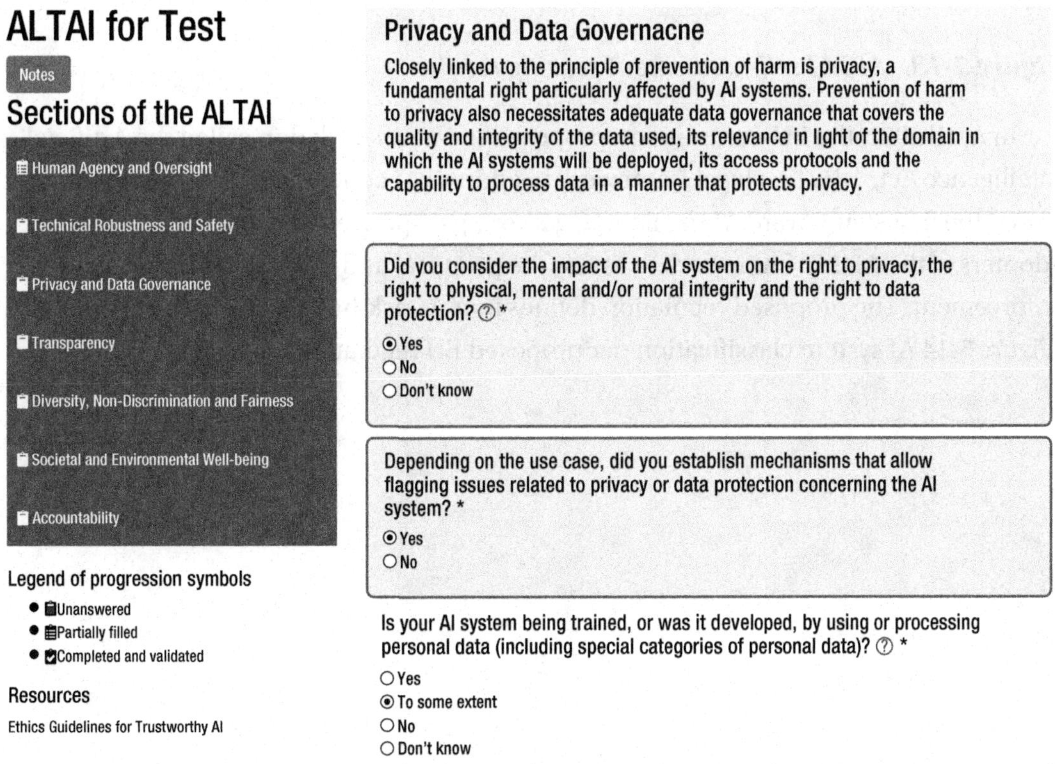

ALTAI for Test

Notes

Sections of the ALTAI

▤ Human Agency and Oversight

▤ Technical Robustness and Safety

▤ Privacy and Data Governance

▤ Transparency

▤ Diversity, Non-Discrimination and Fairness

▤ Societal and Environmental Well-being

▤ Accountability

Legend of progression symbols

- ● ▤Unanswered
- ● ▤Partially filled
- ● ☑Completed and validated

Resources

Ethics Guidelines for Trustworthy AI

Privacy and Data Governacne

Closely linked to the principle of prevention of harm is privacy, a fundamental right particularly affected by AI systems. Prevention of harm to privacy also necessitates adequate data governance that covers the quality and integrity of the data used, its relevance in light of the domain in which the AI systems will be deployed, its access protocols and the capability to process data in a manner that protects privacy.

Did you consider the impact of the AI system on the right to privacy, the right to physical, mental and/or moral integrity and the right to data protection? ⑦ *
- ⦿ Yes
- ○ No
- ○ Don't know

Depending on the use case, did you establish mechanisms that allow flagging issues related to privacy or data protection concerning the AI system? *
- ⦿ Yes
- ○ No

Is your AI system being trained, or was it developed, by using or processing personal data (including special categories of personal data)? ⑦ *
- ○ Yes
- ⦿ To some extent
- ○ No
- ○ Don't know

Figure 5-12. *Interactive ALTAI tool for self-assessment*

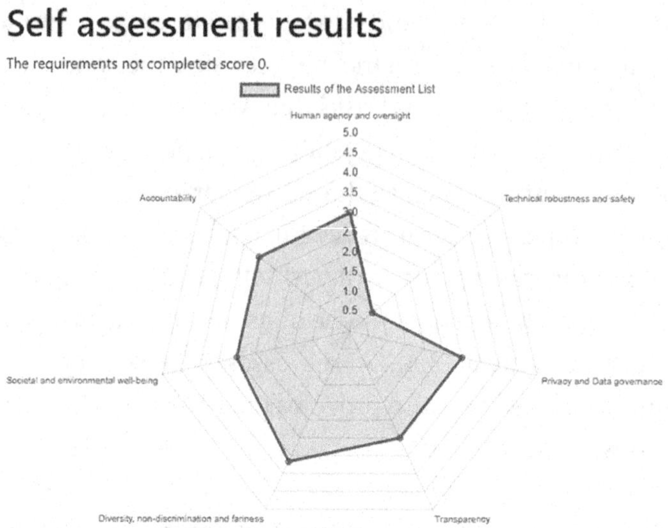

Figure 5-13. *ALTAI self-assessment scoring results*

In April 2021, the EU Commission proposed the new legislation called the Artificial Intelligence Act,[68] the first legal framework to address AI concerns and GDPR limitations. This is the first step toward AI regulation, gathering responses from developers and adopters of the AI/ML framework to assess the proposal and prepare for broad-scale enforcement. The proposed regulation defines four AI risk-based systems categories (Figure 5-14 AI system classification per proposed EU regulation).

---

[68] https://eur-lex.europa.eu/legal-content/EN/TXT/?qid=1623335154975&uri=CELEX%3A52021PC0206

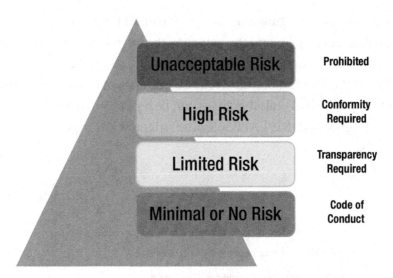

Figure 5-14. *AI system classification per the proposed EU regulation*

Limited- and minimal-risk AI systems include many of the AI applications currently used throughout the business world, such as AI chatbots and AI-powered inventory management.

Unacceptable-risk AI systems include subliminal, manipulative, or exploitative systems that cause harm, real-time, remote biometric identification systems used in public spaces for law enforcement, and all forms of social scoring, such as AI or technology that assesses person's trustworthiness based on social behavior or behavioral predictions. This is the category that will be outright prohibited.

High-risk AI systems include those that evaluate consumer creditworthiness, assist with recruiting or managing employees, or use biometric identification. The systems in this category will be subject to obligatory compliance. It proposes labeling based on existing Conformité Européenne (CE[69]) to indicate that systems meet EU safety, health, and environmental protection requirements. The European Union will be regularly revisiting this category to update the list of systems in this category. Without logo systems will not be accepted on the EU market. To be accepted, systems designed according to five categories of requirements derived from AI ethics principles – *Data and Data Governance, Transparency for Users, Human Oversight, Accuracy, Robustness and Cybersecurity, Traceability and Auditability.*

---

[69] https://ec.europa.eu/growth/single-market/ce-marking/

While the proposed EU regulation is in the transition period, corresponding standards would be developed, and the governance structures would get ready to operationalize the legislation. It is expected that regulation would come into effect in 2024 (earliest) and the EU market would require evidence of conformity assessments.

The United States has several AI policies and best practices activities in development, Figure 5-15 NIST AI Publications depicts key triggers and published papers.

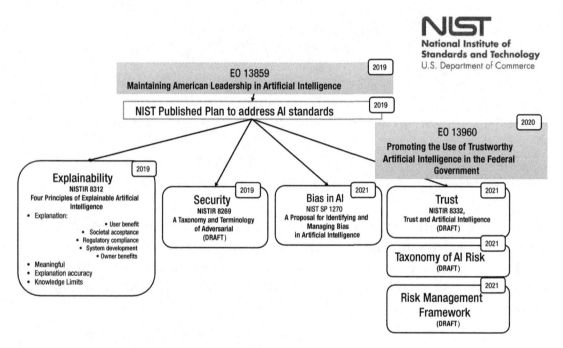

Figure 5-15. *NIST AI publications*

The anchor point for this development is Executive Order (EO) 13859,[70] "Maintaining American Leadership in Artificial Intelligence," issued in 2019. Executive orders are not law, but they influence policy. EO 13859 calls federal agencies to engage in AI standardization to promote US global leadership in AI. Actions to be implemented by agencies include foundational AI research and development to regulate and provide guidance for AI technology deployment and usage.

---

[70] www.federalregister.gov/documents/2019/02/14/2019-02544/maintaining-american-leadership-in-artificial-intelligence

The National Institute of Science and Technology (NIST) is the agency in charge of developing a comprehensive approach to AI standards that could be the basis for a common understanding of how to achieve and measure trustworthy AI. In 2019, NIST published "A Plan for Federal Engagement in Developing Technical Standards and Related Tools"[71] to address the direction of EO's direction and *"ensure that technical standards minimize vulnerability to attacks from malicious actors and reflect Federal priorities for innovation, public trust, and public confidence in systems that use AI technologies; and develop international standards to promote and protect those priorities."* AI Trustworthiness is identified by NIST as an emerging area for standardization and proposed following AI trustworthiness attributes (Figure 5-16 NIST AI Trustworthiness Attributes): accuracy, reliability, resiliency, objectivity, security, explainability, safety, and accountability.

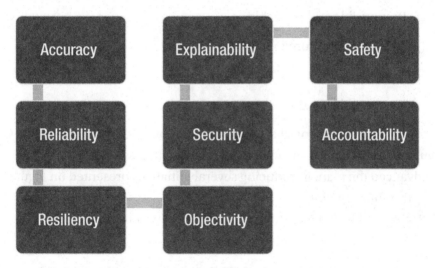

Figure 5-16. *NIST AI trustworthiness attributes*

[71] www.nist.gov/system/files/documents/201"A P9/08/10/ai_standards_fedengagement_plan_9aug2019.pdf

It is also important to mention the US Executive Order 13960 from 2020, "Promoting the Use of Trustworthy Artificial Intelligence in the Federal Government"[72] with the objective *"to ensure they design, develop, acquire, and use AI in a manner that fosters public trust and confidence while protecting privacy, civil rights, civil liberties and American values."* This EO outlines the following principles for use of AI in Government:

(a) Lawful and respectful of our Nation's values

(b) Purposeful and performance-driven

(c) Accurate, reliable, and effective

(d) Safe, secure, and resilient

(e) Understandable

(f) Responsible and traceable

(g) Regularly monitored

(h) Transparent

(i) Accountable

Clearly, there is a strong correlation of principles outlined in the Executive Order with EU guidance and reflection of the NIST trustworthiness principles.

NIST advanced the plan, introducing several initiatives presented on Figure 5-15 NIST AI Publications timeline.

In 2019, NIST published NISRIR 8312[73] that outlines four principles of Explainable AI:

1. AI systems should deliver accompanying evidence or reasons or their outputs

2. AI systems should provide meaningful and understandable explanations to individual users

---

[72] www.federalregister.gov/documents/2020/12/08/2020-27065/promoting-the-use-of-trustworthy-artificial-intelligence-in-the-federal-government
[73] www.nist.gov/system/files/documents/2020/08/17/NIST%20Explainable%20AI%20Draft%20NISTIR8312%20%281%29.pdf

3. Explanations should correctly reflect the AI system's process for generating the output

4. The AI system "only operates under conditions for which it was designed or when the system reaches sufficient confidence in its output."

"A Taxonomy and Terminology of Adversarial Machine Learning" NISTIR 8269[74] report was introduced by NIST in 2019. The data-driven approach of ML introduces additional security challenges in training and inference of AIS operations. Adversarial ML focused on the design of ML algorithms that can resist security challenges, the study of the capabilities of attackers, and the understanding of attack consequences. The taxonomy is arranged in a conceptual hierarchy that includes key types of attacks, defenses, and consequences (Figure 5-17 The Taxonomy and Terminology of Adversarial Machine Learning – NIST 8269).

---

[74] https://csrc.nist.gov/publications/detail/nistir/8269/draft

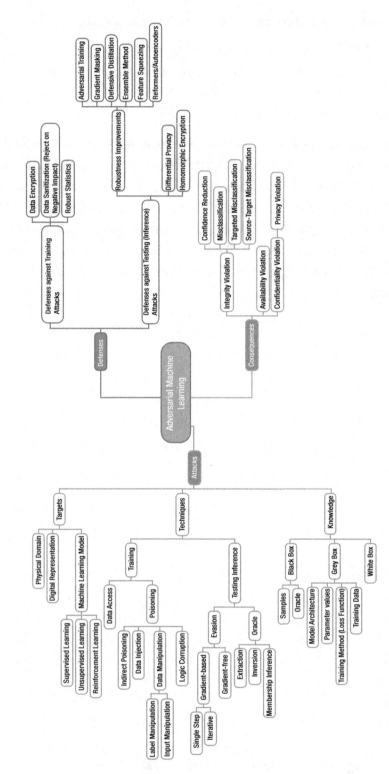

Figure 5-17. The Taxonomy and Terminology of Adversarial Machine Learning – NIST 8269

In 2021, several new reports were presented by NIST. Special Publication 1270 "A Proposal for Identifying and Managing Bias in Artificial 6 Intelligence,"[75] was published in June 2021. Ethical implementation and consequently the use of AI technologies are one of the top societal concerns. To implement AI ethically, it is necessary to ensure that AI is acting within the defined scope, and that its behavior meets the expectation of fairness and potential harm. If an AIS can't fulfill these expectations, then it cannot be trusted and therefore cannot be adopted in public infrastructure. This NIST paper recommends an approach for identifying and managing AI bias that is tied to three stages of the AI lifecycle (Figure 5-18 Example of biases across AI Lifecycle per NIST SP 1270): pre-design, design, and development, and deployment (and post-deployment). Instead of chasing specific biases for individual use cases, for better mitigation and effectiveness, it is suggested to address the context-specific nature of AI implicitly in the life cycle of system development.

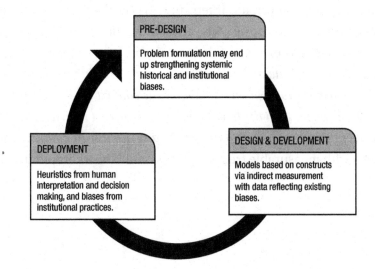

Figure 5-18. *Example of biases across AI Lifecycle per NIST SP 1270*

Finally, NISTIR 8332, Trust and Artificial Intelligence, examines how humans experience trust as they use or are affected by AI systems. NIST has the following proposal. If the AI system has a high level of technical trustworthiness, and the values

---

[75] https://nvlpubs.nist.gov/nistpubs/SpecialPublications/NIST.SP.1270-draft.pdf

of the trustworthiness characteristics are perceived to be good enough for the context of use, then the likelihood of AI user trust increases. According to NIST co-author Brian Stanton, the issue is whether human trust in AI systems is measurable – and if so, how to measure it accurately and appropriately.

NIST is also researching the problem of measurable trustworthiness. NISTIR 8332[76] "Artificial Intelligence and User Trust" is a proposal on how to evaluate user trust in AIS based on nine weighted attributes of AI trustworthiness (Figure 5-16 NIST AI Trustworthiness Attributes), including privacy. The weight of these nine factors may change, depending on the use case, reflecting how the individual is using the AI system and the level of risk involved in that particular use. For example, user trust in a low-risk application, such as a music selection algorithm, may be tied to certain factors that differ from those factors influencing user trust in a high-risk application, such as a medical diagnostic system. Figure 5-19 NIST User Trust Decision[77] illustrates how a person may be willing to trust a music selection algorithm, but not the AI "medical assistant" used to diagnose cancer. It is interesting to note that NISTIR 8332 is the result of cross-disciplinary cooperation, one of the co-authors, Brian Stanton, is a psychologist, and another, Ted Jensen, is a computer scientist. The authors suggest that *"If the AI system has a high level of technical trustworthiness, and the values of the trustworthiness characteristics are perceived to be good enough for the context of use, and especially the risk inherent in that context, then the likelihood of AI user trust increases. It is this trust, based on user perceptions, that will be necessary of any human-AI collaboration."* Thus, building solutions with measurable trustworthiness could be a competitive advantage.

---

[76] https://nvlpubs.nist.gov/nistpubs/ir/2021/nist.ir.8332-draft.pdf
[77] www.nist.gov/news-events/news/2021/05/
nist-proposes-method-evaluating-user-trust-artificial-intelligence-systems

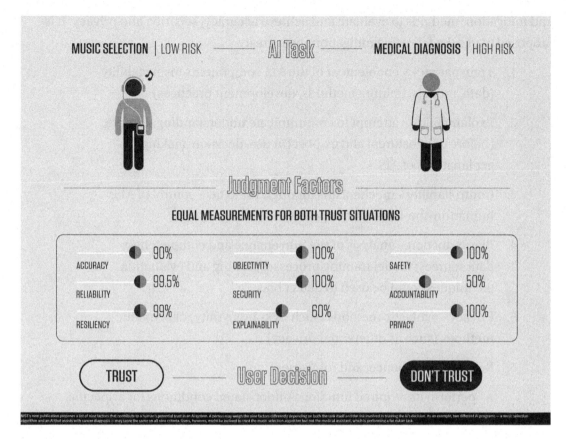

Figure 5-19. NIST user trust decision

As was mentioned before, it is essential to have harmonized international standards, the ISO/IEC SC42[78] subcommittee is the anchor point for international efforts across the definition of AI trustworthiness, bias, safety, performance, risk management, and governance. ISO defines trustworthiness as the *"ability to meet stakeholders' expectations in a verifiable way, requiring a combination of organizational process with KPI and non-functional requirements."*[79] Consumers of AI Systems (AIS) technologies expect trust to be established and maintained at each layer of AIS to sufficiently protect infrastructures for data collection, storage, processing infrastructure, and AIS assets.

ISO/IEC published a technical report "Overview of trustworthiness in artificial intelligence"[80] that surveys methods to establish the trust in AIS, threats, vulnerabilities

---

[78] www.iso.org/committee/6794475.html

[79] www.iso.org/obp/ui/#iso:std:iso-iec:tr:24028:ed-1:v1:en:term:3.42

[80] www.iso.org/standard/77608.html

and mitigation, methods to evaluate and achieve accuracy, security, and privacy. It is proposed to use the following mitigation measures:

1. Transparency – enablement of the AIS components inspectability (data, models, training methods, development practices)

2. Explainability – attempt to communicate understanding; ex-ante (before use, features) and ex-post (in use, decision-making) explanations of AIS

3. Controllability – mechanisms for operator to take control of AIS; human-in-the-loop control points

4. Bias reduction – analysis of the provenance and completeness data sources; model training processes; testing and evaluation techniques could be used to detect bias

5. Privacy – syntactic methods (such as k-anonymity) or semantic methods (such as differential privacy)

6. Reliability, resilience, and robustness

   a. perform its required functions under stated conditions for a specific period of time

   b. recover operational condition quickly following an incident

   c. maintain its level of performance under any circumstances

7. System HW faults – mask or work around failures using hardware (e.g., n-plication at a course or fine grain), information (e.g., check bits), or time (e.g., re-computation at different, usually random times) redundancy; software faults are protected against by software redundancy (e.g., software diversity, or other forms of moving target mitigation)

8. Functional safety – monitor the decisions taken by the AI in order to ensure that they are in

   a. a tolerable range or bring the system into a defined state in case they detect problematic behavior

Among other notable activities in the domain of Trustworthy AI, it is important to mention AI Principles developed by the Organization for Economic Co-operation and Development (OECD).[81] OECD is an intergovernmental organization founded with the objective to stimulate economic growth and world trade. Its AI Policy Observatory focused on multi-disciplinary analysis of AI and produced OECD AI Principles,[82] which became the basis for the G20 AI Principles endorsed by Leaders in 2019[83] and later adopted by many governments around the world. (Figure 5-20 Governments that have committed to the OECD AI Principles [source OECD]).

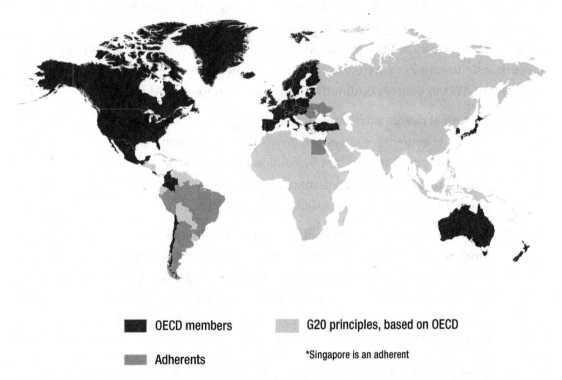

OECD members   G20 principles, based on OECD

Adherents   *Singapore is an adherent

Figure 5-20. *Governments that have committed to the OECD AI Principles (source OECD)*

---

[81] https://oecd.ai/en/ai-principles#:~:text=The%20OECD%20AI%20Principles%20promote, stand%20the%20test%20of%20time.

[82] https://legalinstruments.oecd.org/en/instruments/OECD-LEGAL-0449

[83] https://oecd-innovation-blog.com/2020/07/24/g20-artificial-intelligence-ai-principles-oecd-report/

Additionally, Consumer Technologies Association (CTA) leads two AI standardization efforts for consumer use cases:

- Guidelines for Developing Trustworthy Artificial Intelligence Systems (ANSI/CTA-2096)[84]

- The Use of Artificial Intelligence in Health Care: Trustworthiness (ANSI/CTA-2090)[85]

In 2021, NIST published a draft "Taxonomy of AI Risk"[86] to solicit public input toward building an AI Risk Management Framework (AI RMF). The document categorizes risks outlined in OECD, EU Ethics Guidelines for Trustworthy AI, and US Executive Order 13960 Principles of Trustworthy AI. A hierarchical approach is proposed for categorization to simplify the risk management for the stakeholders and three broad categories of AIS risk sources outlined (Figure 5-21 Taxonomy of AI Risk):

1) **Technical design attributes:** factors that are under the direct control of system designers and developers, and which may be measured using standard evaluation criteria that have traditionally been applied to machine learning systems, or that may be applied in an automated way in the future.

2) **How AI systems are perceived:** mental representations of models, including whether the output provided is sufficient to evaluate compliance (transparency), whether model operations can be easily understood (explainability), and whether they provide output that can be used to make a meaningful decision (interpretability).

3) **Guiding policies and principles:** broader societal determinations of value, such as privacy, accountability, fairness, justice, equity, etc., which cannot be measured consistently across domains because of their dependence on context.

---

[84] https://shop.cta.tech/products/guidelines-for-developing-trustworthy-artificial-intelligence-systems-ansi-cta-2096

[85] www.cta.tech/Resources/Newsroom/Media-Releases/2021/February/CTA-Launches-New-Trustworthiness-Standard-for-AI-i

[86] www.nist.gov/system/files/documents/2021/10/15/taxonomy_AI_risks.pdf

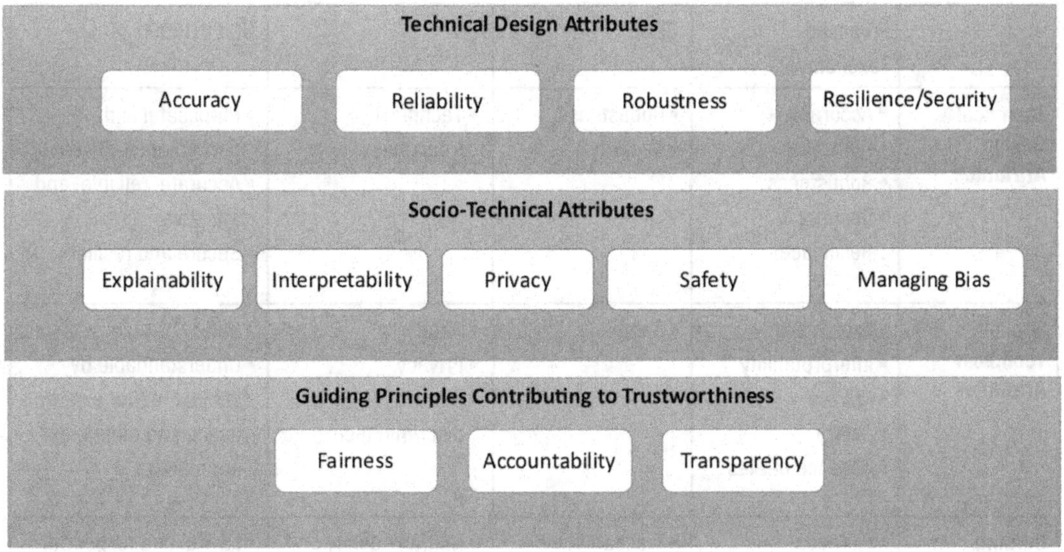

Technical Design Attributes			
Accuracy	Reliability	Robustness	Resilience/Security

Socio-Technical Attributes				
Explainability	Interpretability	Privacy	Safety	Managing Bias

Guiding Principles Contributing to Trustworthiness		
Fairness	Accountability	Transparency

Figure 5-21. *Taxonomy of AI Risk*

NIST not only proposed the taxonomy but also provided the mapping to the relevant policy documents (Figure 5-22 Mapping of proposed Taxonomy to OECD, EU, US EO [source NIST]). At the current stage of emerging cross-Geo policy development, it is important to have developed an approach that can satisfy the global needs while industry is working on harmonizing the policy approach.

	Proposed Taxonomy	OECD	EU	US EO 13960
Technical Design Attributes	• Accuracy • Reliability • Robustness • Security & Resilience	• Robustness • Security	• Technical robustness	• Purposeful and performance-driven • Accurate, reliable, and effective • Secure and resilient
Socio-Technical Attributes	• Explainability • Interpretability • Privacy • Safety • Absence of Bias	• Safety	• Safety • Privacy • Non-discrimination	• Safe • Understandable by subject matter experts, users, and others, as appropriate
Guiding Principles Contributing to Trust-worthiness	• Fairness • Accountability • Transparency	• Traceability to human values • Transparency and responsible disclosure • Accountability	• Human agency and oversight • Data governance • Transparency • Diversity and fairness • Environmental and societal well-being • Accountability	• Lawful and respectful of our Nation's values • Responsible and traceable • Regularly monitored • Transparent • Accountable

Figure 5-22. *Mapping of proposed taxonomy to OECD, EU, US EO (source NIST)*

AI Model and Data Provenance

If simplified, the ML model can be visualized as a function or a program that takes an input as data, applies logic, and produces an output as data. Traditional software programs are developed by humans, and it takes human knowledge as input to produce results. In the case of the AI/ML, the model's logic is driven by its training data and the quality of the data has a paramount impact. Models are only as trustworthy as the data they are built on and contain implicit information about how training data used to create the models was collected, organized, labeled, and processed.

Basic provenance enables a system operator or consumer to know where the model came from and that it has not been tampered with. This provenance data is essentially a cryptographic hash of the model which has been cryptographically signed by the creator or publisher that can be verified with the publisher's public key provided by a certificate authority. In addition, because the model is an embodiment of the training data, being able to verify the source and integrity of the training data gives the system operator or consumer deeper trust.

The highest level of transparency for model provenance includes more information about the training data and the training environment. How the training data was gathered, labeled, and how it was pre-processed for AI model training can be known by also providing provenance metadata for the training data. The annotation tools, statistical analyses, division into training, test, and evaluation subsets, mini-batches used for smaller training epochs, hyperparameter selection, and the security configuration of the platform also can contribute provenance for even more trust. This level of transparency can be used for system operators, customers, regulators, and compliance certifications that require the highest level of transparency and trust. The provenance of the source, labeling, and pre-processing of the training data can provide transparency for bias and discrimination reduction and verification to foster fairness and equity.

When the data that is input to the AI inferencing algorithm has provenance metadata, the system operator has the assurance that the data came from the source that signed it and that it has not been tampered with. This can help mitigate manipulation of the input data to produce false positives or false negatives and can help protect against oracle attacks that are attempting to reverse engineer the model or the training data. AI algorithms that are doing the training while deployed for inferencing (e.g., reinforcement learning) are particularly susceptible to manipulation, so the value of provenance on the input data is multiplied for these algorithms.

Provenance applied to the AI output data allows consumers of that data to verify the integrity and source of that content. If that output data is signed by the model and by the system operator, with the provenance of the input data also available, the consumer has all of the information available to trace the provenance of the entire system to gain the highest level of trust in that output data.

Data provenance and data lineage are evolving and there are two important vectors of development:

- Automation of data provenance practices. Given the amount of data required for ML, manual operations and practices are no longer a viable and ultimately present a bottleneck for ML solution scaling. Therefore, automated tools for data provenance and, most important, integration of those tools into the ML lifecycle.

- Metadata schema definitions are the starting point for the data provenance. This includes machine-readable structures to capture the provenance of all aspects that apply to the AI output. Standardization and harmonization of the metadata schema will greatly influence the ecosystem of ML solutions.

- Metadata efficient processing is another critical factor as it might become a barrier of the adoption of the provenance tooling. The cryptographic workload for provenance metadata generation and processing is not negligible and is overhead for the main "useful" data processing functions. Hierarchies and (secure) linkages can help to minimize the overhead when the trust in the source and risk factors do not require a deep dive into provenance.

- Security best practices must be applied to the data provenance tools and metadata, integrity of the processing and integrity of the metadata are critical factors.

One of the organizations that work on defining the best practices for provenance is Coalition for Content Provenance and Authenticity (C2PA),[87] a joint development foundation project, formed through an alliance between Adobe, Arm, Intel, Microsoft, and Truepic. This project was motivated by the problems in digital media, where the ability to trace the provenance of media has become critical. C2PA focuses on developing technical specifications for establishing content provenance and authenticity.

The C2PA defines a Provenance Manifest as a series of statements that cover asset creation, authorship, edit actions, capture device details, bindings to content, and many other subjects. These statements, called Assertions, make up the provenance of a given asset and represent a series of trust signals that can be used by a human to improve their view of trustworthiness concerning the asset. Assertions are wrapped up with additional information into a digitally signed entity called a Claim. These assertions, claims, credentials, and signatures are all bound together into a verifiable unit called a C2PA Manifest (see Figure 5-23 A C2PA Manifest)

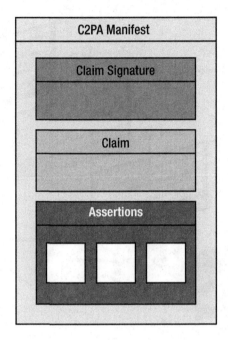

Figure 5-23. *A C2PA Manifest[88]*

Figure 5-24 C2PA elements demonstrate the C2PA architecture for image transformation, origin as a camera type, location and time, transformation in form of the filter and compression, and final digital content with asset metadata.

---

[88] https://c2pa.org/specifications/specifications/1.3/specs/C2PA_Specification.html

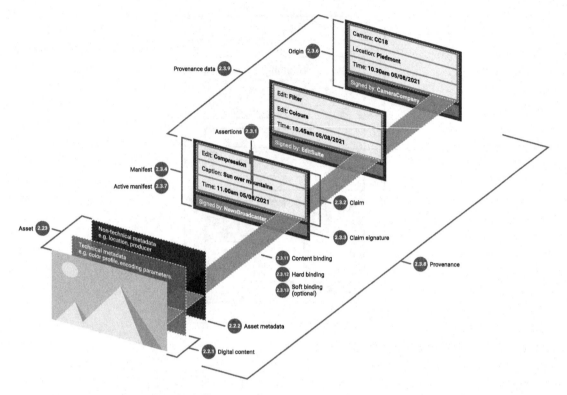

Figure 5-24. *C2PA elements*[89]

AI Risk Management

As mentioned before, the goal for policymakers, standardization bodies, and broad industry stakeholders is to address the risk of AI/ML systems and solutions and remove barriers for broad deployment and scale. ISO 31000[90] defines the general-purpose practical guide risk management method, provides principles, a framework, and a process. According to ISO 31000, risk management is defined as *"coordinated activities to direct and control an organization with regard to risk,"* where risk is *"effect of uncertainty on objectives"* with the following notes[91]:

---

[89] https://c2pa.org/specifications/specifications/1.3/specs/C2PA_Specification.html
[90] www.iso.org/iso-31000-risk-management.html
[91] www.iso.org/obp/ui#iso:std:iso:31000:ed-2:v1:en

- *An effect is a deviation from the expected. It can be positive, negative, or both, and can address, create or result in opportunities and threats.*

- *Objectives can have different aspects and categories and can be applied at different levels.*

- *Risk is usually expressed in terms of risk sources, potential events, their consequences and their likelihood.*

The IMSS and AIS supply ecosystem are very complex, it spreads beyond a single organization and includes developers, distributors, solution providers, customers, their partners as well as human society. The risk management for this complex ecosystem should evaluate and address the concerns of all stakeholders. ISO/ IEC 242028 outlinesthe risk management process of the AI system, starting with the identification of risk sources based on the trustworthiness principles (see AI/ML Trustworthiness), translating those to control objectives and corresponding mitigation, and further mapping of those to set for guidelines or measures according to the policy (see Figure 5-25 Risk Management Process). Well-established risk management is a continuous process that includes validation, assessments, and measurements of the approaches, including performance metrics and field trials.

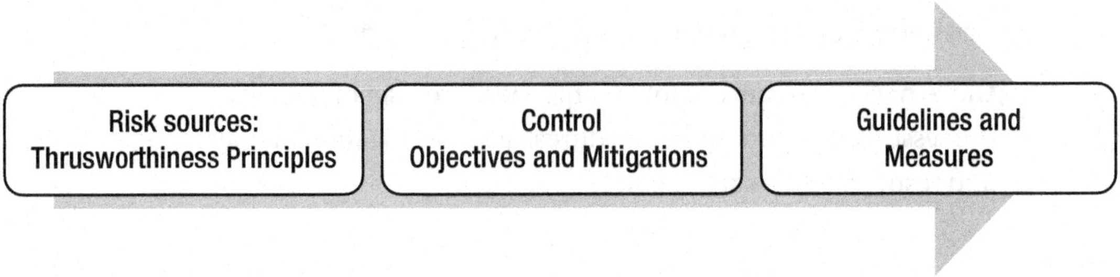

| Risk sources:
Thrusworthiness Principles | Control
Objectives and Mitigations | Guidelines and
Measures |

Figure 5-25. *Risk Management Process*

As a part of the broad plan for Federal Engagement in AI standards, (Figure 5-15 NIST AI Publications) NIST works on the development of AI Risk Management practices. The goal is to stimulate the development of methods to address the trustworthiness of the AIS (see Figure 5-16 NIST AI Trustworthiness Attributes). Again, this framework should encompass principles during the entire life cycle of AI systems, design, deployment, use, and evaluation of AI systems, hence establishing trustworthiness. NIST published the concept paper for public input.[92] This paper describes the synergy between AI RMF and NIST Cybersecurity Framework[93] and Privacy Framework.[94] It is important for IMSS/AIS developers to realize the dependency between Security, Privacy, and AI Trustworthiness. An AI RMF is required to be maintained continuously throughout the life cycle entireness, see Figure 5-26 Risk Management Throughout the AI System Life Cycle with four sample categories to be implemented during Pre-design, Design and Development, Test and Validation and Deployment:

1. **Map**: Context is recognized, and risks related to the context are enumerated.

2. **Measure**: Enumerated risks are analyzed, quantified, or tracked where possible.

3. **Manage**: Enumerated risks are prioritized, mitigated, shared, transferred, or accepted based on measured severity.

4. **Govern**: Appropriate organizational measures, set of policies, processes, and operating procedures, and specification of roles and responsibilities are in place.

---

[92] www.nist.gov/system/files/documents/2021/12/14/AI%20RMF%20Concept%20Paper_13Dec2021_posted.pdf

[93] www.nist.gov/cyberframework

[94] www.nist.gov/privacy-framework

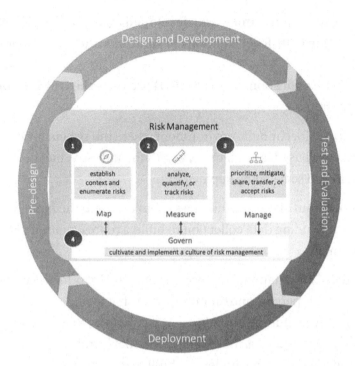

Figure 5-26. *Risk Management throughout the AI System life cycle (NIST RMF)*

The AI Risk Management process helps to alleviate challenges that arise from the broad and evolving AI use cases. As we mentioned earlier, the AI ecosystem is complex with a multitude of diverse stakeholders, including developers, users, deployers, and evaluators. This makes risk management even more complicated when entities must identify, assess, prioritize, respond to, and communicate risks across business and social boundaries at scale. Adoption of a consensus-driven framework such as the one proposed by NIST, can address regulation, establish trust in AI systems, and unleash business opportunities.

IMSS with ML Protection

Regulatory, Policy, and Standards development demonstrates the need for a holistic approach when assessing the security, privacy, and trustworthiness of AI/ML-based IMSS.

AI systems classification framework, developed by OESD[95] **could help stakeholders to define high-level elements of solutions and** map implications for key policy areas.

Figure 5-27 AIS Classification (source OECD) **presents the OECD framework which has** four key dimensions:

- **Context:** Socioeconomic environment where the system is being deployed and used. For example, what's the industry, business function, and scale of the deployment.

- **Data and Input:** The data that the system uses and the input it receives, including data collection to build a representation of the environment.

- **AI Model:** Computational representation of real-world processes, objects, ideas, people, and/or interactions that include assumptions about reality, including underlying AI technology, that makes up the AI system. For example, the type of the model (symbolic, statistical, or hybrid), and how the model was built (e.g., supervised or unsupervised learning).

- **Task and Output:** Tasks the system performs and the outputs that make up the results of its work (for example, recognition, personalization, etc.) and resulting action.

---

[95] https://wp.oecd.ai/app/uploads/2021/06/OECD-Framework-for-Classifying-AI-Standard-deck.pdf

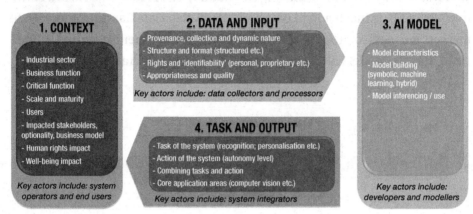

Source: OECD.AI

Figure 5-27. *AIS classification (source OECD)*

Why is this important? Different types of AI/ML systems raise unique policy considerations in their use context. This framework allows cataloging and organizing the AI system. In the context of measurable trustworthiness having such a classification will be a critical factor for building scalable solutions.

Here is the OECD definition of the AIS[96] that can be directly applied to ML IMSS:

An AI system is a machine-based system that is capable of influencing the environment by producing an output (predictions, recommendations, or decisions) for a given set of objectives. It uses machine and/or human-based data and inputs to (i) perceive real and/or virtual environments; (ii) abstract these perceptions into models through analysis in an automated manner (e.g., with machine learning), or manually; and (iii) use model inference to formulate options for outcomes. AI systems are designed to operate with varying levels of autonomy.

---

96 https://oecd.ai/en/ai-principles

Generic ML IMSS architecture includes the collection of data from the Sensors (data ingestion), and an ML models that operates on the ingested data and produces results that will feed into decision-making (Actuators), see Figure 5-28 AI/ML Flow. The distinctiveness of ML is the fusion of data and ML Model. Data has dual importance as training sets are used to produce the model at the development stage and, upon deployment, the ML Model will be used for inferencing to generate insights.

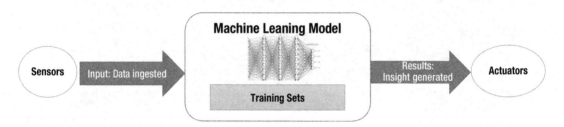

Figure 5-28. *AI/ML flow*

To address the problem of the protection and ML security risks, first we must comprehend the IMSS solution lifecycle, including development, distribution, and execution. Here is the definition of AI lifecycle per OESC (Figure 5-29 AIS Lifecycle (source OECD):

> *AI system lifecycle phases involve: i) 'design, data and models'; which is a context-dependent sequence encompassing planning and design, data collection and processing, as well as model building; ii) 'verification and validation'; iii) 'deployment'; and iv) 'operation and monitoring'. These phases often take place in an iterative manner and are not necessarily sequential. The decision to retire an AI system from operation may occur at any point during the operation and monitoring phase.*

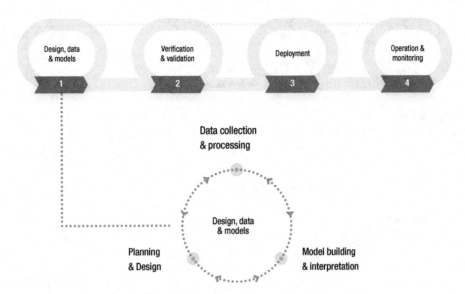

Figure 5-29. *AIS Lifecycle (source OECD)*

AI/ML applications can be narrowed down to 2 major functions: *Training* and *Inferencing*. IMSS solutions are greatly leveraging compute resources from edge to cloud. The Figure 5-30 IMSS with Machine Learning summarizes ML solution scenarios with corresponding data/IP flows:

1. Training in the Cloud using data supplied from the Edge

2. Inferencing in the Cloud based on the data received from the Edge

3. Inferencing at the Edge based on Model developed/distributed from the Cloud and the data received from multiple End Nodes

    3.1. Inferencing on End-Node at the Edge

    3.2. Inferencing on-Prem at the Edge

4. Training based on Federated Learning approach where models get trained locally on-premises without revealing the data to the central cloud entity

    4.1. Federated Learning on End-Node at the Edge

    4.2. Federated Learning on-Prem at the Edge

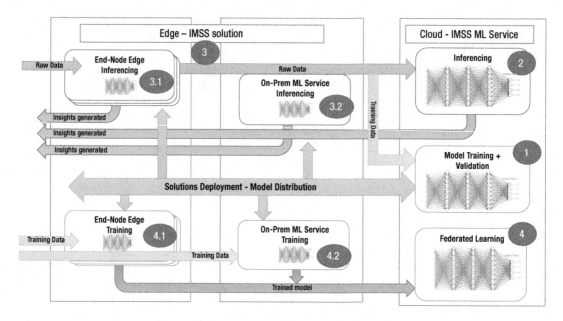

Figure 5-30. *IMSS with machine learning processing nodes and flows*

The preceding flow identifies three major types of processing nodes: 1) End-Node at the Edge (smart camera, robots, drones); 2) On-premises Edge (IoT gateways or servers) that resides within premise within close proximity to the End-Nodes; and 3) ML services that are usually deployed in the cloud environment.

As it is stated above Organizations should embrace risk management practices throughout the entire lifecycle and across diverse stakeholders to establish the trustworthiness of their solutions and scale through the markets. In the case of the IMSS risks should be extended to include the consequences of data or model bias, new security threats such as adversarial inputs, threats to privacy due to leakage of personally identifiable information, and the lack of explainability and accountability.

Stakeholders and Assets

Risk management practices require scope and classify the system's stakeholders and assets. Stakeholders cover all parties (organizations and individuals) who are involved in, or affected by, systems, directly or indirectly. Some stakeholders can play an active role in the life cycle, being directly responsible in the deployment and operation of the

IMSS. ISO/IEC TR 24028:2020[97] defines following stakeholders for the AI value chain that can be directly applicable to the IMSS, see Table 5-1 ML ecosystem stakeholder per ISO/IEC TR 24028:2020.

Table 5-1. *ML Ecosystem Stakeholder Per ISO/IEC TR 24028:2020*

Stakeholder entity	Description
Data source	An organization or an individual providing data that is used to train an ML system.
System developer	An organization or an individual that designs, develops, and trains an ML system.
Producer	An organization or an individual that designs, develops, tests, and deploys a product or a service that uses at least one ML system.
User	An organization or an individual that consumes a product or a service that uses at leastone ML system.
Tools and Middleware Developer	An organization or an individual that designs and develops AI tools and pretrained ML building blocks.
Test and evaluation agency	An organization or an individual that offers independent testing and possibly a certification.
Governance organizations	An organization chartered to monitor and study the usage of AI, including national governments and international organizations

The Technical report also outlines the AI assets that need to be protected. The Table 5-2 ML Assets per ISO/IEC TR 24028:2020 summarizes tangible and less tangible assets that might be impacted by the IMSS ML product.

---

[97] www.iso.org/standard/77608.html

Table 5-2. *ML Assets per ISO/IEC TR 24028:2020*

Tangible assets	Less tangible assets
Data used to train an ML system	Reputation of, and trust placed in, a stakeholder involved in developing, testing, or operating an ML product
A trained ML system – including Model IP	Time • saved by the user or producer
Product of service that uses one or more ML components	• time wasted by user in reacting to an inappropriate recommendation from an ML system
Data used to test the ML product or service	Skills • this could become less valued due to automation enabled by an AI system
Raw data fed to a product or service operation, based on which ML-based decisions are made	Autonomy: • enhanced by more efficient provisioning method for ML system
Computing resources and software used to train, test, and operate ML systems.	• eroded, e.g., using ML profiling for individual usage

Threats

Threat analysis is a key element in the design and development of a secure solution, and getting the threat taxonomy defined is a key factor for building trustworthy solutions. IMSS ML inherits the traditional cybersecurity threats for Edge and Cloud deployments and at the same time introduces new threats that are not addressed by traditional security measures.

Edge deployments require strong physical security, which cannot depend on the assumption of physical perimeter security such as monitoring the environment for access control and surveillance. Edge devices operate in potentially hostile environments and require physical defense mechanisms built into edge system designs. The levels of a physical defense vary based on the market segment use cases. Additionally, cloud services customers may be concerned about physical threats even though there is an expectation that the service providers practice perimeter security.

Security technologies that mitigate physical threats are also seen as a benefit to the cloud services providers in that it not only provides better security assurance, but also reduces their liability for losses and breaches. Physical attacks are also reflected in the following diagram that provides Microsoft Azure vision for the Edge threats.[98]

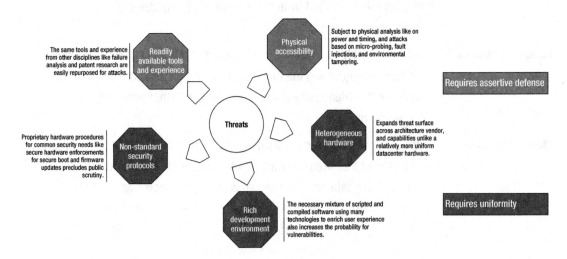

Figure 5-31. *Security threats at the edge (Source: Microsoft)*

In addition to edge threats and traditional vulnerabilities, an IMSS ML system must address new attack methods. The Adversarial ML Threat Matrix project,[99] led by Microsoft, with participation from other industry leaders, MITRE, Bosch, IBM, NVIDIA, and others, developed the knowledge base of ML systems attacks. The motivation here is to leverage the ATT&CK[100] framework for ML attack enumeration. Definitional starting point is the categorization of the machine learning attacks across inferencing and training use cases (see Table 5-3 ML System Attack Categories (source: GITHUB).

[98] https://azure.microsoft.com/en-us/blog/securing-the-intelligent-edge/
[99] https://github.com/mitre/advmlthreatmatrix
[100] https://attack.mitre.org/

Table 5-3. *ML System Attack Categories (source: GITHUB)*

Attack	Overview	Type
Model evasion	Attacker modifies a query to get a desired outcome. These attacks are performed by iteratively querying a model and observing the output.	Inference
Functional extraction	Attacker is able to recover a functionally equivalent model by iteratively querying the model. This allows an attacker to examine the offline copy of the model before further attacking the online model.	Inference
Model poisoning	Attacker contaminates the training data of an ML system in order to get a desired outcome at inference time. With influence over training data, an attacker can create "backdoors" where an arbitrary input will result in a particular output. The model could be "reprogrammed" to perform a new undesired task. Further, access to training data would allow the attacker to create an offline model and create a Model Evasion. Access to training data could also result in the compromise of private data.	Train
Model inversion	Attacker recovers the features used to train the model. A successful attack would result in an attacker being able to launch a Membership inference attack. This attack could result in compromise of private data.	Inference
Traditional attacks	Attacker uses well established tactics, techniques, and procedures to attain their goal.	Both

These categories were fed into the Adversarial ML Threat matrix to produce a meaningful tool for the security analyst to navigate the complex landscape of ML threats. This framework is populated with a curated set of vulnerabilities and adversarial behaviors that Microsoft and MITRE have vetted to be effective against production ML systems (Figure 5-32 Adversarial ML Treat Matrix (source: Github)). There is an axis with seven tactics, though in this case, they are focused in the area of ML: Reconnaissance, Initial Access, Execution, Persistence, Model Evasion, Exfiltration, and Impact. Each column has the techniques, categorized into two types: orange techniques are unique to ML systems, and white/grey techniques that apply to both ML and non-ML systems and come directly from Enterprise ATT&CK.

Reconnaissance	Initial Access	Execution	Persistence	Model Evasion	Exfiltration	Impact
Acquire OSINT Information: (Sub Techniques) 1. Arxiv 2. Public blogs 3. Press Releases 4. Conference Proceedings 5. Github Repository 6. Tweets	Pre-trained ML model with backdoor	Execute unsafe ML models (Sub Techniques) 1. ML models from compromised sources 2. Pickle embedding	Execute unsafe ML models (Sub Techniques) 1. ML models from compromised sources 2. Pickle embedding	Evasion Attack (Sub Techniques) 1. Offline Evasion 2. Online Evasion	Exfiltrate Training Data (Sub Techniques) 1. Membership inference attack 2. Model inversion	Defacement
ML Model Discovery (Sub Techniques) 1. Reveal ML model ontology – 2. Reveal ML model family –	Valid account	Execution via API	Account Manipulation		Model Stealing	Denial of Service
Gathering datasets	Phishing	Traditional Software attacks	Implant Container Image	Model Poisoning	Insecure Storage 1. Model File 2. Training data	Stolen Intellectual Property
Exploit physical environment	External remote services			Data Poisoning (Sub Techniques) 1. Tainting data from acquisition – Label corruption 2. Tainting data from open source supply chains 3. Tainting data from acquisition – Chaff data 4. Tainting data in training environment – Label corruption		Data Encrypted for Impact Defacement
Model Replication (Sub Techniques) 1. Exploit API – Shadow Model 2. Alter publicly available, pre-trained weights	Exploit public facing application					Stop System Shutdown/Reboot
Model Stealing	Trusted Relationship					

Figure 5-32. *Adversarial ML Treat Matrix (source: Github)*

Berryville Institute of Machine Learning (BIML) Threats took a different approach in their "An Architectural Risk Analysis of Machine Learning Systems: Toward More Secure Machine Learning."[101] The BIML conducted the risk analysis of generic ML system decomposed to individual components that are associated with various phases of ML lifecycle, such as 1) raw data in the world, 2) data set assembly, 3) data sets, 4) learning algorithm, 5) evaluation, 6) inputs, 7) model, 8) inference algorithm, and 9) outputs. After identifying risks in each component, the aggregated risks for ML system as a whole were identified what they believe are the top 10 ML security risks presented in the Table 5-4.

---

[101] https://berryvilleiml.com/results/ara.pdf

Table 5-4. *BIML Top Ten ML Security Risks*

1. Adversarial examples	Provide malicious input with very small perturbations that can cause the system to make a false prediction or categorization.
2. Data poisoning	Attacker intentionally manipulates the training data being used by an ML system in a coordinated fashion.
3. Online system manipulation	Attacker to influence the "still-learning" system in the wrong direction through system input and slowly "retrain" the ML system to do the wrong thing. Requires data provenance, algorithm choice, and system operations to properly address it.
4. Transfer learning attack	In many cases in the real world, ML systems are constructed by taking advantage of an already-trained base model which is then fine-tuned to carry out a more specific task. A data transfer attack takes place when the base system is compromised (or otherwise unsuitable), making unanticipated behavior defined by the attacker possible.
5. Data confidentiality	This is a traditional data protection problem, but a unique challenge in ML is protecting sensitive or confidential data that, through training, are built right into a model. Extraction and membership attacks against an ML system's data are an important category of risk.
6. Data trustworthiness	Data provenance and integrity are critical for ML systems, quality of data, reliability of data sources, data integrity preservation.
7. Reproducibility	Hyper-rapid growth of ML results in often under-reported, poorly described, and otherwise impossible to reproduce results.
8. Overfitting	Overfitting happens when a model learns the detail and noise in the training data causing it to not generalize well. Overfit models are not robust to data inputs outside of the domain of the training data. Overfit models are also easier to attack with input perturbations found by generative Adversarial Networks. This is the opposite to underfitting, when models overgeneralize and exhibit similar confidence for overlapping decisions.
9. Data pre-processing integrity	Data pre-processing (e.g., encoding, filtering) can cause loss of data quality and integrity that will alter the model results.
10. Output integrity	Lack of ML operation's traceability makes attack on the output integrity easy since the intrusion will be hard to detect.

Threats for the Training Process

There are IMSS use cases that perform training in edge devices, which brings the direct training threats into the inferencing environment.

The training data itself may be subject to data confidentiality and privacy constraints that can be exposed during inferencing by classic cybersecurity, property inference, membership inference, or model inversion attacks. Following the cybersecurity basics in this text will help with the classic cybersecurity attacks; however, the latter three attacks occur because of having control of the input and access to the output data during normal operation. The risk is primarily for the application developer, but system operators and their integrators and contractors may be required to provide cybersecurity controls to minimize their responsibility.

Also, the trustworthiness of the inference algorithm depends in large part on the trustworthiness of the training data. As you learned in the policy and standards section, the training data and resultant algorithms must be legal and ethical to use, and the system operator must ensure that.

Machine Learning algorithms are often trained with generic data that may not be representative of the deployed IMSS. This is a very common problem leading to poor accuracy in a deployed IMSS.

See the section on protection solutions for methods to improve performance, accuracy, and reduce risk.

Threats for the Inferencing Process

Real world data sampling is turning actual events into a digital form that can be processed by a machine learning algorithm. The performance will only be accurate and trustworthy anchored on the expectation that those sensors and subsequent data processing are secure.

In addition, real world deployed systems often exhibit noise, distortion, and artifacts that are not present in the training data. And in some cases, called transfer learning, algorithms are used outside of the scope they were trained for. Sometimes this works well, but some of the algorithms will randomly produce wildly inaccurate results when presented with data that they were not trained for.

The Machine Learning applications must also be trustworthy. The applications may carry malware trojans or backdoors that will compromise IMSS, leading to ransomware, functional failures, or data manipulation that produces false positives or negatives. Or they may be tampered with within the inferencing system.

The hyperparameters that control Machine Learning applications at runtime can cause the models to be overconfident (producing false positives) or underconfident (softening the probability distribution leading to classification errors).

It is rare for an IMSS to run in a complete air gapped network with only highly secured devices on the network. For example, most systems allow a remote user to access data via a phone, tablet, or laptop which can allow access to the secure network. If the inferencing is being done in a public cloud, the models and the input and output data may be exposed to untraceable attackers posing as cloud tenants due to poor security, misconfiguration, and misplaced inherent trust. Zero Trust protocols provide layered protection for these use cases. The main concept behind zero trust is elimination of implicit trust and continuously validating every stage of a digital interaction. The core principle of Zero Trust is "never trust, always verify." The Zero Trust objective is to protect compute environments using strong authentication methods, use least privileged access, and minimize the exposure. NIST recently published "Zero Trust Architecture" SP 800-207,[102] which provides an abstract definition of zero trust architecture (ZTA) and gives general deployment models.

In the same manner that the integrity and provenance of the input sensor information is critical for trustworthiness, the outputs must also be secure and trustworthy.

Methods to mitigate these threats are described in the ML-based IMSS Protection section of this chapter.

Training at the Edge

Edge training as a use case is driven by data compartmentalization requirements of various industries. There are regulations in Health and Life Sciences, Public Sector, and Finance technology (FINTECH) markets that drive training at the edge (especially Federated Learning). In some parts of the world, national data sovereignty laws do not allow data to be exported beyond the borders of that nation.

---

[102] https://csrc.nist.gov/publications/detail/sp/800-207/final

And there are a growing number of jurisdictions with privacy laws, such as the EU General Data Protection Regulation, similar laws in many other nations, recommendations for NIST in the United States, and local state laws in the United States. These are coming from a general desire for privacy which results in consumer demand for privacy-preserving analytics that benefit the consumers while preserving their privacy.

Federated Learning meets the goals of highly accurate analytics based on large diverse data sets, with the individual's privacy being protected. Federated learning is a distributed machine learning approach that enables organizations to collaborate on machine learning projects without sharing sensitive data, such as, patient records, financial data, or classified secrets (McMahan, 2016[103]; Sheller, Reina, Edwards, Martin, & Bakas, 2019[104]; Yang, Liu, Chen, & Tong, 2019[105]). The basic premise behind federated learning is that the model moves to meet the data rather than the data moving to meet the model. Therefore, the minimum data movement needed across the federation is solely the model parameters and their updates.

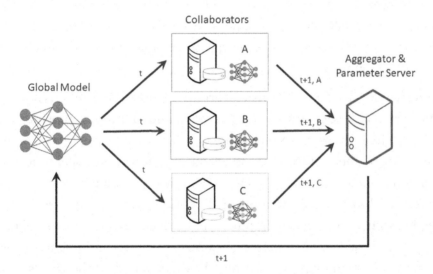

Figure 5-33. *Federated learning (source Overview — OpenFL 2022.2 documentation)*

---

[103] [1602.05629] Communication-Efficient Learning of Deep Networks from Decentralized Data (arxiv.org)

[104] Multi-Institutional Deep Learning Modeling Without Sharing Patient Data: A Feasibility Study on Brain Tumor Segmentation (nih.gov)

[105] Federated learning in medicine: facilitating multi-institutional collaborations without sharing patient data | Scientific Reports (nature.com)

Figure 5-33 present Federated learning systems with new components introduced to the AIS data pipeline.[106]

- **Collaborator**: A collaborator is a client in the federation that has access to the local training, validation, and test datasets. By design, the collaborator is only component of the federation with access to the local data. The local dataset should never leave the collaborator.

- **Aggregator**: A parameter server sends a global model to the collaborators. Parameter servers are often combined with aggregators on the same compute node. An aggregator receives locally tuned models from collaborators and combines the locally tuned models into a new global model. Typically, federated averaging (a weighted average) is the algorithm used to combine the locally tuned models.

- **Round**: A federation round is defined as the interval (typically defined in terms of training steps) where an aggregation is performed. Collaborators may perform local training on the model for multiple epochs (or even partial epochs) within a single training round.

Reinforcement Learning and Transfer learning are other ML methods that conduct training on the edge system or gather data from the edge, to provide accuracy improvements while performing inferencing.

Both learning methods are fundamentally different from traditional supervised learning methods, conducted in an isolated environment, traditionally on cloud systems.

Reinforcement learning is the training method when learning happens from the interaction within the target environment, either real or simulated, that allows he production of versatile models for specific usage. In this scenario, action will be evaluated for a positive or negative outcomes, based on an established reward. Upon receiving feedback, the model "learns" whether that decision was good or bad and gets self-adjusted.

Transfer learning is a method of reusing a pre-trained model for a new problem when the model was trained on one dataset and then fine-tuned to work with another dataset and perform modified tasks. This is especially important for the broad scale

---

[106] Overview — OpenFL 2022.2 documentation

deployments, when models developed based on the traditional supervised methods stored and distributed through "Model Zoo"s, still require tuning to operate in specific use cases.

When the IMSS models are developed using sensor data based on reinforcement or transfer learning, poisoning the training data provides a new pathway for the threats. It can amplify spurious correlations, cause the model to drift, amplify bias, and intensify general inaccuracies and, as a result, compromise the IMSS produced outcomes.

The security required for these use cases is unique. It includes confidentiality and privacy requirements for data involved in a training or retraining path. Depending on the Context (see Figure 5-27 AIS Classification [source OECD]), it might be required to use different keying and protocols to protect and isolate the inferencing data from the data originally used in training, or different stages of training. More importantly, it brings new considerations for data poisoning and provenance protection that are not present in a traditional enterprise feed-forward training environment.

ML-based IMSS Protection and Trustworthiness Framework

Considering cross dependency in addressing security, privacy, and trustworthiness risks of ML-based IMSS, defense in depth strategy should be employed with layered approach to protect IMSS assets and establish trust for stakeholder. Figure 5-34 Layered ML Protection shows composed defense layers. The proposed model uses an OSI (Open Systems Interconnection Model)-type, bottom-up layers.

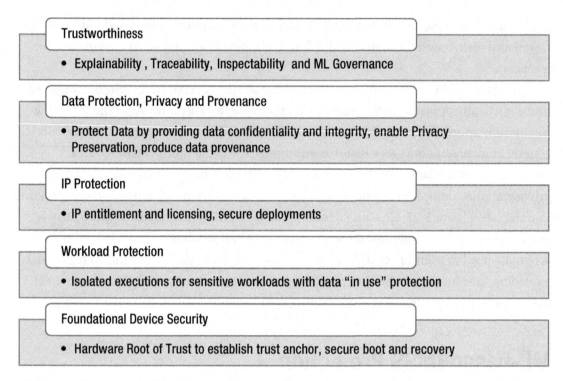

Figure 5-34. *Layered ML Protection and trust*

Foundational Device Security

Any security solution requires foundational or baseline security capabilities to be built-in on the device. The concept of the baseline is aligned with the industry momentum on defining the IoT cybersecurity capabilities (NIST, ENISA, ISO/IEC). With increased attention to the high level of software, attackers are drilling down into the platform stack, exploiting vulnerabilities in the platform firmware and hardware.

Hardware-enabled security techniques can help mitigate these threats by establishing and maintaining platform trust – assurance in the integrity of the underlying platform configuration, including hardware, firmware, and software. The Root of Trust (RoT) is the anchor for establishing trust, it provides protection for identities and workloads, hardened data crypto services, and authentication for a variety of applications. A Hardware-based RoT is an immutable foundation for establishing platform integrity. Platform attestation or verifiable evidence is the basis of creating a trusted platform, where the measurement of platform firmware and configuration chained with the rest of the Software Bill of Material (BOM) verify the boot loaders and then OS, hypervisor, or container runtime layers. The transitive trust described here is consistent with the concept of the chain of trust (CoT), a method where each software module in a system boot process is required to measure the next module before transitioning control. Hardware-rooted platform integrity and trust strengthen and complements the extension of the CoT and can be extended even further to include data and workload protection, critical protection problems for the IMSS ML.

Hardware-based protections lay the foundation for protecting multi-tenant data and workloads in edge compute devices. And in systems that do not have multiple tenants, the compute contexts themselves rely on foundational hardware security and the CoT to provide robust isolation so the different contexts are secure from each other.

Workload Protection

Machine Learning Analytics models and applications represent a wide range of development costs. These costs range from free-to-use open-source pre-trained models to custom models trained from proprietary data sets using custom processing layers and custom topologies costing millions of dollars to develop. The data sets themselves may be expensive to gather or may contain proprietary information or trade secrets. On top of the data, most ML training methods require annotation of the data, which involves a human providing the annotation. For example, in an application such as MRI images, a highly paid specialist spends on average seven minutes per image. And the data may be subject to privacy laws and regulations requiring the subjects to approve the use of their personal data. These add more elements of cost and value to the curated input data.

Training an algorithm can take lots of time on a server, and if the model topology and layers are also being developed, it may take many trial iterations to arrive at an optimal solution. There is no guarantee as to how many iterations it takes for the training to converge – or even a guarantee that they will converge.

Finally, the current market expectations, and hype are heightening the perceived market value of analytics solutions. Because they can be relatively faster and more reliable than humans, they may represent significant cost savings or quality improvements. And in some cases, the reduced response latency, accuracy, and reliability may save lives compared to traditional systems.

These factors mean that developers are highly motivated to protect their investments. They want to prevent integrators or end users from copying or cloning the applications, and from reverse engineering them.

IP Protection

ML Intellectual Property (IP) is the core of ML systems and introduces the specific challenges related to IP opportunities and pitfalls. Traditional IP Protection tools include copyrights, patents, contracts, and trade secrets. ML innovation targets are ML algorithms/models, model evaluations and optimization, data pre-processing and post-processing. Extensive high-quality, representative training datasets are extremely important for reliable performance of an AI model when processing new data. Business value can be found in the following:

- Protecting AI/ML models and/or algorithms

- Software and systems with embedded models/algorithms

- Training, evaluation, and/or optimization strategies

- Training data

- Results data

Institutions around the world are addressing a variety of issues associated with AI/ML IP protection to obtain legal exclusivity to secure assets. Patents may be attained for application of ML in solving a technical problem. In October 2020, the US Patent and Trademark Office released the report "Public Views on Artificial Intelligence and Intellectual Property Policy."[107] The objective of this report was to seek feedback on whether the current patent-related laws are adequate for AI IP protection. It is interesting to note that the report highlighted many of the concerns raised around AI and IP rights as the technology of AI evolves.

Gartner's Hype Cycle for Legal and Compliance Technologies[108] (Figure 5-35 Hype Cycle for legal and Compliance Technologies, 2020 (Source: Gartner)) provides vision for legal and compliance technologies to anticipate, evaluate the impact of emerging legal technology and business innovations. It is interesting to see the several AI/ML-related aspects highlighted in the analysis, specifically AI governance is on the rise and Explainable AI reaching the peak of expectations.

---

[107] www.uspto.gov/sites/default/files/documents/USPTO_AI-Report_2020-10-05.pdf
[108] www.gartner.com/smarterwithgartner/4-key-trends-in-the-gartner-hype-cycle-for-legal-and-compliance-technologies-2020

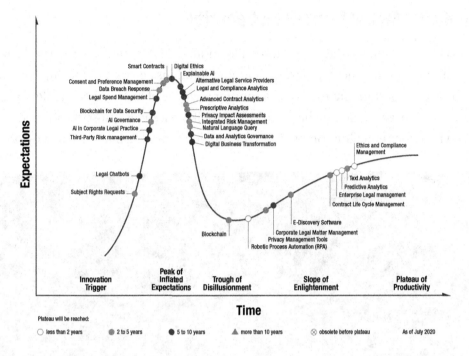

Figure 5-35. *Hype Cycle for legal and compliance technologies, 2020 (Source: Gartner)*

To rely on trade secret protection mechanisms, an owner must implement related internal policies and adequate protective measures. However, the democratization of the Edge and cross-industry collaborative execution model makes this unattainable. Besides the drawbacks of complexity, traditional IP protection tools might jeopardize existing and novel business models. These drawbacks are critical impediments for high-scale AI/ML usages across Edge to Cloud for multi-tenant IMSS deployment.

There is an emerging analytics-as-a-service market where cloud service providers enable tenants to bring their data to be processed in the cloud. In this environment, not only do the tenants distrust other tenants, but also, distrust the service providers, their personnel, or the service provider's infrastructure. Consequently, to gain business benefits, service providers want to reassure that they can enforce IP Protection mechanisms.

OpenVINO™ Model Protection Security

OpenVINO™[109] is an Intel initiative and toolset to address the Machine Learning industry fragmentation, optimize and deploy deep learning solutions across multiple Intel platforms, and maximize the performance of applications for any type of Intel-provided inference engine. The Intel Distribution of the OpenVINO™ toolkit packages a host of tools and optimized functions enabling computer vision and deep learning inference deployment.

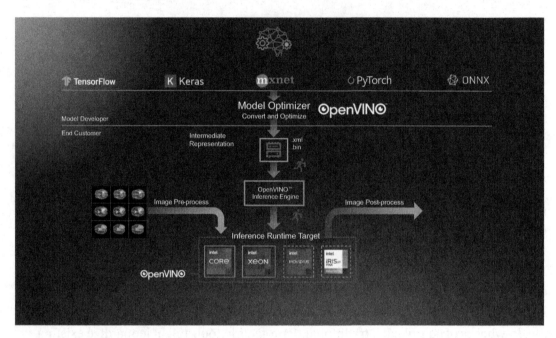

Figure 5-36. *Inference Workflow with OpenVINO™*

OpenVINO™ supports more than 100 public machine learning topologies and custom models, and it accepts models from standard frameworks such as Caffe, TensorFlow, MxNet, and others.

With reference to Figure 5-36 Inference Workflow with OpenVINO™, a model is built and trained with a common framework (left side). Next, models are imported into the model optimizer, a Python-based tool that converts and optimizes them for performance, accuracy, and power efficiency. This can occur on the development machine or the target hardware for deployment. Intermediate representation files, or IR files, are then sent to the inference engine. This is a common API interface with dynamic

---

[109] www.intel.com/content/www/us/en/developer/tools/openvino-toolkit/overview.html

plugins to easily deploy across multiple hardware types. The model optimizer allows for performance comparison or tuning across different accelerators without having to recode. The inference engine also allows heterogeneity – for example, by providing fallback from custom layers on an FPGA to a CPU. The toolkit also contains optimized OpenCV,[110] media encode and decode functions, OpenCL[111] drivers, pre-trained models, and a host of samples for full workload pipeline integration.

ML Model developers Often make a significant investment in the training data set and in the actual training of the models. So, they are concerned that the models might be copied, cloned, or reverse-engineered during runtime.

The OpenVINO Security Add-on (OVSA) (see Figure 5-37) is an end-to-end IP security solution that applies to analytics models developed using Intel's OpenVINO™ toolchain that enables retargeting pre-trained models for optimal execution on various Intel HW accelerators (or back-ends). OVSA cryptographically protects IP at the Model Developer (or ISV) location, through delivery, and while in use by customers or the Model User (i.e., during run time).

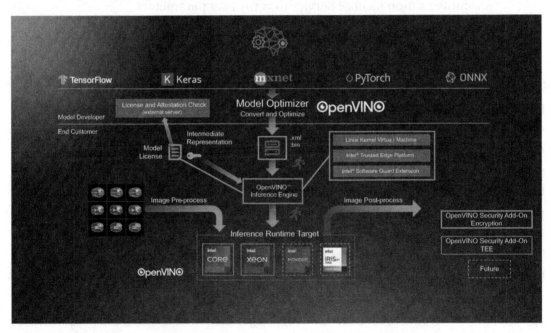

Figure 5-37. *OpenVINO Security AddOn*

---

[110] https://opencv.org/
[111] www.khronos.org/opencl/

OVSA applies cryptographic confidentiality and integrity protection to the model's Intermediate Representation (IR) and binds it to a customer license that describes the terms of use of the model. Licenses are specified on a per-customer basis. A model is usable by a customer, as long as the terms of use specified by the license are valid. Once these terms of use are exceeded, the model is no longer usable.

The OpenVINO™ Security Add-on along with the OpenVINO™ Model Server (OVMS) provide solutions for Model Developers to use secure packaging and model execution to enable access control to the OpenVINO™ models, and for model Users to run inference within assigned limits.

The OpenVINO™ Security Add-on consists of three components[112]:

- **OpenVINO™ Security Add-on Tool:** As a Model Developer or Independent Software Vendor, you use the OpenVINO™ Security Add-on Tool to generate an access-controlled model and master license.

- **OpenVINO™ Security Add-on License Service**: Use the OpenVINO™ Security Add-on License Service to verify user parameters.

- **OpenVINO™ Security Add-on Runtime**: Users install and use the OpenVINO™ Security Add-on Runtime on a virtual machine.

Figure 5-38 OpenVINO™ Security Add-On for Deployment demonstrates the IP protection during the model deployment. Protected models are launched in a model container of OpenVINO™ Model Server. It can load multiple models into memory and customer applications can submit analytics jobs to Model Server for processing by a specific model. The OVSA license checks are performed when a protected model is loaded into OVMS. Protecting cryptographic keys is essential in security protocols. OVSA protects the encryption key by wrapping it with the customer's public key and binding it to the platform Trusted Platform Module or to Intel® Platform Trust Technology.[113] The customer's private key decrypts the model inside a trusted execution environment (TEE). OVMS and OVSA execute within a TEE to ensure the model is protected at run time. The TEE provides isolation from other applications, including the calling application that invokes the model. OVSA leverages the Linux Kernel Virtual Machine

---

[112] OpenVINO™ Security Add-on — OpenVINO™ documentation

[113] www.intel.com/content/www/us/en/developer/articles/code-sample/protecting-secret-data-and-keys-using-intel-platform-trust-technology.html

(KVM)[114] hypervisor and virtual machine isolation mechanisms or a hardened type 1 virtual machine environment.[115] For modern Xeon platforms, OVSA also supports Intel® Software Guard Extensions (SGX)[116] and in the future, Intel® Trusted Domain Extensions (TDX)[117] HW enforced Virtual Machines. TDX is a future technology, the details are beyond the scope of this document.

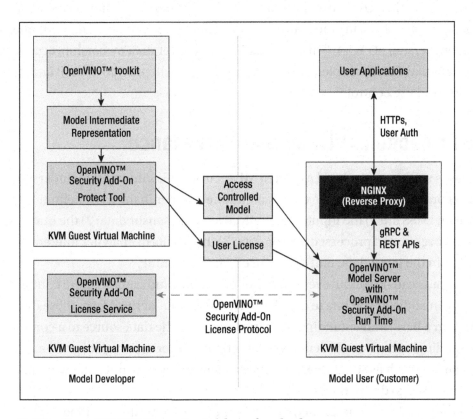

Figure 5-38. *OpenVINO™ Security Add-on for deployment*

---

[114] www.linux-kvm.org/page/Main_Page

[115] Type 1 Vs Type 2 Hypervisor - What's The Difference? (technewstoday.com)

[116] www.intel.com/content/www/us/en/developer/tools/software-guard-extensions/overview.html

[117] www.intel.com/content/www/us/en/developer/articles/technical/intel-trust-domain-extensions.html

When OpenVINO targets an accelerator with a back-end plug-in, the trusted execution environment is extended to the accelerator by encrypting the interface over the PCIe bus. So, the models never appear in plaintext, they are always protected by encryption or by trusted execution environments.

The focus of OVSA is the cryptographic IP protection and IP licensing mechanism. As mentioned earlier, OVSA uses existing run-time isolation mechanisms. The same cryptographic and licensing mechanisms will be applied to protected data streams in a subsequent version of OVSA. This will enable control over data ownership, access, use, and provenance. Once complete, the OVSA framework will provide both IP and data protection and use controls.

Data Protection, Privacy, and Provenance

Data makes up the most critical aspect of ML security. It is important to understand the data categories in ML systems. As it was mentioned earlier in the asset definition, data assets in an IMSS are 1) the inputs: generally, event and sensor data; 2) the outputs: processed events, and processed sensor data; 3) the results of analytics inferences derived from the input data; and 4) data used for the training.

The inputs can be simple events like a door opening indicator to more complex data from an audio or still image or video systems. Output derived from these data ranges from a basic understanding of characteristics of the data source to a complex understanding with narrowly defined differentiating criteria, to high cognitive understanding such as situational awareness. Many different input data types and sources are used to derive the output.

The value of the data assets depends on the cost of gathering, curating, and producing the data and the benefit derived from its use. Some data has obvious value, such as proprietary company data or trade secrets. Other types of data may be expensive to gather, such as Magnetic Resonance Imaging data.

The value of the output data is higher than that of input data because of the additional knowledge provided by the analytics. The benefits of high accuracy, high throughput, and the amount of information that can be processed can save lives, provide improved outcomes, enable faster response, and more complete understanding based on more data than was possible until now.

Additionally, for some systems, the data must be kept private or confidential, it must also be protected from tampering. US federal jurisprudence rules of evidence allow for "self-authenticating" evidence that includes proof that it has not been altered from the time of capture. The emerging tools for manipulating images and data are getting good enough that it is becoming difficult to prove intrinsically whether data is true, so it is beneficial to authenticate the data itself combined with encrypting data streams to maintain their confidentiality.

Sensor outputs and their analytical product are generally the property of the system owner. In some cases, laws confer ownership to the subject that the data is gathered from, and the system owner is a custodian of the data with legal responsibilities and limits for how it can be used or made public. This is particularly true for privacy-related data under the growing body of laws and regulations such as the EU General Data Protection Regulation (GDPR), US state-level legislation, such as the California Consumer Privacy Act (CCPA). These laws reflect how much people value their privacy and want to control personal data.

Classic cybersecurity methods grounded in a hardware Root of Trust will assure that the data came from a source that can be trusted and that the data has not been tampered with as well as maintain confidentiality and privacy of the data. Provenance methods employ cryptographic integrity and authentication methods that prove the data comes from a particular entity (that digitally signs the data) and that the data has not been altered since it was signed.

The threats section introduced specific threats to training and inferencing processes that are beyond the reach of traditional cybersecurity methods. Here are specific data and IP protection methods for those threats that will enhance the trustworthiness of the machine learning results.

Inaccurate data can be signed, authenticated, and subsequently verified. When using data to train machine learning, there must be an independent way to establish the veracity of the training data, essentially a ground truth reference. The ground truth reference must be reserved from the training process to use in the evaluation phase to establish the accuracy of the model. For in-loop training algorithms like Federated Learning and Reinforcement Learning, that same reference must be used periodically in a field evaluation to prevent model drift and thereby maintain trust.

The training dataset has to be large enough and the sampling has to be representative of the real-world diversity that will be experienced during inferencing. There is a necessary phase of processing the training data to eliminate redundancies, incomplete data, etc. During this process, developers may be tempted to manipulate the data samples to give better accuracy figures by, for example, eliminating anomalies. Proper use of statistical sampling methods to measure sampling error vs. the population, and randomness of the selection of training, test, and evaluation data sets will mitigate manipulation and provide data-based estimates of the true accuracy of the fielded algorithm. Using a FIPS-140-3 approved random Number Generator provides truly random numbers to mitigate the introduction of errors due to poor dataset sampling randomization.

Expert legal and ethics reviews are recommended to ensure the training set is legal and that the data has the necessary diversity, and the data, especially the annotation, is free from bias.

There are tuneable hyperparameters that are adjusted by developers during the training process. These are used to reduce false positives or false negative, and to control the confidence of the results. Overconfident or overfitted algorithms that have essentially memorized the training data will be more brittle when fielded and the results will be easier to manipulate with small perturbations of the input data. Adjusting the other way makes the algorithms more resilient but also less discriminating and more likely to produce alternate results with high confidence.

While system operators may not be directly responsible for this work, this must be included in the algorithm selection process because operators are responsible for selecting a trustworthy machine learning application.

Federated Learning

Federated learning applies to usages where the data must be compartmentalized, but the overall accuracy of the inferencing application requires a larger data set than the compartmentalized data contains. The compartmentalization can be driven by privacy considerations such as data sovereignty regulations at a national level, privacy regulations such as HIPAA or GDPR or the CCPA (and many others), compartmentalization for national security such as defense intelligence data, or as a general privacy preservation technology providing privacy-sensitive customers the greater assurance of privacy. In some cases, data transmission and storage constraints may also lead to a federated learning solution.

Because of the data compartmentalization, the data cannot be brought to a cloud backend, so the training must go to the local data domain. The edge devices used for federated learning range from high-performance server class computers to the IoT edge devices themselves, essentially where the sensors are.

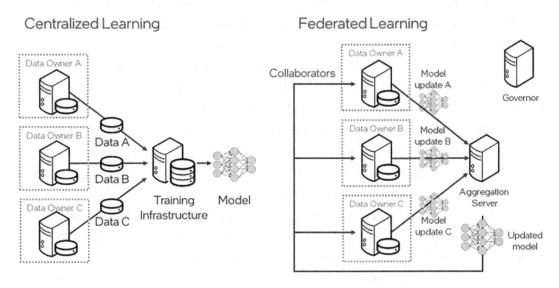

Figure 5-39. *Centralized vs. Federated Learning*

The centralized or federated training process receives machine learning parameters from the edge collaborator nodes and combines them to gain the benefit of a large training data set represented by the multiple edge node collaborators.

Intel® Open Federated Learning is a github[118] project that demonstrates Python 3 library with two components: the collaborator, which uses the local dataset to train a global model, and the aggregator, which receives model updates from collaborators and combines them to form the global model. The aggregator is framework-agnostic, while the collaborator can use any deep learning framework, such as Tensorflow or PyTorch. Additional documentation is available at openfl.readthedocs.io/en/latest/index.html.

While Federated learning enables dynamic collaboration while maintaining collaborator node data privacy, establishing trust and providing end-to-end security and privacy safeguards are critical to deployment and adoption of Federated Learning.

---

[118] https://github.com/intel/openfl

Data and the model both should remain confidential and private, protected from multiple threats, including theft and manipulation that could lead to data leaks or model tampering that would undermine the accuracy and integrity of the solutions, damaging the trustworthiness of the AI/ML system. Intel published a paper on "Federated Learning through Revolutionary Technology,"[119] where the role of hardware-rooted security technologies and Trusted Execution Environments (TEE) are employed to protect Federated Learning system nodes and connectivity to ensure trustworthiness.

TEE provides a mechanism for hardware-based isolation with memory encryption for code and data during execution. In the context of federated learning, foundational security functions provided by a TEE are confidentiality of the execution to mitigate attacks such as model IP stealing out of memory as the training process executes, the integrity of the execution to mitigate attacks that alter the behavior of the code, and remote attestation of the execution, wherein a TEE can provide some measurements as a proof for participating entity trustworthiness.

Intel® Software Guard Extensions (SGX) is a hardware-based TEE that is available on the market and helps to protect against data and code snooping and manipulation by malware. As Figure 5-40 Intel® SGX shows, technology is rooted in the hardware with a minimized trusted computing base that limits the attack surface and is more robust than pure SW methods. This follows a basic principle of cybersecurity and complexity, that is, the lower the complexity (the amount of code in the TCB) the better the security of the system is.

---

[119] www.intel.com/content/www/us/en/financial-services-it/federated-learning-solution.html

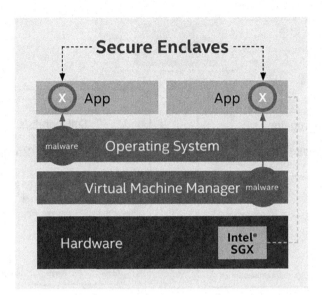

Figure 5-40. *Intel® SGX*

Intel® SGX can be integrated at both collaborator nodes and aggregation engine. This will ensure that both aggregated model, data used to construct the model, and communication will be confidential and protected from tampering. Figure 5-41 Federated Learning system with SGX enclave protection shows how SGX enclaves are used in the aggregator, collaborator, and governor nodes to provide confidentiality, and execution integrity, with robust attestation and isolation from the OS and Virtual Machine in each processing node.

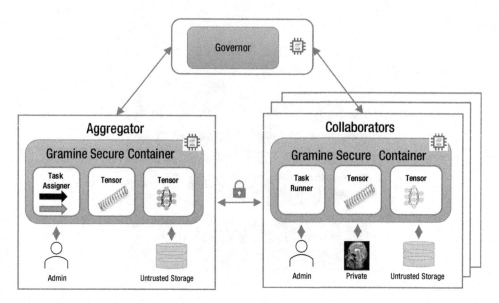

Figure 5-41. *Federated Learning system with SGX enclave protection in Gramine containers*

During federation, data of a collaborator remains with the collaborator node for local training and never leaves it. Instead, model updates from each collaborator node are sent to an aggregator node so that they can be combined into a global "aggregated" model. The global model is returned to the collaborator nodes for a further round of local training. Thus, secure communication is a critical element for establishing secure federated learning systems. Two-way TLS[120] is a well-known method of establishing secure communication. SGX TEE requires significant modifications to enable the execution of the ML training code inside a TEE that increases development efforts in a user's application. To address this extra overhead, lightweight, open-source library OS Gramine[121] was developed for running unmodified user applications inside Intel SGX. This method allows users to run OpenFL code seamlessly without any modifications within TEE.[122] For more information on how to integrate gramine to OpenFL see OpenFL GitHub.

---

[120] https://en.wikipedia.org/wiki/Mutual_authentication

[121] https://gramineproject.io/

[122] https://medium.com/openfl/a-path-towards-secure-federated-learning-c2fb16d5e66e

Homomorphic Encryption

Another method to address data privacy protection is Homomorphic Encryption (HE) which allows ML computation to be performed over the encrypted data without the need to be decrypted. However, the usage of HE-encrypted data is limited to only simple types of machine learning models, which are not proven efficient and accurate with more practical and advanced datasets. HE acceleration is a promising and prospective solution to enable HE for traditional training methods. The Intel® Homomorphic Encryption Toolkit (Intel® HE Toolkit)[123] is designed to provide a well-tuned software and hardware solution that boosts the performance of HE-based cloud solutions running on the latest Intel® platforms. The vision is to lead the homomorphic encryption transformation by providing advanced HE technology on Intel® architecture, allowing customers to gain valuable insights while protecting highly private and sensitive data.

Intel is enabling the emerging HE ecosystem by accelerating HE to meet commercial performance requirements on real-world future use cases. The toolkit has been designed as an extensible solution to take advantage of the latest Intel® Advanced Vector Extensions 512[124] (Intel® AVX-512) acceleration instructions. The toolkit can also be combined with future purpose-built accelerator technology.

In the Trusted Zone, data is encrypted using a homomorphic encryption scheme and sent to the Central Non-Trusted Zone for computation (Figure 5-42 HE solution). In the case of IMSS, edge components will generate data and implement Trust Zone, and send it to the cloud for processing (training or inferencing).

---

[123] Intel® Homomorphic Encryption Tookit (Intel® HE Toolkit)
[124] Intel® Advanced Vector Extensions 512 (Intel® AVX-512) Overview

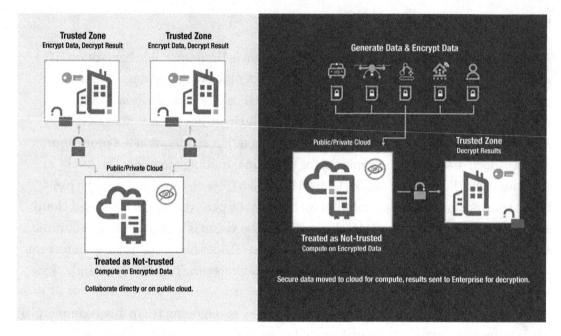

Figure 5-42. *HE solution*

Data Provenance

As mentioned earlier, Data Provenance solutions are developing and fast growing. There are solutions both from market leaders such as Microsoft and IBM as well as from novice visionary companies.

IBM DataStage[125] is a data integration tool that combines analytics, on prem or cloud environments, governance, and data warehouse in a single platform built for AI development.

Microsoft Purview[126] unified data governance solution to help manage and govern data on-premises, multi-cloud, and software as a service (SaaS) data, mapping data with automated data discovery, sensitive data classification, and end-to-end data lineage.

---

[125] www.ibm.com/products/datastage

[126] https://azure.microsoft.com/en-us/products/purview/#overview

Trustworthiness

As it was stated earlier, Trustworthiness is the most complex category as it covers several aspects that need to be assessed, and measured for an ML solution implemented with values-based principles. As standards are getting developed and policy is getting more and more mature, what does the technical community have to do to stay ahead of the curve and remove barriers to broad adoption of IMSS technologies? The first question for organizations who are developing and deploying systems would be to determine the right time to intervene.

Here we face a well-known problem of uncertainties for emerging technologies. In 1980, David Collingridge, a renowned researcher, published *The Social Control of Technology*,[127] where he introduced "The Collingridge Dilemma"[128] to explain the difficulty of controlling risks with given uncertainties, the dichotomy between insufficient information and power problems.

> *"When change is easy, the need for it cannot be foreseen; when the need for change is apparent, change has become expensive, difficult, and time-consuming."*

According to Collingridge, at the conceptual development stage, there is more ability to influence innovation, whereas, at the same point, there is limited information on the knowledge on the impact. When technology reaches maturity, we would have sufficient information on impacts but will have a lesser ability to control. This dilemma directly applies to AI. There is increased consensus that AI technology is at a juncture, and this is the right time to embrace the opportunity to start exploring the tools for trustworthiness. Deployment of these tools, integrated with IMSS will increase customer trust and adoption of solutions, remove the regulatory market entry barriers, and differentiate the solution on the market.

The following are examples of some industry trustworthiness tools that address fairness, explainability, interpretability, and robustness:

---

[127] *The Social Control of Technology* (New York: St. Martin's Press; London: Pinter) ISBN 0-312-73168-X

[128] https://en.wikipedia.org/wiki/Collingridge_dilemma#:~:text=The%20Collingridge%20 dilemma%20is%20a,face%20a%20double%2Dbind%20problem%3A&text=A%20power%20problem% 3A%20control%20or,the%20technology%20has%20become%20entrenched.

- AI Fairness 360 (AIF360)[129] – IBM has released this open-source library containing techniques developed by the research community to help detect and mitigate bias in machine learning models throughout the AI application lifecycle.

- Microsoft Fairlearn[130] – Open-source toolkit that empowers data scientists and developers to assess and improve the fairness of their AI systems.

- Explainable Artificial Intelligence (XAI)[131] – Program by DARPA has the goal of developing a toolkit library consisting of machine learning and human-computer interface software modules that could be used to develop future explainable AI systems.

- InterpretML[132] – An open-sourced code by Microsoft toolkit to improve explainability. It can also be used to explain predictions and enable auditing to meet compliance with regulatory requirements.

- Adversarial Robustness Toolbox (ART)[133] – An LF AI Foundation project that provides tools that enable developers and researchers to defend and evaluate Machine Learning models and applications against the adversarial threats of Evasion, Poisoning, Extraction, and Inference.

---

[129] www.ibm.com/blogs/research/2018/09/ai-fairness-360/

[130] www.microsoft.com/en-us/research/publication/fairlearn-a-toolkit-for-assessing-and-improving-fairness-in-ai/

[131] www.darpa.mil/program/explainable-artificial-intelligence

[132] https://interpret.ml/

[133] https://github.com/Trusted-AI/adversarial-robustness-toolbox

CHAPTER 6

Sample Applications

Putting It All Together – What Does It Take to Build a System?

Goal: Based on the foundations in system architecture and security practices, create pragmatic E2E IMSS systems. The key concepts are:

- Define Cloud to Edge system requirements and expectations
- Define key system metrics – accuracy, throughput, latency, power
- Define key system blocks and architecture, concept of resource graph
- First order system analysis and derived system attributes
- Identify key security vulnerabilities and mitigations

This chapter will examine three different IMSS system applications, starting with the least sophisticated and progressing to more sophisticated systems.

IMSS WORKSTATION (NVR Light, IMSS 3.0) – 4 Dumb cameras and storage only, < 8 video streams of data, alerts based on light analytics in host, action taken by humans reviewing display: Solution: Intel® Core™ x86, TGL class device + 3 screens, forward videos to corporate office under operator control

IMSS Enterprise (Video Analytics, IMSS 4.0) – 32 smart camera – performs detection, forward ROI and metadata to Video analytics node; Video analytics node performs classification and feature matching. Solution: Xeon™ Edge server with AI enhanced instruction set class accelerator

IMSS Smart City (Video accelerator, IMSS 4.0) – 1000 smart cameras, object detection and attribute classification for multiple object classes; real time and historical correlations, Solution: Xeon™ rack server, 1000 streams in 1000 watts, PCIe card based AI class accelerator, edge processing for low latency response as needed

---

The original version of this chapter was previously published without open access. A correction to this chapter is available at https://doi.org/10.1007/978-1-4842-8297-7_9

© Intel 2023, corrected publication 2023
J. Booth et al., *Demystifying Intelligent Multimode Security Systems*,
https://doi.org/10.1007/978-1-4842-8297-7_6

Resource Graph

Previously, we introduced the concept of the task graph, a sequence of tasks connected to accomplish an overall result. A task graph is an abstract object. To execute a task graph requires mapping the tasks to an infrastructure composed of components such as hardware, software, and firmware. A single task graph can be mapped to multiple resource graphs. Figure 6-1 is an example of the application we will use for this section.

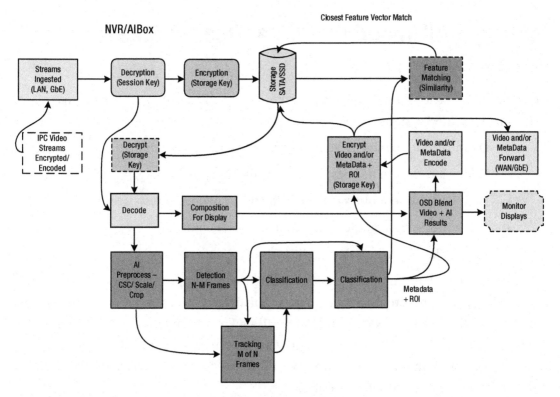

Figure 6-1. *Example task graph for IMSS 4.0 system*

The components of a resource graph can be characterized in terms of key building blocks, connections, and metrics. Figure 6-2 shows an example of a resource graph for an NVR/VAA Node. A resource graph is historically shown in the format of a block diagram, which is the notation we will use here. The blocks correspond to the nodes of a graph and the interconnects correspond to the connections between graph nodes. In this example, the functions enclosed in the box are assumed to be a single physical device, connected to other physical devices. Common interconnects between physical devices are listed, each of which has an associated bandwidth, latency, and power per bit transmitted. Each interconnect will also have an associated Bit Error Rate (BER). Internal to the physical device there will be one or more interconnect techniques. Commonly a Network on Chip (NoC) will interconnect internal components. Additionally, dedicated interconnects are often used for low-speed devices, shown here as the Peripheral subsystem (PSS) and High-Speed IO Subsystems (HSIO SS).

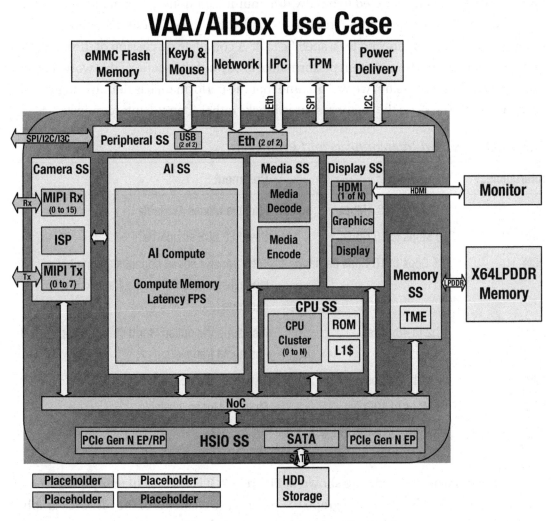

Figure 6-2. *Resource graph WORKSTATION example*

A key difference between external and internal interconnects is accessibility. External interconnects can be more easily accessed and intercepted than internal interconnects. This does not mean internal interconnects are immune to disruption and probing, but do require more sophisticated techniques and higher levels of skill.

Some properties of the resource graph are independent of the task graph or provide upper bounds. Table 6-1 shows a very simplified set of interconnects and restricted to bandwidth only. Even restricted to bandwidth, multiple options are available spanning a wide range of values. In addition to the raw bandwidth, the different interconnects often have protocols optimized for a specific task. A complete discussion of the detailed impact of interconnects on system performance is beyond the scope of this work. For the remainder of this discussion, we will assume that the performance is dominated by the execution of the tasks on the major resource blocks rather than the interconnects.

Table 6-1. *Selected Interconnects and Properties*

Interconnect	Bandwidth	Comment
I2C	100 kbps to 3.4Mbps	Multiple Modes Available
EtherNet	10 Mbps to 10 Gbps	See IEEE 802 standards
PCIe	2.5 Gbps to 16 Gbps per lane	Total transfer speed depends on number of lanes instantiated. X1, x2, x4 and x16 are common.
HDMI	10.2 to 48 GB/s	Also supports options for different bits per pixel and audio transport
MIPI	Up to 11.6 Gbps per lane	1–4 lanes are common
USB	1.5Mbps to 10Gbps	Multiple Modes Available
LPDDR Memory	400 Mbps to 6400 Mbps	

The major resource blocks are shown in Figure 6-2. It is feasible in many instances to assign an element from the task graph to one or more elements of the resource graph. As an example, the media decode task could be mapped either to a CPU or to a media decoder HW block. However, the performance and other metrics will not be the same between the two choices.

In this section, we will use the task graph in Figure 6-1 as a reference and map it to different resource graphs as the requirements become more stringent and the system scales in both the number of streams and the analytics requirements. The primary rationale for this discussion is to highlight the security aspects of the IMSS systems, hence we will look at a simplified set of parameters. Table 6-2 contains the default parameters used in the remainder of the analysis. It is based on a 1080p30 video stream and a representative estimate for the compute required for video analytics during the classification and detection phases discussed in Chapter 3. The compute for the analytics is given in GigaOperations per second (GOPs), where 1 GOP = 1 Billion ($1x10^9$) operations. The storage assumption here is that each storage device supports 8TB (8 x 10^{12} bytes). The general principles used in the analyses can be extended to other situations by modifying the following parameters.

Table 6-2. *Default Parameters for Purposes of Analysis*

Video bps/ stream	30 days → Seconds/mo	Classification GOPs/ stream	Detection GOPs/ stream	Storage/HDD (TB)
5.00E+06	2592000	7	40	8

Using these parameters, we will examine three different scenarios as described in Table 6-3. The applications shown are representative and are not meant to be exhaustive. These correspond roughly to IMSS 4.0 systems for Small businesses (SMB), an enterprise or critical infrastructure scale system (Enterprise) and a metropolitan deployment (Smart City). These scenarios correspond to systems based on workstations, edge servers, and data centers, respectively. The architecture applied to each summarizes the types of resources that will be used in constructing a solution. The scenarios are distinguished primarily by the number of video streams being processed and the assumption that all video streams are being analyzed. In practice, only a subset of the video streams may be analyzed, in which the subsequent values for video bandwidth, storage and analytics compute would be adjusted. A further assumption is that in Figure 6-1, the object tracking function is invoked. This block has a parameter where M of N frames use an object tracking algorithm rather than perform classification and detection on every frame. This is very critical in practical systems to balance the memory and compute requirements vs. the required accuracy. In the compute values for Table 6-3, we assumed an M of N frames value of 1 of 2, that is, object tracking is performed on every other frame. This results in a reduction in classification and detection compute requirements of a factor of 2 relative to performing these operations on every frame. Note the values for Compute are given in TOPs = Trillions of Operations per second (1×10^{12} operations per second).

Table 6-3. *Scenarios for IMSS 4.0 Systems Examination*

	Architecture	# Streams (1080p30)	Video bandwidth (bps)	Video storage TB (30 days)	Classification compute TOPs	Detection compute TOPs
SMB IMSS System	Workstation: Intel® Core™ x86® PC based	5	2.50E+07	8	0.5	3
Enterprise	Edge Server: Intel® Xeon™ + accelerator	100	5.00E+08	162	10.5	60
Smart City	Data Center: Distributed Intel® Xeon™ + accelerator	2000	1.00E+10	3240	210	1200

Also note that TOPs is a very crude estimate of the computational requirements and is also *very* architecture-dependent. An accelerator optimized for video analytics tasks can perform a given neural network model with many fewer operations than a compute unit optimized for another task, say graphics. The difference **can be up to 3x fewer TOPs** required by the accelerator compared to the non-specialized units. In practice, *always use the performance on the actual workloads* when sizing systems and comparing options.

Crawl – Starting Small – Workstation: An SMB IMSS System

We will begin our examination of the SMB IMSS system by explicitly reprising the calculations used to arrive at the values in Table 6-3. These can be used as a guide for the reader in modifying the results to adapt to your needs.

Table 6-4. *Calculations for SMB IMSS 4.0 System*

Parameter	Formula	Calculation	Comments
Video Bandwidth	# of streams X Video bps/stream	5 streams x 5.00E6 bps = 2.5E7 bps	Adjust for actual bps for actual stream resolution
Video Storage	Video Bandwidth x Storage time (in seconds)	Video BW (2.5E7) bps X 30 days (60*60*24*30)/8 (bits/byte) =8 E12=8 TB	Adjust for storage retention time; note this is for *compressed* video streams
Classification Compute	# of streams x GOPs/stream x M of N X frames per second	5 streams * 7 GOPs/stream * (1 of 2=0.5) * 30 = ~0.5 TOPs	Adjust for actual GOPs/stream or preferred, actual # streams empirically determined per engine
Detection Compute	# of streams x GOPs/stream x M of N X frames per second	5 streams * 40 GOPs/stream * (1 of 2=0.5) * 30 = ~3 TOPs	Adjust for actual GOPs/stream or preferred, actual # streams empirically determined per engine

The estimate given for the Classification compute implicitly assumes there is one object per frame to be identified. In practice, the number of objects per frame may vary depending on the application and the estimate will need to be adjusted. An example may be a monitoring of an entrance to a business where, depending on the time of day, there may be zero, one, or multiple persons in the camera view. In this case, one can either size the system for the worst case (highest number of expected people at once) or allow some latency in the system and store the items to be classified and process the excess detections at a chosen rate such as one per frame. The architectural trade-off between provisioning for worst case compute and acceptable latency is one we will encounter in all the scenarios examined.

Figure 6-3 shows the critical external connections of an SMB system block diagram (resource graph) built using the device shown in Figure 6-2. Refer to Figure 6-1 for the task graph described here. The compressed video streams from the external camera(s) are ingested through a Gigabit Ethernet (GbE) port via an Ethernet switch. The first step is to decrypt the video streams with a session key using either a dedicated hardware engine or software decryption on the CPU. The choice will depend on the number for streams and encryption protocols; however, it is preferred to use the HW encryption engines when available to reduce host compute loads. It is then recommended to re-encrypt the video streams using a persistent key for storage. Once ingested into the x86° system, the video streams may be stored on one or more SSD or HDD devices via PCIe or SATA, respectively. For the example shown, 8TB storage are required for 30 days retention, which can be satisfied by a single HDD unit or multiple SSDs. Additional streams and/or longer retention periods will require additional storage units and usage of additional PCIe/SATA lanes from the host.

Many applications will require local display of the video data on one or more monitors as shown at the top of Figure 6-3. The GPU can be used to decode the video streams desired for display and composite the video streams on the desired monitors(s) alongside operator control and system status information. Core™ x86° systems supporting up to three displays or more are commonly available. Connection to the displays may be via either DisplayPort, HDMI, or Type C USB/ThunderBolt° connections.

An SMB system may run stand-alone without any external Ethernet connections (i.e., it may be "air gapped" from the public Internet). Optionally, an external connection, shown as Ethernet2 in Figure 6-3, to an enterprise or public cloud may be added to leverage cloud storage, processing, or to enable viewing from devices via the public Internet. We'll discuss the security implications of this option later in this section.

The video analytics requirements in Table 6-4 can be approached in several ways depending on the specific x86° system chosen and the details of the detection and classification networks chosen. The simplest approach is to assign the video analytics to the CPU complex. The CPU will often have the broadest coverage in terms of models supported and developer familiarity. In these cases, the decoded video streams will be sent from the GPU to the CPU for processing. If the CPU is not able to perform all the video analytics, then the next candidate will be the GPU. The decoded video is already present in the GPU subsystem and memory; however, the GPU analytics tasks may also be competing with the display functions for compute and memory resources.

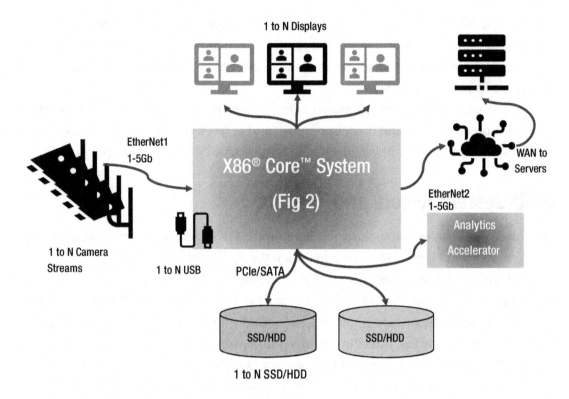

Figure 6-3. *SMB system block diagram*

For a moderate number of video streams and moderate levels of video analytics, the CPU and/or GPU will often suffice. It should be noted that modern Core™ x86 systems can decode up to 32 video streams, depending on the video stream resolution and scene complexity. This will substantially exceed the video analytics capabilities of the base Core™ x86 systems if all or even a substantial fraction of the streams require analysis. There are two fundamental approaches in this situation. The first is to forward the compressed, unanalyzed streams to a remote processing capability in the cloud via the second EtherNet port connected to a WAN. While relieving the immediate local pressure, the system does not scale well when the total system involves large numbers of cameras as we will see in subsequent discussions. The second approach is to add an external analytics accelerator via either an M.2 or PCIe form factor card. These accelerators are much more efficient at performing the analytics task both in terms of performance per dollar and performance per watt. The accelerators are available in a range of capabilities from as low as 5 TOPs to over 100 TOPs. These accelerators have the added advantage of freeing up the CPU/GPU complex for other application tasks. When using an accelerator for video analytics, it is strongly recommended to ensure a video codec is incorporated in the accelerator. Uncompressed video has a memory and BW footprint anywhere from 25x to 150x larger than compressed video and can quickly strain interconnect bandwidth, memory capacity, and even system power as the number of streams/analytics complexities grows.

From a security viewpoint, all external connections must be addressed with multiple levels of protection. Data and models in transit and at rest must be encrypted and authenticated for integrity using the techniques described in previous chapters.

SMB System Assets and Threats

To provide the right level of security for this simple SMB system, let's break it down to the basics: Assets and Threats. Then we can design the right level of security.

The primary assets in this system are the video streams, the detection and classification processing that is being performed on those streams, and the results of the processing. As the streams are generated, processed, and stored, they may be exposed to various threats. The first threat to streams is in the network connecting video cameras and the core system which is functioning as a smart digital video recorder (DVR). The second threat is when the streams are stored on the SSD/HDD volumes. The third is when the streams are displayed, and the fourth threat is when they are sent on via the Wide Area Network (WAN) to a video storage server.

The analytics applications performing the detection and classification are loaded into the system by a system administrator with the rights to add or update applications on the system. These may be provided by the OEM that manufactured the system, by a third party, or by the system operator themselves. The applications can be copied, cloned, reverse engineered, or tampered with when they are sent to the system operator, into storage in the device, or when they are running on the system.

And finally, the results of the analytics processing can either be stored in a separate file structure to the stream storage, inserted into the stream data channel, or may be used to generate graphics that is composited with the video stream and re-encoded for storage and transmission over the WAN. This data may be more privacy-sensitive and therefore may have a higher security requirement than the video stream itself.

Note the assumption that all the assets are protected inside the system. Let's discuss those threats as well to understand what is being relied on inside the system to protect the assets. Anytime instructions or data are decrypted in storage, in DRAM, and in various caches or buffers in internal processing, they must be protected. In this environment, the threats may come from anything that is assumed to be trusted inside the system – other user mode applications, middleware, and drivers; the system software (Drivers, Operating System, hypervisor); and the infrastructure that controls access to the assets, including the users and administrators themselves. Also assumed is that the system administrators have a maintenance process that monitors for vulnerability citings, updates from the systems' software and firmware suppliers, and installs those updates promptly.

Using Information Security Techniques to Address These Threats to an SMB IMSS System

Booting a system with a secure, cryptographically authenticated root of trust is the foundation of system security. Extending that chain of trust through the BIOS, FW, and OS ensures all of the SW bill of materials up to user-loaded applications has not been tampered with.

The video streams from cameras attached with USB-A, USB-B, or USB-C cannot be secured. There is no standard native protocol that provides encryption. The only solution to this would be a proprietary solution that encrypts the packet payloads in the camera and decrypts them in the system. For all the ethernet interfaces, the standard ONVIF protocol allows link encryption to be applied to keep the video confidential in transit (using Secure Real Time streaming Protocol). S-RTSP also allows for stream hashing to detect any errors in the stream (particularly due to tampering). This is initiated with a secure key exchange between the camera and the DVR. As mentioned previously, the video security is terminated (decrypted) in the network layer and must be re-encrypted to store it on the SSD/HDD volume. Disk encryption protects the confidentiality and privacy of the video stream in storage from removal of the storage volume. Depending on how the disk encryption key is stored and its use is controlled, it may also protect from some software attacks.

Protecting applications when they are sent to the system administrator, when stored on the platform, and when they are running involves several different security implementations. Encryption will provide confidentiality when the application is deployed to the end user. Some license managers will do that. To protect the application from being copied or cloned from storage, it also must be stored encrypted, and the decryption authorization must be performed by the license manager.

In the most basic context, faith that an application will do what it is supposed to do and not do what it is not supposed to do depends on whether the supplier of the application is trustworthy. The company that wrote the application needs to be reputable and have a secure design lifecycle process that mandates secure coding practices and tests for vulnerabilities. Using digitally signed applications (and verifying the signatures) ensures through a third party signature authority that the application came from the signing company, that it stands behind the application, and that it has not been tampered with.

The results of the detection and classification can also be protected using the same methods as video streams: link encryption and device (i.e., hard disk) encryption.

These methods provide basic security with the assumptions about the system being physically secured, the entire software stack trustworthy, and that the people with access to the system (especially the administrators) are trustworthy. You will read in the enterprise and smart city sections what can be done if these assumptions are not true.

Walk – Let's Get Enterprising – Edge Server: Critical Infrastructure

The next application to be considered is an enterprise-level system, an increase of approximately one order of magnitude in video streams. These applications require the processing of a hundred to a couple of hundred video streams, almost always requiring that all video streams be analyzed, and the analytics occur in real time. Critical infrastructure, industrial processes, and factories all require real time responses and usually analytics across the entire web of video feeds. The interrelationships between the information in the different video streams is as critical as the analysis of the information in a single video stream.

Referring to Table 6-3 for the Enterprise system, the compute, bandwidth, and storage requirements exceed what the system described in the previous section can support requiring a fundamental change in architecture. Figure 6-4 introduces the resource graph for an enterprise-level system in the form of a server class product, using the Intel® Xeon™ product line as an example; similar considerations would hold for alternative products. In addition to the requirements noted earlier, at this level of workload consolidation, it is not unusual for the resources to be shared among multiple entities. Virtualization and security therefore become more critical considerations in addition to raw performance metrics.

In comparing the SMB resource graph in Figure 6-2 to the Enterprise resource graph in Figure 6-4, critical architectural choices quickly become apparent. In the SMB system, considerable functionality is devoted to interacting with the specific environmental sensors such as video (note the MIPI, for example, and the I2s for audio) as well as interacting with the operator (note the graphics and display functions). To support the graphics and display functions requires the media blocks as well. The overall result is to place limits on the compute, memory and storage capabilities to observe constraints on cost and power.

In the Enterprise Device, Figure 6-4, the greyed-out blocks indicate many of these functions have been eliminated. This frees up power, die area, and package interface pins to focus on compute, memory, and storage functions. These are exactly the features required to support the higher density video loads that the Enterprise systems will see. The number of CPU clusters is increased to support the 4–8 CPU cores in an SMB system to the 12–50+ cores of a server type system. In addition to increasing the number of cores, the Instruction Set Architecture (ISA) of the cores is extended to support the operation required for video analytics, including both training and inferencing. At a minimum, the CPU should support vector instruction set extensions and preferably tensor instruction set extensions. The Intel x86° Xeon™ cores have extensions to support both types of operators. In addition, from Table 6-3, we note that HDD capacity on the order of 160 TB of storage is required. At 8 TB per HDD, approximately 20 HDD drives are required. This requires a similar number of PCIe/SATA lanes potentially with SATA port multipliers. Overall, substantially more high-speed IO lanes are required than supported by a Core™ level device.

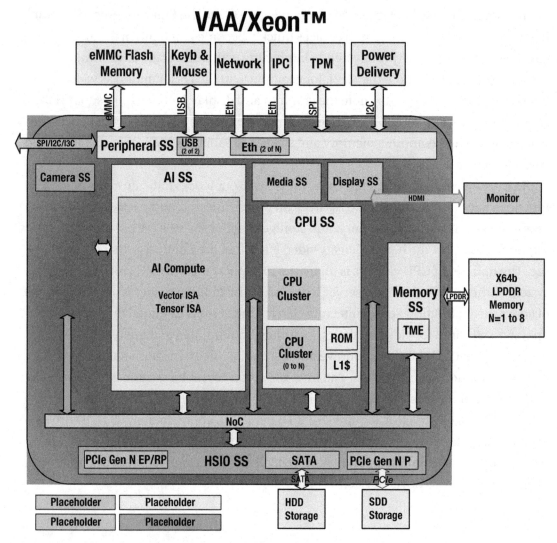

Figure 6-4. *Resource graph for enterprise device*

Next, recall that the relationships between video streams is as important as the information in the individual streams in order to understand the entire context of the environment and the actions taking place. Referring to Figure 6-1, this is where the feature-matching function becomes critical. Seeking pattens and correlations among the inference results from multiple video streams across time and the different locales monitored by the cameras is how the context is understood. This requires accessing data across the entire stored data base and holding a substantial fraction in working memory so these correlations can be made in real time. The multiple memory channels in the Intel® Xeon™ devices make this feasible. Table 6-5 shows potential memory configurations with a device supporting 8 memory channels. Each channel is 64b at up to 6400 MTS, resulting in up to 50GB/s memory BW per channel. The memory configuration will determine the database size which can be addressed for the feature matching function. A common configuration would be in the 1 to 2 TB range for system with 100 cameras. This would allow access to several hours of video across all cameras per the description in Table 6-2 of 160 TB over 30 days of video storage (~4 ½ hours of video per TB).

Table 6-5. *Server Class Memory Configurations*

Module Size	16DIMMs (8 per CPU)	32 DIMMs (16 per CPU)
16GB	256GB	512GB
32GB	512GB	1TB
64GB	1TB	2TB
128GB	2TB	4TB
256GB	4TB	8TB

Figure 6-5 describes an Enterprise class system architecture based on the enterprise device of Figure 6-4. Video streams may be ingested from a cloud type of interface, either from the SMB systems described in the previous section or directly from cloud connected cameras. The enterprise solution requires great compute flexibility because the number and types of video streams ingested may not be known ahead of time or may change over time. The content of the video streams may also be quite diverse with some video streams having no processing, some such as those from the SMB type systems having partially analyzed data to the detection phase or through the classification phase (See Figure 6-1). Table 6-6 indicates the extreme range of video ingestion data rates and hence impact on both storage in HDD/SDD and number of video stream accessible for processing in working memory as indicated in Table 6-5. For the example shown in Table 6-6, if an input system has performed the detection phase, then only Region of Interest (ROI) is sent to the Enterprise system; if the input system has performed classification, then only a feature vector is sent.

Table 6-6. *Video Data Ingestion Rate vs. Analytics Stage*

Source sends:	Raw Video	Detection	Classification
Data Structure	Compressed Video	ROI = 224 pixelsx224 pixelsx1.5x8 b/ Byte x30 fps @ 20:1 compression	Feature Vector 512B * 30 fps * 8b/Byte
Bits/sec per Video Stream	5E6	9E5	1.2E5
Dumb Camera	Yes	No	No
Smart Camera	Optional	Yes	Maybe
SMB System	Optional	Yes	Yes

A similar consideration holds when considering the relationship between the incoming streams and the compute requirements for the system. (See Table 6-2 for classification and detection parameters). The following table demonstrates the impact on the overall system architecture performing the detection and classification operations at different points in the enterprise system. The typical enterprise system will be fed by some combination of dumb cameras, smart cameras and SMB (or the equivalent) sources.

Table 6-7. *Server Class Compute Requirements vs. Analytics Stage*

Source sends:	Raw Video	Detection	Classification
Compute	Detection (40 GOPs/ frame) + Classification (7 GOPs/Frame)	Classification (7 GOPs/frame)	Feature Matching (~0.01 to 0.1 GOPs/frame, DB size dependent)
GOPs/ Video Stream)	(40+7) * 30=1400	7*30=210	~0.3 to 3
TOPs @100 streams	140	21	0.3
Dumb Camera	Yes	No	No
Smart Camera	Optional	Yes	Maybe
SMB System	Optional	Yes	Yes

Clearly the compute requirements are even more strongly influenced by the source processing than the memory bandwidth and storage requirements.

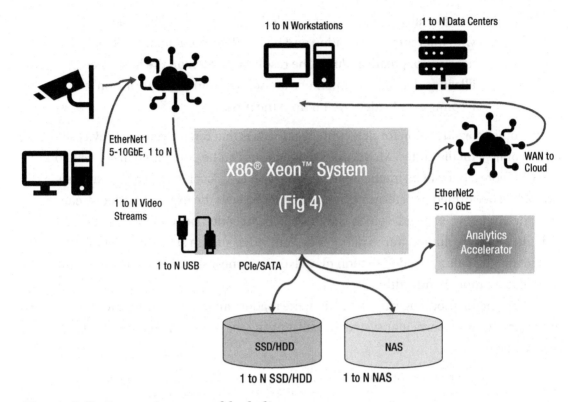

1 to N Workstations

1 to N Data Centers

EtherNet1
5-10GbE, 1 to N

X86® Xeon™ System
(Fig 4)

WAN to
Cloud

EtherNet2
5-10 GbE

1 to N Video
Streams

Analytics
Accelerator

1 to N USB   PCIe/SATA

SSD/HDD   NAS

1 to N SSD/HDD   1 to N NAS

Figure 6-5. *Enterprise system block diagram*

Depending on the configuration and model of the server CPU selected, it is possible to set a few guidelines for selection based on a 100-stream scenario, in which all video streams are analyzed.

- All server class devices will have sufficient compute to perform feature matching.

- Some server class devices will have sufficient compute power to perform classification.

  - Even in these cases, an accelerator may prove more cost effective and power efficient from a TCO viewpoint and should be considered. Analysis should be performed.

- Few, if any, server class devices will have sufficient compute power to perform detection plus classification and will require accelerator(s) to achieve the necessary performance.

- Video analytic accelerators should integrate the media codec with inference acceleration and have a dedicated memory. This accelerator greatly reduces the resource burden on the host since all video decode and inference are self-contained, requiring only a compressed video stream from the host.

Another consideration for detection workloads is that few server class devices incorporate a media codec. Media decode functions can be performed in software on the CPU cores, but will be inefficient compared to a HW accelerated codec. Analysis should be performed to determine the performance with the expected video streams; historically, between 2 and 8 video streams can be decoded per core depending on the original video resolution, frame rate, codec, and video stream structure. It should be noted that the video decode function may also consume a significant fraction of the available memory bandwidth.

Using the methodology in this section, the reader can estimate compute requirements for a particular system by substituting the appropriate values for the key system factors:

- Number of compressed video streams

  - Frames per second...

- Number of compressed Regions of Interest

  - Frames per second, ROI size, Compression ratio...

- GOPs per Detection inference

- GOPs per Classification inference

The better the understanding of the types and structure of the incoming sources and the processing which has previously occurred, the lower the risk of either under-provisioning or over-provisioning the system. Again, best practice is to perform a proof of concept on the proposed system using the actual workloads; however, an analysis at this level of granularity may narrow the scope of system configurations to be tested. Many vendors will also report performance of common inference models through the MLCommons organization (mlcommons.org/en for the English language version). In addition to reporting results in different categories, the organization also supplies open datasets and tools for use. MLCommons is supported by a broad cross-section of leading players in the field of AI and machine learning.

Server class devices (Figure 6-4) used in Enterprise systems (Figure 6-5) support a substantially higher number of high speed I/Os. These IOs can often be configured to support multiple protocols, the most common being the PCIe and SATA standards. SATA is more often associated with HDD; PCIe with SSD and peripherals, including accelerators. The processing of the incoming video streams as described in Table 6-6 will also impact the use of the storage resources. Within a single 2U rack (3.5" height) it is possible to mount up to 20 3.5" HDD. Assuming each drive supports 8TB of storage, then we estimate a nominal total of 160 TB of storage located within the same rack. (Of course, HDD density is increasing over time, so this estimate should be verified at the time of system architecture analysis).

Table 6-8. *Storage Requirements vs. Analytics Stage*

Source sends:	Raw Video	Detection	Classification
Data Structure	Compressed Video	ROI = 224 pixelsx224 pixelsx1.5x8 b/Byte x30 fps @ 20:1 compression	Feature Vector 512B * 30 fps * 8b/Byte
Bits/sec per Video Stream	5E6	9E5	1.2E5
Hours of Video/TB of storage @100 streams	4.5	24	180
TB to store 30 days	(24x30)/4.5 =160 TB	(24x30 days)/24=29 TB	(24 x 30days)/180=4 TB
Dumb Camera	Yes	No	No
Smart Camera	Optional	Yes	Maybe
SMB System	Optional	Yes	Yes

Based on these estimates, a 2U server rack would easily support an ingestion of 100 streams if the source performed detection with about eight 8TB, the data sent were ROI and only classification was done at the Enterprise system; if the source had performed both detection and classification so only feature matching was required, then as little as 4 TB, or a single 8TB storage unit would suffice. Conversely, if raw video were sent, then the storage requirements may exceed the capabilities of a single rack, and Network Attached Storage (NAS) architectures are required. In the example shown, the storage requirements are at the edge of what a single 2U rack system can support.

Operator interaction is typically through remote workstations via a cloud interface rather than a local interface. The operator interaction will consist of some combination of compressed video streams, analytics results, and user interface functions. Because the remote operator workstation may support multiple displays, the forwarded information may comprise a few to several tens of video streams. There may also be multiple operators or client's workstations supported, in some cases, including the workstation that initially forwarded the video data to the edge server. The methodology used to estimate video ingestion based on Table 6-6 can also be used to estimate video egress bandwidths. The final egress destination for data will often be to a datacenter for further processing of the video data. Because there are multiple points of consumption for the data generated at this stage, depending on the number of clients and the types of data sent, the data *egress BW may be substantially larger* than the data ingress. In addition, the data egress BW may be substantially more variable than the ingress BW. In this critical infrastructure example, the ingress is dominated by the cameras monitoring the facility throughout the day, representing a relatively constant load. Conversely, the operators and clients may only be present during a single shift for both workstation type clients and those accessing via a data center.

From a security perspective, the edge server application adds multi-tenancy as a feature. While the server may have a single owner, multiple tenants will reside on the edge server, as shown in Figure 6-5. The video streams entering the edge server may need to maintain isolation and authentication. If an endpoint is breached, then the malicious code must be confined at a minimum, detected, and eradicated, if possible. A similar consideration applies to the data and telemetry egressing the edge server to the operators and the data center. As part of the communications protocol, these entities will certainly be sending messages and data requests back to the edge server which could be corrupted. Virtualization and memory encryption techniques are critical to maintaining confidentiality on a multitenant environment.

A second class of challenges is that in contrast to the workstation environment, the edge server is often in a physically unsecured location. This makes the edge server vulnerable to physical attacks such as use of interposers, bus snooping, power supply and pin glitching, and clock manipulation attacks. Systems located in remote or off-site locations are particularly susceptible. Memory encryption and IO channel encryption can mitigate against these attacks that attempt to intercept and/or corrupt data.

Edge Server Critical Infrastructure System Assets and Threats

To provide the right level of security for an edge server critical infrastructure system, the primary assets in this system (like the SMB system) are the video streams, the detection and classification processing that is being performed on those streams, and the results of the processing. Please refer to the SMB System Assets and Threats section for the details.

The system environment is significantly different. On the enterprise premises side of the edge server, there are more types of devices networked into the system. Figure 6-5 shows local DVR workstations connect to the edge server. Proper network security practices would have those devices on a separate physical network, or on a VPN using managed switches. This may not always be the case; not only might there be many other types of devices that have a physical security role but also general office devices might be connected to the network without being realized. These all provide more ways that access can be gained to the assets from devices inside and outside the LAN. In Figure 6-5, there are also remote workstations (or on cellphones, tablets, and personal computers) for emergency access to time- sensitive data on the edge server over the WAN. Those external devices, including the local networks they are on, are yet another risk that can allow unauthorized access to the assets. Furthermore, the open ports for WAN access are an attack point.

In addition, because this class of system is expected to have multiple users at a time, the threat environment is different than for an SMB system. Not only do more users represent more threats simply due to the numbers of users, it also is more difficult to track behaviors to determine whether the assets are under attack and more difficult to attribute a data leak to a particular user. Unless there is high certainty that the multiple users can be trusted and that they will not make naïve mistakes like fall for phishing schemes, employing zero trust security principles is the best way to manage risk.

Using Information Security Techniques to Address the Threats to an Edge Critical Infrastructure System

Foundational security, as described in the Small Business threat mitigation section, is the basis for all system security and must be applied to Edge Critical Infrastructure systems.

For enterprises where the value of the assets is high enough to warrant risk mitigations, the critical applications should be run in trusted execution environments such as virtual machines. These will help protect against inevitable vulnerabilities in the OS and applications as well as protect against users of the system that are naive, or inattentive. Malicious attackers that appear to be authorized through phished or stolen credentials also will have more difficulty gaining access to system assets. Those agents may also escalate their privileges to administrator for which zero trust methods like barring administrators from viewing, copying, or modifying the assets help to protect these assets.

Run – Forecast: Partly Cloudy – Data Center: Building Blocks for a Smart City

The final application class we will examine is that of a data center, an increase of another order of magnitude in the number of video streams comprehended to a thousand to several thousands. Data center architectures are required when the processing required exceeds that contained in a single server or single rack of servers. Typically, this will involve both the analysis of the video streams and also incorporation of other enterprise-level workloads. These enterprise-level workloads may or may not be directly related to the video analytics task. Common enterprise level workloads are diverse comprising recommendation engines for e-commerce, logistics and inventory, remote gaming, accounting and applications specific to the clients of the data center. For these reasons, a data center will contain a much more diverse set of resources consisting of at least CPUs, GPUs, dedicated storage elements, IPU (infrastructure processing units), NIC (network interface card), and analytics accelerators.

The basic compute building block for the data center remains the server architecture previously described in Figure 6-4. However, because of the order of magnitude increase in the data volume, the interconnect, as reflected by the networking component, becomes much more critical. The data center architecture is dominated by how the compute server elements, storage elements, and the external world are networked together. The data center architectures continue to evolve and are vendor specific. A complete discussion of all the data center architectures is beyond the scope of this work. A representative data center architecture is given in Figure 6-6.

The data center connects to the external world through the core network shown at the top of the diagram. The network elements at this layer connect to the external world. In general, there will be more than one router at the core level which communicate data from the outside world to the layers below it. In principle, the core layers can connect to any of the networking layers below it, represented here as the Aggregation Network. In this example, the aggregation network is composed of clusters, in this example, two aggregation nodes in each cluster.

Aggregation Nodes within the same cluster can communicate with each other as well as the Core Network layer and the compute resources at the next level. The connections in the aggregation layer may take a variety of forms – mesh, star, ring, and bus are the most common topologies. The selection of a specific topology for connectivity will be based on a balance of scalability, fault tolerance, quality of service, and security.

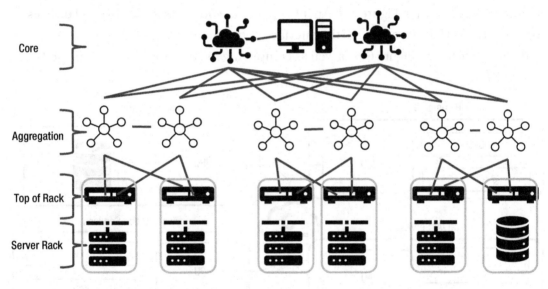

Figure 6-6. *Data center architecture*

The next layer down comprises the compute and storage resources which are physically arranged in racks. Each rack will consist of several rack units which can be either compute, storage, or some combination. The rack units are similar in concept to the edge server described in Figure 6-4 in the previous section. The difference is primarily one of scale. In contrast to the edge server, the scale of the workload has grown beyond the ability of a single device or a single group of devices in a rack to address. In the example shown here, the connection between the aggregation network layer and the racks are through a router at the top of the rack (ToR) router. The ToR mediates all communication between the components in the rack and the aggregation layer.

The components in the rack may be populated according to the specific needs projected for the data center as a whole. In Figure 6-6, the server racks to the left and center are primarily composed of computational elements, as described in Figure 6-4. The server racks on the right-hand side are a mix of computational elements and storage elements.

From the preceding discussion, it is apparent that connectivity of the elements through the tiers in Figure 6-6 is the critical emergent property in data centers. An important emerging trend in data center architecture are Infrastructure Processing Units, devices which are specialized to perform infrastructure tasks such as routing, scheduling, and allocating tasks to resources. An example of an IPU-based data center architecture is shown in Figure 6-7. An intelligent network links the IPU-based devices together. The IPU devices provide the interface between the processing units and the network described in Figure 6-6 as well as comprising the tiers for Aggregation and Core Network functions.

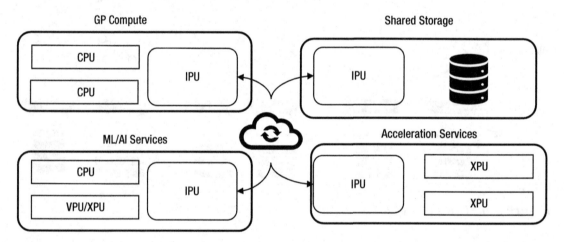

Figure 6-7. *IPU-based data center*

The IPU is optimized for network functions only with no compromises for general compute or specialized compute functions such as analytics, graphics, or storage. The software controlling the data center infrastructure is isolated from the client application software, providing a high degree of isolation. A common IPU architecture for the data center network enables a common software stack for the infrastructure applications and services. The IPU instruction set architecture and accelerators for network functions can be accessed uniformly and efficiently. The data center operators can configure the core, aggregation, and ToR (or equivalent) topologies and operations independently of the impact of client application code resource contention and security considerations. The client code runs on the CPU/GPU/XPU/VPU, and the data center provider code runs on the IPU. In summary, the benefits of an IPU-based data center are to provide 1) a highly optimized network infrastructure; 2) system level security, control, and isolation; 3) common software frameworks – for infrastructure functions; and 4) flexibility via SW programmability to implement a wide variety of data center architectures.

Smart City Data Center System Assets and Threats

In addition to the video and applications assets described previously, Smart Cities often collect many more types of data than a typical physical security system does. Audio may be collected to provide a more complete situational awareness or to enable citizens to interact with city services by talking at a services kiosk. Audio data can locate gunshots, thunder, car crashes, and crowds at events. Other city services may require environmental sensors for air or water quality, motion or vibration sensors, sonar, radar, or lidar for distance measurements to locate objects. In addition, many city services are installed and supported by data carriers, so the communications are often included in these systems, not only for the city services but also for their direct customers. For some of these use cases, secure time as an input to the system is also critical data, especially when using data from different edge devices or when using heterogeneous types of data to get more accurate results.

The actions taken by these services also represent critical assets. Traffic controls, emergency services, law enforcement, and health services can improve our quality of life and even save lives. Particularly due to the latter, the proper function of the sensor devices, software, and outputs of these systems must be reliable and trustworthy.

These geographically distributed devices communicate over private or public networks. The edge devices and local aggregation servers are often in physical locations that are difficult to physically secure. This makes the devices and the networks more vulnerable than SMB or Edge infrastructure systems generally are.

The services for a smart city may be publicly funded, but often they are leased equipment and services that one entity has provided the capital for, in exchange for profits from the data and services. In both cases, reliability and trust are required;

however, for the latter, there is a complex relationship between the city, the data owners, data consumers (the entities whose business depends on that data and provide services), and the citizens (who benefit from the services and may also be consuming that data). Privacy laws and regulations may be applicable to some of the data as well.

To maximize the value of the data, it must be broadly available via the public Internet through web browsers, applications, and through data APIs. The data value also makes it an attractive target for exploitation and theft. And public availability means not only are poorly secured devices accessing the data, but also enterprises eager to profit by manipulating citizens, manipulating the services, or manipulating the data itself for profit (legal or otherwise).

So, to summarize, a smart city represents the worst case scenario for security – a very complex geographically distributed system with little physical access control; a lot of valuable applications and data; complex ownership, use, and control of the applications and data; public access over the Internet; with lives depending on its proper behavior. It is a high threat environment, vulnerable to physically present and remote agents.

Using Information Security Techniques to Address the Threats to a Smart City System

As always, foundational security is essential to providing protection for the primary assets: applications and data. Devices must employ secure boot, have authenticated firmware, OS, and drivers and services, and applications.

When possible, applications should be run in SGX secure enclaves to provide the highest level of hardware enforced isolation and cryptographic protection. If the devices are not capable of running an enclave, then they should be run in a launch authenticated virtual machine that is running on a type 1 hypervisor. The applications must be encrypted when they are transmitted and stored and only decrypted in the virtual machine. Likewise, input and output data must be encrypted in transit and in storage, and only decrypted in an authenticated enclave or virtual machine.

The OpenVINO Security Add-on[1] will do all of this with a secure protocol that protects the encryption keys and uses a secure method of attesting the secure boot and enclave or virtual machine launch measurement.

---

[1] GitHub - openvinotoolkit/openvino: OpenVINO™ Toolkit repository

Zero trust authorization protocols should also be employed to minimize the risk of gaps in security protocols and lapses by personnel. Access to any valuable asset should be limited to the actions required and only be granted at the time that action is needed. For example, an administrator needs to install or uninstall applications, but rarely needs to see the binary executable code. The authorization should be granted for only that one task and once completed, the authorization should be terminated automatically. The authorizations need to be multi-factor authenticated, fine grained, and time limited.

Employing these techniques will keep the risk of loss, penalties, and damage to the system operators reputation as low as possible.

In the next chapter, you will learn how to keep IMSS cybersecurity capabilities up-to-date as threats evolve and as standards and laws change to keep up with technology.

CHAPTER 7

Vision – Looking to the Future

Understanding the trends in Intelligent Multi-Modal Security Systems (IMSS) will enable manufacturers, consultants, and system integrators to anticipate the requirements at the time of deployment. For system operators, knowing the trends keeps systems current to reduce risk. Here are several key trends to monitor.

The Evolution of Intelligent Multimodal Security Systems

As we progress from distributed systems with distributed machine learning with end-to-end security and enter the age of predictive analytics, augmented humanity,[1] telepresence, mirrorworlds,[2] and transhumanism,[3] security capabilities must anticipate the confidentiality, privacy, integrity, trustworthiness, and availability requirements for IMSS.

Intelligence at the edge

Fundamental economics and response speed requirements are driving intelligence to edge devices. Not only does that mean that Edge devices are more expensive due to the cost of Machine Learning (ML) applications and cost of specialized hardware to make them efficient enough to be useful but also increases edge device value in terms of

---

[1] 13th Augmented Human International Conference | ACM Other conferences
[2] AR Will Spark the Next Big Tech Platform—Call It Mirrorworld | WIRED
[3] Transhumanism - Wikipedia

The original version of this chapter was previously published without open access. A correction to this chapter is available at https://doi.org/10.1007/978-1-4842-8297-7_9

© Intel 2023, corrected publication 2023
J. Booth et al., *Demystifying Intelligent Multimode Security Systems*,
https://doi.org/10.1007/978-1-4842-8297-7_7

risk because of reliance on the intelligent edge devices. The devices are more valuable because the loss has a bigger impact on the overall security objective.

More intelligence on the edge means not only more need for cybersecurity but also more need for ML-specific security. As ML-fueled machine-on-machine attacks evolve, defense must also stay in front so the benefits of the investment in intelligent edge devices can be realized and be beneficial to mankind.

Chapter 5 informed us how machine learning is rapidly evolving not just in algorithm development for utilitarian use cases, but also evolving as a threat, and as defenses against classic cybersecurity threats as well as threats specific to machine learning.

Multimodal

Emerging IMSS that perform machine learning on multiple sensors to extract a full situational awareness are also subject to errors and manipulation from each of these inputs. Sensor fusion must account for the security, accuracy, and resilience of each input and apply more confidence to the more resilient inputs and apply increased skepticism to the less resilient inputs.

Mobility

Edge devices for IMSS are going mobile. Dashboard cameras, body cameras, and drones are all not only pushing the boundaries of where IMSS can reach but also exposing the systems to more threats because of the lack of physical protections for these devices. The energy constraints of battery technology place stress on the budget for cybersecurity. Yet, coupled with technologies like GPS, Wi-Fi communications, and location services, and cellular communications with e-911 services, it also means more information can be exposed if the systems are not properly secured.

Threats

In Chapter 4, the evolution of threats was discussed. Attackonomics will provide incentive for this for the foreseeable future, and malware, tailored malware, targeted threats, weaponization of research, and machine learning will continue to evolve. New and valuable assets as components of or protected by IMSS will also drive this trend.

Most of today's encryption is based on the difficulty of solving certain classes of math problems, for which brute force solutions take years to complete. Quantum computers can break today's encryption methods in seconds, not years. Quantum computers are still in research today, but are expected to be able to break today's encryption by 2030.

Defenses

Defenses are also evolving. Defense in depth, quantum resistant cryptography, advances in privacy preservation, robustness, transparency and ethics in machine learning, machine learning performing specific defensive functions, and zero trust methods are all helping to solve problems making IMSS increasingly secure, robust, and resilient.

Trust

We are in an age of a bimodal divergence of trust. Trust in technology, government, news media, business, the 1%, the other 99%, and even the integrity of documentary evidence has been deteriorating for many years. The emergence and proliferation of what manifests as insider attacks (usually remote attackers aided by phishing, malware with privilege escalation) also erodes the underpinning assumptions of trust in colleagues, networks, and devices in the enterprise.

Privacy

Another value proposition of edge device intelligence is improvements in privacy protection. Take the case where a security system camera is detecting and identifying people. Applying security principles, the output video feed should be redacted to preserve identities and unredacted identifying information transmitted with encryption in a side band data channel so authorized parties with permission can access the identifying information. This provides improved system privacy protection over systems that send unredacted video everywhere (even if it is encrypted in communication links) by making sure that unredacted video is never available except when in a controlled authorized environment. However, if the security of the camera is poor, a remote hacker can turn off the redaction and the privacy benefit is lost. Once again, value in IMSS edge devices depends on corresponding security for the benefit to be realized.

It is common for technology to run ahead of regulatory and standards activity. Certainly, the open market will arrive at solutions that would never be invented by regulating them into existence, though that same open market inadvertently enables harm from unethical use and unforeseen consequences. Regulations and Standards, and even new technologies respond to ameliorate negative consequences, but the response takes time.

The growing body of privacy and data sovereignty legislation from municipalities, states, nations, and federations of nations requires not only rigor in system design and integration, but also continued vigilance. Fielded systems may have architectures or capabilities that must be modified or retracted in the future. And data laws can require data to be moved or removed entirely from systems.

National and International standards that apply to IMSS and Machine Learning applications are primitive today.

Given all this change, what should you be doing?

What Should You Do?

If you are reading this, it is out of date.

The speed at which technology evolves, and laws, regulation, and standards emerge means that Component and Software suppliers, IMSS Equipment Manufacturers, systems integrators, consultants, and system operators must actively monitor progress to properly maintain their systems.

So, pay attention! Manually searching out all this information would be a full time job for a good sized team. Fortunately, today there are many information and news aggregator services that feature relevant cybersecurity, legal, policy, and standards threads.[4, 5, 6] The Washington Post issues daily newsletters[7] on many relevant topics.

---

[4] `www.scmagazine.com/`

[5] `https://thehackernews.com/`

[6] `https://ranenetwork.com/`

[7] `https://subscribe.washingtonpost.com/newsletters/?itid=nb_front_newsletters#/newsletters`

On standards and recommendations, ANSI,[8] ISO,[9] IEC,[10] and NIST[11] provide regular newsletters. Start your day with a cup of your favorite morning beverage and a browse of cybersecurity news.

Laws, Regulations, and Public Policy are mandatory for IMSS operators to comply with to avoid liability and penalties. IMSS legislation comes from topical areas of physical security, cybersecurity, information security, privacy, and specific topics around the use of Computer Vision, Artificial Intelligence, and Machine Learning. Laws and legal precedent from judgments lag technology. So, while tracking these is necessary, it is not sufficient to manage risk. Trade associations are helpful, not only to stay informed, but also trade associations monitor and actively participate in the creation of laws and public policy to improve their applicability and quality. ASIS International,[12] the Security Industry Association (SIA),[13] and the PSA[14] are physical security trade associations that publish information on Laws and Regulations.

Laws and policies are mostly written by lawyers, not engineers, and they take long enough to get passed that technological details would not be applicable by the time they are enacted. Consequently, Manufacturers and System Integrators need to understand and monitor progress in technical standards. IMSS are members of the family of Internet of Things (IoT) devices. The leading relevant IoT standards and recommendations are:

- NISTIR 8259[15] Foundational Cybersecurity Activities for IoT Device Manufacturers

- ISO/IEC 27402[16] Cybersecurity – IoT security and privacy – Device baseline requirements

---

[8] www.ansi.org/resource-center/publications-subscriptions

[9] https://committee.iso.org/sites/tc211/home/standards-in-action/newsletters.html

[10] www.ieci.org/newsletters

[11] https://public.govdelivery.com/accounts/USNIST/subscribers/qualify

[12] ASIS Homepage (asisonline.org)

[13] Security Industry Association (SIA) -www.securityindustry.org/

[14] Home - PSA Security Network –https://psasecurity.com/

[15] https://csrc.nist.gov/publications/detail/nistir/8259/final

[16] www.iso.org/standard/80136.html

- ETSI 303 645[17] Cybersecurity for Consumer Internet of Things: Baseline Requirements

- CTA 2088[18] Baseline Cybersecurity Standard for Devices and Device Systems

Your system started its life with appropriate security. To keep it secure, you must make sure you are able to efficiently maintain your system. First, make sure your suppliers can contact you with notifications and updates. Some OSs and applications have an automatic update feature that is helpful. Even some OEMs will have an update service for the SW stack and applications sourced from them. Your firewall, anti-malware, and anomaly monitoring tools should also automatically update themselves. Also, some security maintenance applications will automate this for you. Device Authority[19] and Razberi[20] supply good examples of complete lifecycle management tools, from onboarding onward. And, don't neglect your hardware – drivers are SW components, but are generally associated with the hardware components, so make sure they are included in your maintenance portfolio.

For all of these, (securely!) use the computerness of your computer and the Internetness of the Internet, and leverage applications created by experts in cybersecurity to accomplish these essential tasks with the best speed and the minimum amount of manual effort.

---

[17] www.etsi.org/technologies/consumer-iot-security
[18] https://standards.cta.tech/apps/group_public/project/details.php?project_id=594
[19] www.deviceauthority.com/
[20] www.razberi.net/

CHAPTER 8

As We Go to Press

He that will not apply new remedies must expect new evils; for time is the greatest innovator.

—Francis Bacon, in "Of Innovations," in Essays (1625)

The threat economy continues to evolve rapidly, as well as the technology, standards, and regulations that impact Intelligent Multi-modal Security Systems. Yogi Berra said, "it's tough to make predictions, especially about the future." Nonetheless, the people that look around the corner are the ones that are less likely to be surprised. To conclude this text, we will discuss emerging IMSS trends to watch to help you understand your needs for maintaining existing systems and specifying and designing new ones.

Growth of IMSS

While the days of 25% market growth may be behind us, market forecasts have the Physical Safety systems market growing at 6.7% to 8.5% over 2022 to 2026 and 2028. [1,2,3] The analytics market is estimated to grow even faster than that, at 16.3% according to Omdia.[4] Both the number of devices and the growth of analytics applications engender

---

[1] https://omdia.tech.informa.com/OM024672/Video-Surveillance--Analytics-Database-Report--2022-Data

[2] Video Surveillance Market Size, Share, Trends | Report [2026] (fortunebusinessinsights.com)

[3] Global Security & Surveillance Market Growth Booming At A CAGR of 8.50% During 2022-2028: Latest Trend Analysis, Industry Demand Status, Size Estimation, Top Players Strategies, Forthcoming Development, Revenue Expectation, & Forecast 2028 (yahoo.com)

[4] Video Surveillance & Analytics Database Report – 2022 Data :: Omdia (informa.com)

The original version of this chapter was previously published without open access. A correction to this chapter is available at https://doi.org/10.1007/978-1-4842-8297-7_9

© Intel 2023, corrected publication 2023
J. Booth et al., *Demystifying Intelligent Multimode Security Systems*,
https://doi.org/10.1007/978-1-4842-8297-7_8

corresponding attractive targets for ransom, denial of service, and targeted attacks on valuable assets. Outside of the direct function of physical security, IMSS can be corroborated as attack vectors in botnets and as weak security entrance points into networks.

Cybersecurity General

These aren't the droids you're looking for

—Obi-Wan Kenobi – Star Wars IV

It turns out that hackers aren't just asocial, hoodie-clad, 30-somethings living in their parent's basement; the leaked records from the Conti Group showed us that the collectives can be run like legitimate businesses with HR departments, an R&D group, and an employee of the month award. The 350 members made $2.7B in cryptocurrency in two years.[5] This illustrates that exploit development takes special skills, but the actual deployment can be done by low skilled workers – the smart cow problem,[6] that is, it only takes one smart cow to unlatch the gate, and all the other cows can follow. This was accomplished in a corporate setting, but the same exploit development and malicious deployment economies apply generally, enabled by the anonymity of dark web marketplaces and digital currency.

The Digital Shadows Photon Research team reported in June 2022 that there are over 24 billion credentials for sale on the dark web.[7] This report shows that the market for selling these credentials is effective, providing services for purchasing the credentials.

Despite many botnets and nefarious tools markets that have been taken down, [8, 9, 10, 11] Distributed Denial of Services attacks continue to grow and the DDOS as a service

---

[5] Conti ransomware leak shows group operates like a normal tech company (cnbc.com)

[6] Smart cow problem - Wikipedia

[7] Account Takeover in 2022 (digitalshadows.com)

[8] Feds take down Kremlin-backed Cyclops Blink botnet • The Register

[9] Actions Target Russian Govt. Botnet, Hydra Dark Market – Krebs on Security

[10] Southern District of California | Russian Botnet Disrupted in International Cyber Operation | United States Department of Justice

[11] Notorious cybercrime gang's botnet disrupted - Microsoft On the Issues

marketplace offers services at $100 per day or $10 per hour.[12] This article from Spiceworks[13] and the science direct paper[14] have helpful best practices to prevent your systems from being participants in botnet attacks.

In 2021 and 2022, there were increasing Cyberattacks on critical infrastructure, attacking the basis of public safety, health, and the economy. In 2016, an elaborate multiple vector, coordinated attack sabotaged a Ukrainian power plant and several hundred thousand people suffered loss of power.[15] The ransomware attack on the Colonial Pipeline Company in 2021, on a Florida water protection plant,[16] many destructive attacks on Ukrainian systems and network infrastructure in the 2022 Military conflict[17] all illustrate the trend in critical infrastructure attacks. IMSS that are an element in perimeter protection or are connected to the Internet and to internal networks of critical infrastructure facilities are a necessary security component that can be an entry point for cyberattacks. Note these systems often have access via the Internet for devices like tablets and cellphones that may serve as another entry point into critical infrastructure networks.

Even attacks against individual consumers can have life-threatening consequences, as demonstrated by the "swatting" attacks on Ring doorbell owners.[18]

Zero Trust has become a buzzword that people have come to distrust. The term is over-hyped, poorly defined, and often costly or even impossible to implement. Having to constantly prove you are who you say you are and that you have a legitimate need to access assets impedes business and information flow, not to mention it is annoying to be mistrusted. That said, technology is providing solutions in better identity verification such as passwordless access using cryptographically strong Multifactor Authentication (e.g., FIDO2[19]) that mitigates the classic data theft where an attacker gains access to a

---

[12] Distributed denial of service attack prediction: Challenges, open issues and opportunities - ScienceDirect

[13] Botnet Attack Examples and Prevention (spiceworks.com)

[14] Distributed denial of service attack prediction: Challenges, open issues and opportunities - ScienceDirect

[15] Cyberattack on Critical Infrastructure: Russia and the Ukrainian Power Grid Attacks - The Henry M. Jackson School of International Studies (washington.edu)

[16] Florida Water Plant Hack: Leaked Credentials Found in Breach Database | Threatpost

[17] Destructive HermeticWiper Malware Targets Ukrainian Entities (cyclonis.com)

[18] Ring doorbell owners raided by SWAT teams in nationwide "swatting" spree | Digital Camera World

[19] FIDO2 - FIDO Alliance

system via phishing, logon credential stuffing, or man in the middle attacks, followed by network exploration. Defense in depth adds behavioral anomaly detection (bonus points for AI-based detection) to monitor for unusual compute activity and unusual network activity to thwart the exploration and exfiltration phases of an attack.

According to the 2022 Verizon data breach incident Report,[20] depending on the industry, financial motivation accounts for 78% to 100% of the breaches. Attackonomics, the cost of an attack vs. the return, will always be relevant. Until the costs are greater than the gains, market forces will continue to provide easy-(easier)to-use tools with which to demand ransom or steal assets that can be marketed for financial gains.

Technology

In the next few years, it is expected that there will be a diffusion of compute from cloud services throughout the network infrastructure. Infrastructure computing can provide lower latency compute resources that provide real world response times that cloud computing cannot guarantee. And networking providers will compete with Cloud Service Providers and with each other for this expanded market. IMSS that take real-world actions based on analyzing sensors can benefit from moving from proprietary on-premise compute resources to the network infrastructure when response times and economies of scale provide lower cost solutions that meet these stringent performance requirements. In this networking infrastructure, the infrastructure itself can become an attack vector. Consequently, the IMSS workloads, the data being processed, the analytics results, and corresponding actions must be securely protected against denial of service, tampering, and data exfiltration.[21, 22, 23]

Piloted and pilotless balloons and airplanes have been used for reconnaissance and warfighting by the military for more than 100 years.[24, 25, 26] Modern Unmanned Aerial Vehicles (UAVs) or drones reduce the cost of aerial surveillance and make it easier to do, bringing these capabilities to border patrol, local law enforcement, emergency services,

---

[20] 2022 Data Breach Investigations Report | Verizon

[21] Confidential Computing for 5G Networks (intel.com)

[22] Arm Confidential Compute Architecture – Arm®

[23] Future network trends – intelligent infrastructure (ericsson.com)

[24] History of military ballooning - Wikipedia

[25] History of aerial warfare - Wikipedia

[26] History of unmanned aerial vehicles - Wikipedia

security services, and commercial enterprises[27, 28, 29] and individuals. AI is being used for navigation, real time route planning, and the data gathered from on board sensors are used for classic object detection, identification, and tracking,[30] enabling UAVs to function as an IMSS. Designing and operating these systems requires security planning for potential hacking, signal jamming, and AI tampering and manipulation that will not only be an availability or accuracy problem but also could even turn the UAV in to a threat itself.

Artificial Intelligence and Machine Learning

The advancements in AI/ML (ChatGPT) highlight the growth of the capabilities of AI/ML. Nonetheless, we are still a long way from creating machines that have general knowledge and can think in the sense that humans are able to.[31] While ChatGPT has guardrails from preventing it from writing malware explicitly, this class of generative AI can be used to increase the efficacy of email Phishing and SMS Smishing attacks.[32] And ChatGPT has been used to improve and help generate working malware [33, 34, 35] and hacking tools.[36] It is not improbable that a worm whose destructive power will eclipse the NonPetya worm from 2017[37] could be inadvertently created with ChatGPT assistance and released into the wild. Basic cybersecurity hygiene, using workload and data provenance, and defensive AI-based tools all can be used in IMSS for layered defenses.

Another important aspect of the new generative AI models is the amount of data they are trained with and the size of the models. The models aren't big because of the type or amount of data they produce, they are big because of the complexity of the information being processed. For IMSS applications, that means that models that can ingest multiple

---

[27] 2018 Commercial Drone Industry Trends | by DroneDeploy | DroneDeploy's Blog | Medium

[28] How AI-Based Drone Works: Artificial Intelligence Drone Use Cases | by Vikram Singh Bisen | VSINGHBISEN | Medium

[29] The role of AI in drones and autonomous flight - Datascience.aero

[30] Image Processing: Principles and Applications | Wiley

[31] Enterprises: Beware Of 'Coherent Nonsense' When Implementing Generative AI (forbes.com)

[32] What Cybersecurity Attack Trends Should You Watch Out for in 2023? - Databranch

[33] ChatGPT Artificial Intelligence: An Upcoming Cybersecurity Threat? (darkreading.com)

[34] ChatGPT is enabling script kiddies to write functional malware | Ars Technica

[35] Hackers are using ChatGPT to write malware | TechRadar

[36] ChatGPT-built hacking tools found in the wild (techmonitor.ai)

[37] Petya and NotPetya - Wikipedia

types of information from multiple sources and could potentially provide full situational awareness of large public venues or even cities in the near future. These models are very large, the biggest being 100s of billions of parameters, so the systems running those models will have to scale accordingly.

Being aware of the legal and ethical implications of not only the AI algorithm but also the training data behind it is becoming increasingly important because of privacy sensitivity, fair use vs. copyright laws, and new laws and regulations. See the Regulations section for more detail.

Applications developers and data providers now have a standardized way to include provenance information for their products. The Coalition for Content Provenance and Authenticity[38] has defined a standard that consumers can use to trace the origin and verify the authenticity of different types of media. Using provenance verification tools, consumers can be assured that the content came from the source it appears to have come from and that it has not been altered in any way. These tools can also be integrated with web browsers and social media applications, raising trust in the veracity of content and reducing misleading information online.

In 2022, we learned that cyberwar is already a component of conventional war.[39] In the future, AI weaponized attacks, generative adversarial attacks, AI for defenses against said attacks, and weaponized defensive AI as a counterattack[40] will all be increasing in use. And once again, basic cybersecurity hygiene, using workload and data provenance, and defensive AI-based tools all can be used in IMSS for layered defenses.

You may want to revisit the exhortations from Chapter 5 on AI/ML Transparency, privacy, responsibility, and trustworthiness. Not only will these recommendations help your IMSS to be more robust and accurate, as you will read in the next section, they will help IMSS stay current with regulations.

Regulations

With the rapid advancement and adoption of IMSS, and extensive use of the AI/ML Technologies, there is a growing recognition of the need for comprehensive policies and regulations to address the many ethical, legal, and social issues raised by the use of the

---

[38] Overview - C2PA
[39] Cyber Warfare Is Getting Real | WIRED
[40] Defensive vs. offensive AI: Why security teams are losing the AI war | VentureBeat

technology. The European Union and the United Nations are some of the international organizations that are developing policies and guidelines to govern the development and use of AI. In the United States, some states have begun to pass laws addressing the use of AI in areas such as law enforcement and hiring.

Because IMSS inherently may be used in identification, laws and regulations regarding privacy are a paramount design constraint for IMSS manufacturers. In addition, system operators must consider applicable legislation in the region where a system is located, and multiple regions where systems are interconnected across regions. Privacy laws and regulations have been enacted at national, and in the United States, at state and local jurisdictions.[41] Since the GDPR went into effect in 2018, many other nations have enacted similar legislation. In addition to the EU nations, at least 30 other nations have some form of privacy legislation.[42, 43] As of January 2023, the United States does not yet have national privacy legislation, but there are five states that have laws, all of which come into effect in 2023.[44, 45] Four more states have active bills, and 23 additional states have bills introduced or in committee. The article from the National Law Review provides a comprehensive comparison of the enacted state laws.[46]

Some US states have laws specifically on surveillance.[47, 48] California, New York, and Rhode Island do not allow video cameras where a person has a reasonable expectation of privacy. Hotel rooms, rest rooms, and changing rooms are examples of prohibited areas. Some states allow exceptions to that as long as customers are notified. Surveillance in the workplace is used by many employers to mitigate violence, theft, abuse, and sabotage. Regulating workplace surveillance is mostly left to the states as well. Workplace surveillance must be used with the privacy rights of workers and state regulations in mind. The use of drones for surveillance present new significant considerations for privacy as well.[49, 50]

---

[41] Data privacy laws: What you need to know in 2023 | Articles | Osano

[42] 17 Countries with GDPR-like Data Privacy Laws (comforte.com)

[43] A Guide to Privacy Laws by Country - Free Privacy Policy

[44] As data privacy laws expand, businesses must employ protection methods | VentureBeat

[45] US State Privacy Legislation Tracker (iapp.org)

[46] Summary Of Current State Privacy Laws (natlawreview.com)

[47] Video Surveillance Laws by State: Everything You Need to Know (upcounsel.com)

[48] Security Camera Laws, Rights, and Rules | SafeWise

[49] Surveillance Drones | Electronic Frontier Foundation (eff.org)

[50] Drones and Aerial Surveillance – EPIC – Electronic Privacy Information Center

Negotiating the complex legislation mapping is a dynamic problem and future proofing systems by monitoring legislation in process can give manufacturers, consultants, and integrators a competitive edge.

The European Union AI Act[51] is proposed to address the "risk or negative consequences to individuals or society" due to the use of AI. Like the GDPR is an example used in privacy regulations in many domains, the EU AI Act may also be exemplary or even become a global standard. Additionally, like the GDPR, the proposed legislation levies large fines for violations. The AI Act not only defines a methodology to define risk, it also mandates requirements and conformity assessment for trustworthy AI when high-risk AI is used in the EU. See this[52] article from the MIT Technology Review for an informative overview of the proposal.

There are cyber-resiliency acts in both the EU and the United States. In 2019, the EU enacted a cybersecurity act[53] that strengthens the European Union Agency for Cybersecurity (ENISA) and establishes a framework for voluntary cybersecurity certification of products. The EU Cyber Resilience Act[54] in proposal addresses all the hardware and software elements in systems, requiring manufacturers to reduce vulnerabilities at launch and throughout the lifetime of products. It also requires greater transparency, enabling consumers to take cybersecurity into account when making purchasing decisions. In the United States, the Cyber Incident Reporting for Critical Infrastructure Act (CIRCIA) of 2022 requires 16 critical infrastructure sectors (defined here[55]) to report cybersecurity incidents. Also, in 2022, the Securities and Exchange Commission proposed a rule requiring publicly listed companies to report cybersecurity incidents.[56] As of January 2023, Congress.gov reports 2414 house or senate bills on cybersecurity,[57] too many to even list here. The May 2021 Executive Order on Improving the Nation's Cybersecurity[58] orders the US government and private sector cooperation to protect public and private sectors and American citizens from malicious cyber actors. In

---

[51] The Artificial Intelligence Act |

[52] A quick guide to the most important AI law you've never heard of | MIT Technology Review

[53] EUR-Lex - 32019R0881 - EN - EUR-Lex (europa.eu)

[54] European Cyber Resilience Act (CRA) (european-cyber-resilience-act.com)

[55] Presidential Policy Directive %2D%2D Critical Infrastructure Security and Resilience | whitehouse.gov (archives.gov)

[56] SEC.gov | SEC Proposes Rules on Cybersecurity Risk Management, Strategy, Governance, and Incident Disclosure by Public Companies

[57] Legislative Search Results | Congress.gov | Library of Congress

[58] Executive Order on Improving the Nation's Cybersecurity | The White House

addition to specific orders for federal government agencies, this order specifically calls for enhancing software supply chain security.

In October 2022, the US White House released an Office of Science and Technology Policy white paper on a Blueprint for an AI Bill of Rights.[59] This is not yet law, but it describes a future where citizen's rights are protected from potential harms from improper design and use of AI. It provides "a set of five principles and associated practices to help guide the design, use, and deployment of automated systems to protect the rights of the American public in the age of artificial intelligence."[60] For IMSS AI providers and integrators and consultants, adopting these principles will help futureproof your applications and systems.

The US Clarifying Lawful Overseas Use of Data (CLOUD) Act[61, 62] was enacted in 2018 to amend the 1986 Stored Communications Act allowing federal law enforcement with warrants or subpoenas to compel data and communications companies to provide data stored in their systems. This FAQ[63] from justive.gov can help to understand the law. This is similar to the 2017 National Intelligence Law of the Peoples Republic of China[64]; however, the Chinese law lacks judicial oversight in the form of warrants or subpoenas and there are no exceptions for cross international border data that fall under foreign jurisdictions.[65, 66]

The US–EU trade and Technology Council[67] released a statement[68] on December 05, 2022 establishing ten international working groups, portions of which may impact IMSS. The corresponding US White House statement[69] summarizes areas where these agreements may impact IMSS, such as evaluation and measurement tools for trustworthy AI, privacy enhancing technologies, post quantum encryption, and Internet of Things.

---

[59] Blueprint for an AI Bill of Rights | OSTP | The White House
[60] What is the Blueprint for an AI Bill of Rights? | OSTP | The White House
[61] H.R.4943 - 115th Congress (2017-2018): CLOUD Act | Congress.gov | Library of Congress
[62] CLOUD Act - Wikipedia
[63] The Purpose and Impact of the CLOUD Act - FAQs (justice.gov)
[64] National Intelligence Law of the People's Republic of China - Wikipedia
[65] Beijing's New National Intelligence Law: From Defense to Offense - Lawfare (lawfareblog.com)
[66] Administrative Enforcement in China - Yale Law School
[67] International Trade Administration
[68] U.S.-E.U. Trade and Technology Council (TTC) | United States Trade Representative (ustr.gov)
[69] U.S.-EU Joint Statement of the Trade and Technology Council | The White House

It's important to note that IMSS-related policy is still in development, and it is expected to evolve as the technologies such as AI develop and impact on society becomes more apparent.

Standards

Standards play an important role in addressing regulations providing a common framework for the development, deployment, and use of IMSS systems. Standards can help regulators and other stakeholders to understand the capabilities and limitations of IMSS systems, as well as the risks and benefits associated with their use.

The state of the art in AI standards is constantly evolving as new research and developments are made. ISO/IEC, ETSI, CEN/CENELEC, IEEE develop set of standards related to AI/ML. It is expected that by 2025, conformity assessment schemes will be delivered based on the harmonized AI standards that cover a broad range of topics, such as functional concepts, data standards, interoperability, frameworks, etc.

The following are some ISO/IEC AI/ML related published standards[70]:

- ISO/IEC 23053:2022 Framework for Artificial Intelligence (AI) Systems Using Machine Learning (ML)

- ISO/IEC 22989:2022 Information technology – Artificial intelligence – Artificial intelligence concepts and terminology

- ISO/IEC 38507 – Information technology – Governance of IT – Governance implications of the use of artificial intelligence by organizations

- ISO/IEC TR 24029-1:2021 Artificial Intelligence – Assessment of the robustness of neural networks – Part 1: Overview

- ISO/IEC TR 24030:2021 Information technology – Artificial Intelligence – Use cases

---

[70] www.iso.org/committee/6794475.html

- ISO/IEC TR 24029-1:2021 Artificial Intelligence – Assessment of the robustness of neural networks – Part 1

- ISO/IEC TR 24028:2020 – Information technology – Artificial intelligence – Overview of trustworthiness in artificial intelligence

C2PA[71] addresses another critical problem of the modern systems, the prevalence of misleading information via developing and promoting technical standards and best practices for the protection of digital content, such as digital rights management, content protection, and content authentication. Technical specification is progressing, and the latest version can be found at C2PA Specification site.[72]

Final Exhortation

There is a lot of change in cybersecurity, technology, regulations, and standards to keep up with. Automating the process – indeed an AI that automates it for you – will make maintenance as efficient as possible.

IMSS are used broadly and the risks depend on the environment they are used in. Not all of the trends cited earlier will impact all IMSS, but especially when valuable assets or high risks are at stake, it is important for system operators, consultants, system integrators to think about the future – not only the near term when the system is installed, but for the lifetime of the system. Future proofing your devices, software, the systems you recommend or specify, and the systems you operate will future proof your organization as well.

---

[71] C2PA Specifications :: C2PA Specifications
[72] https://c2pa.org/specifications/specifications/1.2/index.html

Correction to: Demystifying Intelligent Multimode Security Systems

Correction to:

J. Booth et al., *Demystifying Intelligent Multimode Security Systems*,
https://doi.org/10.1007/978-1-4842-8297-7

All chapters were previously published non-open access. They have now been changed to open access under a CC BY-NC-ND license and the copyright holders for each chapter updated to "Intel." The book has also been updated with these changes.

An updated version of the book can be found at
https://doi.org/10.1007/978-1-4842-8297-7

© Intel 2023
J. Booth et al., *Demystifying Intelligent Multimode Security Systems*,
https://doi.org/10.1007/978-1-4842-8297-7_9

Index

A

269

© Intel 2023
J. Booth et al., *Demystifying Intelligent Multimode Security Systems*,
https://doi.org/10.1007/978-1-4842-8297-7

E

Printed in the United States
by Baker & Taylor Publisher Services